THE NEW EASTERN EUROPE

The New Eastern Europe

THE KHRUSHCHEV ERA AND AFTER

J. F. BROWN

FREDERICK A. PRAEGER, *Publishers*
New York · Washington · London

FREDERICK A. PRAEGER, PUBLISHERS
111 Fourth Avenue, New York, N.Y. 10003, U.S.A.
77–79 Charlotte Street, London W.1, England

Published in the United States of America in 1966
by Frederick A. Praeger, Inc., Publishers
Second printing, 1966

Library of Congress Catalog Card Number: 65–24939

This book is Number 169 in the series
Praeger Publications in Russian History and World Communism

Printed in the United States of America

Preface

THAT EASTERN EUROPE is a more important factor in world politics today than it was for more than half a century is a truth fast becoming a truism. The great interest in this region shown over the last few years by scholars and journalists has not been "purely accidental," to use a favorite Communist term. It has reflected the growing awareness that Eastern Europe plays a crucial role in the Communist world and is a critical factor in the whole balance of world power.

Eastern Europe's importance has increased in recent years because of changes within individual countries themselves and changes in their relations with the Soviet Union. In this book, I describe how and why these changes came about and discuss their significance.

In Stalin's time, it was possible to generalize about Eastern Europe (although even then this was not always justified). Today, it is very dangerous indeed, for Eastern Europe has reverted to the diversity that had previously always characterized it. Two generalizations of the broadest kind are still, however, permissible: the character of Communist rule in the different countries has radically changed since Stalin, and the changes have rapidly accelerated in the last five years; secondly, it is now misleading to talk about a Soviet Empire in Eastern Europe, it being more correct to speak of an alliance, one that reveals the tensions and problems common to all alliances in history. To strike a fair balance between these general observations and the particular has been one of the great problems in writing this book. I can only say that if I have failed to solve it, it has not been from a lack of awareness that the problem exists.

The book covers what I think are the most important political, economic, and cultural developments within those East European states which, at the time of Khrushchev's fall, were still, to a greater or lesser degree, members of the Soviet alliance. This has meant excluding Yugoslavia and Albania. But in those parts of the book dealing with intrabloc relations, the role of these two countries is covered in some detail, since both the latest *rapprochement* between Moscow and Belgrade and the successful Albanian defiance of the Soviet Union have been two important factors in East European politics in recent years. I also devote a chapter to East European relations with the Western powers, since, for the first time since World War II, the Western presence is reasserting itself in this region. My last chapter is an attempt to sum up the general situation at the fall of Khrushchev and to give a few pointers for the future.

Chapter 6, "Nationalism in Albania and Romania," is based on articles of mine that were published in *Survey* and *Der Monat*; parts of other chapters are also based on material I originally prepared for articles that appeared in various Western journals, primarily *Survey*.

Many people have helped me to write this book; I can only mention a few here. I wish first to thank Walter Z. Laqueur of *Survey* for encouraging me to undertake this work. To my employers, Radio Free Europe in Munich, my debt is very great. RFE not only gave me encouragement and essential "logistic" help, but also supplied much of the information on which this book is based. I am especially grateful to the Director, C. Rodney Smith, and to the former Policy Director, R. V. Burks. The interpretations in this book are, however, my own, as are any mistakes that may disfigure it.

My thanks are due also to Paul Collins; Harry Trend, who helped me generously on the economic section; Dorothy Miller, for her advice on East Germany; and the national staffs of Radio Free Europe's Research Department. Edith Niznansky, my secretary, has been indispensable.

Finally, I must thank my wife, Margaret, to whom I dedicate this book, for her uncomplaining patience while I was writing it.

J. F. Brown

Munich
September, 1965

Contents

THE NEW EASTERN EUROPE

ONE

Political Development

EASTERN EUROPE, blanketed by a gray uniformity when Khrushchev came to power, once again took on the aspect of a patchwork quilt by the time he was so skillfully forced out. The Soviet Union's satellite states had never, of course, been quite identical even during Stalin's time. Their institutions varied, the pace of both industrialization and collectivization differed, as did the severity of police terror and oppression. The fundamental characters of the countries also remained dissimilar. But, in basic aspects of policy, both internal and external, their similarities far outweighed their differences.

The latitude given the East European states under Khrushchev, however, soon led to growing disparities in those fields where the Stalinist *Gleichschaltung* had been most evident. Nowhere was this more clear than in the political sphere. In two countries, Poland and Hungary, the tensions that had built up under Stalin caused serious upheavals in 1956, when entire repressive edifices were torn down in a matter of days or weeks. Yet, in these two countries, the subsequent course of events differed greatly. What had been a successful revolution in Poland in 1956 was slowly eroded, year by year, until by 1964 the sweet taste of success had turned distinctly sour. Still, amid a socialist community, Poland continued to retain its distinctive appearance, with private peasants controlling the countryside and the Roman Catholic Church continuing as a strong alternative center of power. In Hungary, on the other hand, the revolution had been crushed in 1956; eight years afterward, however, people were asking whether it was not enjoying a belated triumph. There was far more optimism and contentment in Budapest in 1964 than in Warsaw, and yet Hungary was more socialized than Poland.

Hungary's northern neighbor, Czechoslovakia, had resisted de-Stalinization as long as it could. But when the dikes finally burst in 1963, it accomplished more in one year than, for example, Bulgaria had in eight. In 1956 and 1962, the Sofia regime made two spectacular attempts to launch de-Stalinization drives. Yet, the final results were extremely disappointing when measured against the flamboyant promises. Romania, to the surprise of many (including, probably, its own regime), found itself on the international stage by 1964. Economically, it was in the first flush of real industrial expansion; politically and culturally, despite the first signs of improvement, it remained a repressive, conservative state. As for the German Democratic Republic, it continued to be, almost by definition, a model of Stalinism. Yet, even here, there were signs of stirring, as Ulbricht strove desperately to make his self-styled state viable and to improve its image in the eyes of the world.

Generalizations about Eastern Europe were still possible then, but, even before Khrushchev's fall, they were becoming more and more dangerous; even the most valid generalization needed at least some qualification. The situation in each country began to demand treatment on its own merits.

The following country-by-country summaries of political development in what were still known as the "satellite states" are not exhaustive. They concentrate on trying to explain and account for the main features of interest.

Bulgaria

The Bulgarian Communist Party came to power after World War II with much in its favor. It had always been a relatively strong Party, and it had an enviable tradition in many respects. Dimitar Blagoev, its founder, was honored internationally as one of the first organizers of Marxist circles in Russia itself (in the 1880's, when he was a student at the University of St. Petersburg). It was the oldest Communist Party in the Balkans, and, besides Blagoev, could boast of such internationally famous figures as Vassil Kolarov and Georgi Dimitrov.

It is true that after World War I, it plunged into a series of failures which were to discredit it for a time with both Moscow and the Bulgarian people. The September Rising of 1923 after the fall of Stamboliski was a fiasco of the first magnitude. The bomb attempt on King Boris in the Sveta Nedelia Cathedral of Sofia in 1925 was a senseless act of violence, all the more censurable because it failed. It led to the outlawing of the Party and, for a time, to its almost complete eclipse. However, in the late 1920's and early 1930's, the Party revived some of its strength and, even in what passed for free elections in Bulgaria, managed to make a strong showing under the guise of certain front organizations.

At the end of World War II, the Party must have looked like the main hope for a better future to many Bulgarians, especially the young and the underprivileged of all ages. It benefited also from the pro-Russian sentiments of the Bulgarian people. There must have been many Bulgarians, not Communists but not hostile to Communism either, ready to place their services at the disposal of the new Communist regime. They were soon to be disillusioned.

Violence and terror have always been among the many unfortunate characteristics of Balkan politics, and Bulgaria had certainly seen enough of both in the interwar years. It was to see even more in the first five years of Communist rule. Once installed in power by Soviet troops, the new regime unleashed a wave of terror against its enemies, real and imagined, which alienated much of the support it might have expected and created a sullen passivity that was hardly conducive to the energetic building of socialism to which the regime ostentatiously dedicated itself.

Worse still, from its own point of view, was the factionalism that immediately broke out in the ranks of the Party itself. Kolarov and Dimitrov were still alive, but Kolarov was an old, sick man, completely out of touch with developments in his own country; Premier Dimitrov, too, was aging and chose to use his remaining energies in schemes for Balkan cooperation that were to be rudely upset by Stalin. Despite Dimitrov's nominal supremacy, the man who actually ran the country in those early years was Deputy Premier Traicho Kostov, a native Bulgarian Communist, hard and fanatical but deserving of respect for his courage and what might be called a "Bulgarian way" of looking at things. Because he was a "home" Communist, his fate was probably sealed anyway, but he apparently hastened his doom by objecting to the extent to which the Soviet Union was plundering the country, and by insisting a bit too strongly on Soviet assistance in the industrialization of Bulgaria. Here was a possible national Communist in embryo, and Stalin had to find a champion to strike him down and take his place. Kolarov and Dimitrov were too old, and Dimitrov, in any case, although Premier, had outlived his usefulness as far as Moscow was concerned. The choice fell on Vulko Chervenkov, who was forty-seven years old in 1949.

Chervenkov was not one of the best-known Communists at the time. The son of a noncommissioned army officer, he had fled to Moscow after taking part in the abortive 1923 uprising. He had received a good education in his native country and had proceeded to improve it in Moscow; he became an expert in Marxism-Leninism and reasonably well read in literature generally. In the 1930's, he taught at the Lenin Comintern school in Moscow, and during the war broadcast to Bulgaria over the Soviet-sponsored Christo Botev radio. He was young, vigorous, Soviet-trained, and Soviet-trusted. The fact that he was Georgi Dimitrov's brother-in-law also worked to his advantage. With Soviet backing, he intrigued successfully against Kostov. In 1949, Kostov first was demoted from his position as Deputy Premier, then tried and executed—one of the most tragic victims of the purge of "native" Communists that took place throughout Eastern Europe after the expulsion of Tito from the Cominform. Dimitrov himself died several months before Kostov's execution, in 1949, and Kolarov early in 1950. Chervenkov, therefore, was the complete master, and he set about ruthlessly to transform Bulgaria in the Soviet, Stalinist image.

By the time of Stalin's death, in 1953, the Communization and

Sovietization of Bulgaria were well under way. But a once vigorous Party had been reduced to debility and near impotence. The Kostov trial and its aftermath—a large-scale purge and the expelling of nearly 100,000 members from the Party—had stripped the Party of some of its most able men. In the monopoly of his power and the terror with which he exercised it, Chervenkov had stifled the initiative of those able men who remained. Probably in no other country was there such total personal dominance. In Romania, Gheorghiu-Dej was at first overshadowed by Pauker and Luca; even after 1952, when he gained full command, there were others like Bodnaras, Apostol, or Stoica who were prominent in the regime. In Hungary, there were Gerö, Revai, and Farkas, as well as Rakosi; in Poland, Bierut had his Berman and his Minc; in Czechoslovakia, Gottwald shared the limelight to some extent with Zapotocky and, earlier, Slansky. In Albania, Hoxha had occasionally to look uneasily at Shehu. Even the all-powerful Tito in Yugoslavia was ready to let men like Djilas, Rankovic, and Kardelj take their places in the sun. But in Bulgaria, Chervenkov dominated everything, as did his model, Stalin, in the Soviet Union.

With the wisdom of hindsight, one can now see that the death of Stalin was the beginning of the slow political demise of Chervenkov; but this was not at all obvious at the time. For the three years following his death, after all, Stalin was still a revered man; so long as there was no question of openly repudiating his legacy, Chervenkov was in no danger. He could adapt himself to the brief "new course" emanating from Moscow and could even accept the division of offices whereby one man no longer held both the Party leadership and the premiership. But it was in his choice of which office to retain that Chervenkov probably made his first big mistake. He decided to remain Premier; at the Sixth Bulgarian Communist Party Congress, in March, 1954, Todor Zhivkov, a young *apparatchik* in his early forties, was elected First Party Secretary. (In imitation of the Moscow model, similar division of offices was taking place throughout Eastern Europe at the time. Bierut, Matyas Rakosi, Walter Ulbricht, and Enver Hoxha chose to retain the Party post. In Czechoslovakia, Klement Gottwald died in 1953 and Antonin Novotny soon used his succession to the Party leadership to assert himself as the most powerful man in the regime. Only Gheorghiu-Dej in Romania did as Chervenkov and retained the Premiership. But, one year later, he wisely took back the post of First Party Secretary and relinquished the other, evidently having realized the dangers of losing his hold on the Party apparatus.)

There seemed to be little danger to Chervenkov at the time. Zhivkov was very much his nominee, even his protégé. An amiable, modest young man, Zhivkov had risen through the Sofia Communist Party machine until he became First Secretary of the Sofia City Committee, an obvious springboard to higher things.* He had entered the Politburo as one of Chervenkov's young men and was thoroughly under his influence and control. His elevation to the top Party post was greeted with a good deal of cynicism in the Party, since it was considered to be a Chervenkov-inspired political maneuver. But it appeared to be very successful. The old master still dominated the scene, and, for a time, Zhivkov remained in a junior role. Party leader though he was supposed to be, he was not even a member of the Bulgarian delegation to the Twentieth Congress of the Communist Party of the Soviet Union in February, 1956.

From the moment he gave up his Party post, however, Chervenkov was no longer in day-to-day touch with the Party machine, while Zhivkov already had had enough experience of Party politics to realize that his new position gave him unequalled opportunities to dispense patronage and build up a loyal following. This he began slowly to do, and, though Chervenkov was not to feel the *final* effects until years later, the first effects were felt quite soon.

Even if Chervenkov had retained the First Party Secretaryship and kept his full grip on the apparatus, it is doubtful whether he could have survived the emergence of Nikita Khrushchev as new leader of the Soviet Union. There is no official documentation of the dislike the two men had of each other, but Sofia gossip—usually more reliable than, for example, Warsaw gossip—lends much support to the belief that Chervenkov held the new Soviet leader in the highest contempt and that the feeling was mutual.

Chervenkov certainly did not make friends easily. Another of his enemies was Marshal Tito. In the years of Tito's ostracism from

* For a biographical note on Zhikov, see Appendix III.

the "socialist camp," Chervenkov had been one of his most bitter assailants; the official Bulgarian invective against Yugoslavia, partly prompted by the traditional animosity between the two countries on the issue of control over Macedonia, was probably equalled only by that coming from Tirana, for the Albanian hatred for Belgrade also was not prompted exclusively by considerations of Marxism-Leninism. Thus, the first Soviet-Yugoslav *rapprochement* which began in May, 1955, was another serious blow to Chervenkov's position. Tito's bargaining power in this first *rapprochement* with Khrushchev was immeasurably stronger than it was in the second, which came eight years later. He was in a strong position internally and knew that his "revisionism" had a considerable following in many of the Eastern European Parties. He had drawn up his list of personal enemies, on which the name of Chervenkov was very high, at least as high as those of Rakosi and Hoxha. At the end of 1955, Chervenkov was in Moscow for several weeks—either trying to restore his position or else being castigated for his sins in much the same way as Rakosi had been two years earlier. The Twentieth Congress of the CPSU, which he attended as chief Bulgarian delegate, was the final factor. After the sensational denunciation of the man after whom Chervenkov had modeled himself, the Bulgarian regime could not have retained Chervenkov as its leader without openly defying Moscow.

He was demoted from the Premiership at the April, 1956, plenum of the Bulgarian Communist Party. This plenum now holds a hallowed place in the Party's history and in its propaganda. It outlined a new policy of reform for the Party and is considered the turning point from the evil era of Stalinism to the good, new era of Leninism and socialist legality. That it produced improvements, no one can deny. After it, living standards slowly improved, investments in light industry and agriculture were slightly increased, more cultural freedom was, for a time, granted, and the old terror of the Stalinist period was considerably diminished. But to call it a real turning point is a gross exaggeration: it marked an improvement in a situation that had been very bad indeed, but some of the advances were reversed when the relaxation produced ferment—a highly dangerous development, from the regime's point of view.

Within the Party itself, the personal changes of 1956 in one important sense actually made things worse rather than better. Chervenkov's one-man iron rule was replaced by a renewed outbreak of bitter factionalism. Chervenkov, though demoted, was far from being disgraced. He remained a member of the Politburo and was appointed Deputy Premier. This reflected his still very strong following inside the Party, especially at the middle and lower levels. The greatest proof of the influence and prestige he retained was his appointment as Minister of Culture and Education in February, 1957, with the duty of quelling the writers' rebellion that had been one of the most important repercussions of the April, 1956, plenum. He did his job with ruthless efficiency and completed it successfully within fifteen months. In several important spheres, the spirit of the April plenum was conveniently forgotten; this meant that Chervenkov, who had been a victim of it, could avoid some of its worst consequences. But, despite his continued strength and influence, he was no longer at the very hub of power, and his failing health made it most unlikely that he could ever return to it.

Chervenkov was replaced as Premier by his old adversary Anton Yugov. A "home" Communist and former associate of Traicho Kostov, Yugov had been Minister of the Interior from 1944 to 1948, which meant that he had played a leading role in perhaps the worst period of repression in Bulgarian history. He entered a period of eclipse after Kostov's execution, having been openly attacked by Chervenkov for not being sufficiently vigilant against the Kostovites while Minister of the Interior. Despite his black record, this dapper little Macedonian had considerable personal charm, a quick intelligence, and some political skill. He quickly began building up his own personal following and put himself at the head of a recognized faction.

Todor Zhivkov, meanwhile, was now to some extent free from the dominating influence of Chervenkov. He had been nominal Communist Party leader for two years, and, aided by the power of patronage that went with his office, he began to assert himself more resolutely. Even more important, he was obviously becoming a favorite of Khrushchev. The weight of the Kremlin, therefore, was thrown behind him in his struggle for more power and authority. He became a man to be reckoned with and steadily enlarged his following.

The fourth faction to move into the vacuum created by Chervenkov's demotion was small and not too significant. It was led by Georgi Chankov, Yonko Panov, and Dobri Terpeshev. The last of these was one of the grand old men of the Bulgarian Communist Party, the sort of revolutionary who had found the transition from barricade to executive desk a little too much to handle. Another "home" Communist who had been relegated to honorary oblivion after the execution of Kostov, he was a popular nonentity. Chankov, the leader of the group, was of much more consequence. As Politburo member and Deputy Premier, he had been number-two man in the Chervenkov regime; after Chervenkov's fall, he had evidently tried to capitalize on the new trends in Eastern Europe by rallying around him the scattered "revisionist" elements in public life. Whether Chankov was motivated purely by personal ambition, of which he certainly had plenty, is hard to say. In any event, he completely miscalculated the situation and, along with Panov and Terpeshev, became one of the first victims in the factional struggle. Accused of both leftist and rightist deviations, the three were purged in July, 1957, immediately after the purge of the anti-Party group in Moscow.

After the purge of Chankov and his group, there were no outward signs of dissension within the Party ranks for more than a year. The Seventh Party Congress, in June, 1958, was a relatively mild affair and produced no surprises. But very soon after the Congress, the Bulgarian version of the "great leap forward" was announced. The economic aspects of this extraordinary development need not detain us here;[1] even more important were the political implications and repercussions.

In a sense, this sudden surge was in the extremist or romantic tradition of the Party; it will probably prove to be the last gasp of this tradition. Ideologically, it was evidently prompted by the realization that in the race toward Communism, Bulgaria was still very much in the rear. As every good Marxist-Leninist knew, the first essential, even for socialism, was a developed heavy-industry base, but, despite the great *quantitative* progress that had been made, the whole Bulgarian economy was still very backward. China, in 1958, was still a respectable member of the socialist community, and the dazzling militancy of Peking must have been attractive to many Bulgarian Communists who saw the Chinese "great leap forward" as an example to follow. Politically, such a move in Bulgaria might also serve to rouse both Party and people from the *malaise* into which they had fallen and to give the Party a sense, a purpose, and a unity which it had clearly lost.

Just whose idea the Bulgarian "great leap forward" was is still a mystery. The philosophy and concrete targets of the program were expressed in the "Zhivkov Theses," published in January, 1959,[2] and it was Zhivkov himself who was the main public exponent of the movement, but many people in Bulgaria saw Chervenkov's hand behind it: in the National Assembly in March, he was to describe the new economic targets as "stupefying but realistic"[3] and to throw his weight behind the new program; and, in the summer of 1958, shortly before "popular pressure" in favor of the "great leap forward" had begun, Chervenkov had visited China. The two events may not have been coincidental. Perhaps this was Chervenkov's last great display of personal influence inside the Party. Still, it was Zhivkov who became identified with the movement, and it is possible that the Zhivkov and Chervenkov factions, between which it was still often impossible to make a real distinction, joined forces in an attempt to push the program through. It was also a chance for Zhivkov, previously under the shadow of more powerful personalities, to capture the center of the stage and to assert himself at last as the nation's leading figure.

That the "great leap forward" had its opponents from the very beginning was quite clear. At the Seventh Party Congress, a five-year plan had already been approved. Like most Communist economic plans, it was ambitious, but not overly so. It had presumably taken a long time and a lot of effort to prepare, and to throw it overboard immediately after it was approved was, to put it mildly, an erratic step disturbing to many of the more sober-minded Party members.* From the charges leveled against Yugov when he was purged in November, 1962, it would appear that he opposed the program from the very beginning. Many of the charges against

* It is possible that the Bulgarian "great leap forward" was connected with the May, 1958, COMECON "summit" meeting in Moscow, at which the economic specialization of member countries was discussed. Bulgaria's decision to scrap the Five-Year Plan may have been a warning that she was not prepared to accept her relegation to the role of an undeveloped, agricultural member in the organization.

fallen Communist leaders are, of course, demonstrably false, and Yugov may simply have been singled out as a convenient scapegoat for the failure of the "great leap forward." Yet it was noticeable even at the time that Premier Yugov very rarely spoke on this subject. It was he who had presented the original Five-Year Plan to the Seventh Party Congress, but thereafter it was Zhivkov who outlined the new economic program, with the Premier taking a back seat.

Opposition was not confined to Yugov alone, however. Strictures in the press against "the doubters"—i.e., those who thought the new economic targets were ridiculous—grew until it was evidently thought expedient to find a victim whose disgrace would act as a deterrent. The victim eventually chosen was very highly placed indeed. It was Boris Taskov, Politburo member and Minister of Trade, who was dismissed from both his Party and government posts in the spring of 1959. The fact that so important a victim was chosen indicates how strong the opposition was, a fact also borne out by the continued grumblings and ominous warnings in the Party press.[4]

If the "great leap forward" had been successful or only half successful, dissension might have diminished. But, despite the regime's specious claims on its behalf, it was obvious to everybody that the program had clearly failed. The whole experiment left a feeling of frustration and anger and made Party morale much lower than it had been before. At the very top of the Party, at the Politburo and Central Committee level, unity was preserved. But purges began to take place at the lower level, and it would not be long before the dissension had its effect higher up as well. It is quite probable that Yugov tried, with some success, to make capital of the discontent left by the failure of the "great leap forward."

In 1961, another divisive factor, perhaps even more important than the failure of the "great leap forward," began to have its effect. This was the quickly developing Sino-Soviet dispute. How large a genuine pro-Chinese element there was within the Bulgarian Communist Party, it is difficult to say. To many of the older, revolutionary Communists, the policies of Mao Tse-tung must have seemed infinitely more correct and familiar than Khrushchev's "revisionist" policy. Moreover, there were still many Stalinists in the Bulgarian Party. These were anti-Khrushchev and anti-Zhivkov (so clearly the Soviet leader's protégé). Everybody also knew of the enmity between Chervenkov and Khrushchev, and that Chervenkov had been the victim of Khrushchev's de-Stalinization policy. It was natural, therefore, that all these disaffected, disconcerted forces should rally around Chervenkov.

Still another divisive factor was the beginning of the new Soviet *rapprochement* with Yugoslavia. There was strong anti-Yugoslav feeling within the Bulgarian Party, on nationalist as well as ideological grounds, and it was natural that the anti-Khrushchev feeling on this issue would also be directed against Zhivkov and work in favor of Tito's old enemy Chervenkov.

Thus, the deceptive appearance of unity at the top could not last. One can say, however, that it was preserved until the very last possible moment. Chervenkov, Zhivkov, and Yugov were all members of the Bulgarian delegation to the Twenty-second Congress of the CPSU, in October, 1961. When they returned, however, Chervenkov's days were numbered. The second wave of de-Stalinization, initiated by Khrushchev at the Congress, and the Soviet leader's dislike for Chervenkov, gave Zhivkov the perfect opportunity to rid himself entirely of the man under whose wing he had matured but who was now the main obstacle to his achieving supreme power in the Party. At a plenum called in November to discuss the results of the Twenty-second Congress, Chervenkov was dismissed from the Politburo and, shortly afterward, from his post as Deputy Premier. He was, of course, a perfect de-Stalinization target; Zhivkov, Yugov, and the whole regime press lost no opportunity in holding him up as the scapegoat for all the crimes and blunders of the previous years.

In the last analysis, it was Khrushchev's support that gave Zhivkov the strength to oust Chervenkov. But, one should not overlook the fact that Chervenkov, highly respected though he might have been in the Party as a whole, was very unpopular in its top echelons. It was also significant that Zhivkov, both during and after the Seventh Party Congress, had greatly strengthened his own position at the top. In particular, a new group of young men had been emerging in the Secretariat whom Zhivkov had handpicked. This group included Stanko Todorov, former Minister of

Agriculture who later became head of the State Planning Commission and Bulgaria's chief Comecon delegate; Mitko Grigorov, Chervenkov's successor as chief Party ideologist; Boris Velchev, who took over responsibility for organization and cadres; Pencho Kubadinski, in charge of agriculture, at first, then of construction, and later of transport; and Tano Tsolov, who became the Party's senior official in charge of industry. Later, Zhivko Zhivkov (no relation to Todor) was to become a powerful figure in both the Politburo and government, and Bulgaria's economic overlord. It was men such as these, backed by young, like-minded brethren in the Central Committee, who gave Zhivkov the domestic strength—and the courage—to move against his old mentor.

But the final ouster of Chervenkov only brought new problems, which showed that the Party was still far from united. Dogmatic, Stalinist opposition remained strong, especially in the provincial Party apparatus, which had lost its leader but could still be a powerful instrument in a factional struggle. After the Twenty-second Congress of the CPSU, a struggle developed between Zhivkov and Premier Yugov, and it was the latter who evidently sought to exploit the old Stalinists, dogmatists, and conservatives for his own advantage. Thus, Zhivkov found himself with the difficult problem of trying to pursue a moderately reformist course in the spirit of the Twenty-second Congress, without the real strength to implement it and faced by an opposition which his chief remaining rival sought to foment for his own purpose. During all of 1962, up to the Eighth Bulgarian Party Congress, the struggle between the moderate reformists, under Zhivkov, and the powerful Stalinist wing continued. Zhivkov sorely needed help from the Soviet Union, and successive visits in the spring and summer of that year from Ilichev, Khrushchev himself, and Kirilenko were designed to bolster his strength.

To support Zhivkov domestically may have been only part of the reason for visits of such top-level personalities from the Soviet Union. There may also have been genuine anxiety among the Soviet leaders that their anti-Chinese policy was meeting with too much opposition in Bulgaria and that the moves toward a new *rapprochement* with Yugoslavia were causing particular unrest. There is no evidence to suggest that Yugov himself was pro-

Chinese; he was essentially an opportunist who would reach for support wherever he could find it. It is possible that he was hoping to gain sufficient support inside the Party either to oust Zhivkov and present the Soviet Union with a *fait accompli*, counting on the probability that Khrushchev would not interfere, or to persuade the Soviets that he had both more strength and more ability than his rival and was, therefore, a better bet for them.

Yugov had two great handicaps, however. Many of the *apparatchiks*, though hostile to Zhivkov and Khrushchev, were not very attached to this old enemy of their idol Chervenkov. He could exploit their dissatisfaction but could not count on their loyalty. Secondly, he had little strength in the Central Committee. What real strength he had lay in the state apparatus, in which he had been able to build something of a following since becoming Premier in 1956. But, as the case of Rudolf Barak in Czechoslovakia showed the same year, a following in the state apparatus is no substitute for real Party strength.

There had been signs before the Eighth Party Congress in November, 1962, to suggest that Yugov's position was weakening, but no one was quite prepared for the manner and the suddenness with which he fell. After fulfilling his duties as Premier right up until the beginning of the Congress, he was denounced by Zhivkov on the Congress' first day and removed from all his Party and government positions. He was expelled from the Party at the same time. With him into oblivion went Georgi Tsankov, Deputy Premier, Politburo member, and, for several years, Minister of the Interior. Another victim was Rusi Christozov, also a former Interior Minister.

Zhivkov carried out these dramatic purges under the banner of "de-Stalinization" and war on the "personality cult"—issues on which all his victims were particularly vulnerable. Yugov had been Minister of the Interior during the bloody years of 1944–48. Christozov had succeeded him and had been followed by Tsankov. The several lesser Party men who were purged at the same time had also once been prominent in the security apparatus. Their removal was, therefore, a popular move with most Bulgarians, and it must have seemed to many that the ground had at last been cleared for a new program of comprehensive reform and liberalization in Bulgaria.

In the twelve months between the Twenty-second CPSU Congress and the Eighth BCP Congress, there had, indeed, already been welcome signs of a thaw. It had been promised that the National Assembly would play a much greater role than before; Tsankov had been removed as Minister of the Interior and kicked upstairs to the Deputy Premiership whence he fell; his successor, Diko Dikov, promptly closed the detention camps, curbed the security forces and the police, and soon succeeded in creating a much healthier atmosphere in the country. A new fillip was given to the satellite Party, the Bulgarian Agrarian Union, and its constructive importance. Of course, such gestures had little political meaning, but they did have some effect on the morale of the population. Finally, whether by accident or design, much greater leeway was given to intellectuals and writers. The ferment of 1956–57 reappeared, and the literary press carried articles that not only showed a complete disregard for "socialist realism" but, in many cases, criticized the regime for its political and economic failures.

At the Eighth Party Congress itself, Zhivkov and many other speakers promised further reforms, and the pardon for political prisoners announced at the end of 1962 looked like a guarantee that they were keeping their word. Zhivkov, who had also become Premier immediately after the Congress, seemed on the way to becoming a Bulgarian Kadar.

But the liberalization that had begun so promisingly ground to a halt within six months, and a period of retrogression began. In April, 1963, in a crude display of anti-intellectualism, Zhivkov himself gave notice that cultural activity should be restricted once again to the strait jacket of Stalinist times.[5] Deportations from Sofia of undesirable political elements were resumed; even convictions and prison sentences for telling anti-regime jokes were widely reported. In December, 1963, Bulgarian-American relations were given a severe jolt by the trial of the "American spy" Assen Georgiev and the consequent violent demonstration outside the American Legation. The repression was, of course, nowhere near as severe as in the Chervenkov days, but in comparison to what was promised—and hoped for—the situation in 1964 was disappointing indeed.

To account for it was not easy. There were three possible explanations, which were not mutually exclusive. The first was that

Zhivkov himself was never really interested in liberalization. Having found it a convenient weapon with which to bludgeon his opponents, he dropped it as quickly as he could when its job was done. The second was more convincing: it was that Zhivkov's triumph at the Eighth Party Congress was more apparent than real. Though he consolidated his position at the very pinnacle of the Party, Zhivkov was still faced, at the middle-cadre level, especially in the provinces, by a fairly solid wall of "dogmatist" (Stalinist) opposition (Chervenkovites, Yugovites) against which he had neither the strength nor the courage to act resolutely. The third explanation was closely linked to the second. In the previous two years, the economic situation in Bulgaria had deteriorated rather than improved. On paper, the regime could point to impressive advances in industrial growth; there was no doubt that a great deal of *quantitative* progress had been made in the twenty years of Communist rule. But more relevant were the serious failures in agriculture and the internal distribution system. These, in a country always noted for its agricultural abundance, caused serious shortages of staple foodstuffs, and the effect on Bulgarian morale was obvious; in the less repressive atmosphere that prevailed in 1963, the mood of dissatisfaction soon expressed itself. It led to nervousness on the part of an essentially weak regime, thereby causing the tightening of controls noticeable in the middle of 1963.

Nowhere in Eastern Europe could the fall of Khrushchev have caused such a shock as in Sofia. Zhivkov's dependence on the Soviet leader had mounted rather than decreased since the Eighth BCP Congress; he had become more dependent both politically and economically. The question was immediately raised, both inside and outside the country, whether Zhivkov could survive the fall of his mentor. He did, of course, survive the immediate aftermath of Khrushchev's fall, but his future remained questionable. He seemed intent on saving himself by pursuing two policies. The first was to continue his complete commitment and loyalty to the Soviet Union. His old ally Khrushchev immediately became a nonentity for him; loyalty was blandly transferred to the new leadership. In internal policy, Zhivkov seemed to realize that his best course was to reactivate the promises of reform made originally at the April, 1956, plenum and later at the Eighth Congress.

Zhivkov's weakness as a national and political leader did not change, however. Indeed, it was markedly revealed in April, 1965, when an anti-regime conspiracy was uncovered in Sofia. The conspirators, including several high-ranking army officers and made up largely of former wartime resistance fighters and "native" Communists, evidently wished to establish a more national Communist regime, along the lines of Yugoslavia's or Romania's. What kind of domestic policies the conspirators stood for is not known; they seemed to be united by impatience over Zhivkov's unimaginative subservience to the Soviet Union. The chief conspirators were tried behind closed doors, and the regime attempted to belittle the incident, ridiculing it as a "Chinese plot" and as having no support whatever among the people.[6] It is probable, however, that there was considerable sympathy for the conspirators. Zhivkov's response was nevertheless a renewed pledge of allegiance to the Soviet Union. In view of his weaknesses and the failures of his regime, it was, perhaps, the only course open to him, but it only succeeded in putting him still further out of touch with popular sentiment.

Czechoslovakia

The Czechoslovak Communist Party came to power in a way completely different from that of the other Communist parties in Eastern Europe. It was not, that is, installed with the help of Soviet troops; it installed itself, by a brilliant *coup* supported, or at least favored, by a strong minority of the population. Its history was also unique. The Party had not been ruthlessly suppressed by the politicians and security police in the interwar period, as were other Communist parties, but had been allowed to operate freely in a democratic Czechoslovakia. It was a mass Party, well versed in the parliamentary methods of the First Republic. This experience and skill in the methods of constitutional government enabled it to bring off the bloodless *coup* of February, 1948—thus destroying the democracy that had allowed it to flourish. Unlike every other Communist Party, it took over a country that was very much a paying proposition. Czechoslovakia had an advanced industrial economy before World War II which had suffered little damage during the war and was in fine working order in 1948.

The Czechoslovak regime, therefore, began its career with many advantages the others lacked. But they were advantages that, for a number of reasons, could not be exploited and that in some respects even worked against the new regime rather than for it. The Party came to power when Stalinism was in full bloom, when Moscow exerted a vice-like grip on every European Communist Party except in Yugoslavia, when complete subservience to the Soviet Union was the only thinkable attitude, when a rigidly centralized and controlled economy was the only one possible, when collectivization was the only policy for agriculture. Had the Party seized power fifteen years later, in 1963, say, it would have enjoyed an utterly different climate, far more conducive to successful administration and government. The basic cause of the Czechoslovak crisis of the early 1960's was her rulers' attempt to graft an underdeveloped system and philosophy of government onto a developed country. What was good for the U.S.S.R. in 1917 was not good for the C.S.R. in 1948.

Klement Gottwald's regime, which took over in 1948, should be seen, therefore, as a typical Communist organization of the time. Its members could hardly have been expected to be anything but the dogmatists they were.

The irony of the Czechoslovak situation was, of course, that dogmatism seemed to pay off for a long time. The economy continued to work with apparent efficiency. Impressive growth rates were chalked up for industry, and if in agriculture the figures were less impressive, they still never reached the crisis or even danger mark. The standard of living continued to be high; both Czechs and Slovaks were relatively well paid and very well fed. Their freedom had been destroyed, but not their well-being. Passive resistance was widespread, but active resistance was minimal—the reign of terror from 1948 to 1953 having rendered it impossible.

It was this success that enabled the regime to withstand the tremors in 1956 and made reform seem both irrelevant and unnecessary. Orthodoxy seemed to be working, and there was neither the need nor the inclination to depart from it. The high point of self-satisfaction and complacency was reached in 1960, when Czechoslovakia triumphantly declared itself a Socialist Republic.[7]

By 1961, however, the effects of the grafting of incompatibles began to show. The economy virtually ground to a halt: industrial production in 1963 was lower than in 1962; serious food shortages began to occur; the long-neglected transport and communications system showed signs of breaking down. Overinvestment in heavy manufacturing projects, rigid centralization of economic control, the failure to rebuild old machinery and plants with its consequent bad effect on productivity, a shortage of manpower, and heavy commitments (for political purposes) in the underdeveloped countries—these were the main reasons for the crisis. The regime had driven an advanced economy into the ground; by the early 1960's, it could take no more.

Such a situation would have caused a crisis at any time. Unfortunately for the regime, the economic disintegration occurred when the second strong wind of change was blowing from Moscow. The Twenty-second Congress of the CPSU in October, 1961, with its onslaught on Stalinism and the vestiges of his system, severely shook the Czechoslovak regime when it could not afford to be shaken. It tried to shrug the whole matter off as it had in 1956, but this time it could not. Willy-nilly, it had to relax the atmosphere, allow more freedom of expression, give people a chance to complain—just when they really had something to complain about. As a result, all the weak and sore points of the nation's life, covered over for so many years, were laid bare. Radical change, long deemed unnecessary, was now urgently demanded; it came—introduced by the same leader who had always opposed it.

In March, 1953, only a few days after the death of Stalin, Klement Gottwald died. His death required realignment in the top leadership of the Party. Antonin Zapotocky became President; Viliam Siroky, a Slovak, became Premier; and Antonin Novotny became First Party Secretary. Zapotocky and Siroky were members of Gottwald's old group. Though completely different personalities, they were both the older, revolutionary type of Communist, well known in Czechoslovak politics before the war. Novotny was a different type, an *apparatchik*, essentially a product of the postwar era. He too was known before the war, since he had risen steadily in the Prague Party organization in the 1930's, but he was never prominent in national politics. Active in the Communist resistance during the war, he was arrested by the Nazis and sent to the

Mauthausen concentration camp. In 1945, he returned to his Party duties in Prague and became First Secretary of the Prague Party Committee, one of the most powerful positions in the Party and a good jumping-off place for the very highest posts. He was elected to the Central Committee in 1946, and soon became the head of the *apparatchik* bureaucratic group within the Party. Though he had little in common with Gottwald and little personal sympathy for him, Novotny assisted him in his struggle against Rudolf Slansky, the powerful Secretary General of the Party, and was one of the main instruments in the latter's downfall. Slansky was hanged in 1952. Before his execution, Novotny had obtained his seats in both the Secretariat and the Politburo and, when Gottwald died in 1953, he took over the leadership of the Party. He was not quite fifty years old at the time.

To most of the population, Novotny was unknown; he lacked the personality to catch the public eye. Gottwald had been very much a public personality; so was Zapotocky, who had a certain rough and ready charm which made him genuinely popular among the working classes. Novotny, however, was and still is shy in public and a wretched platform speaker. Glacially cold, with few apparent leadership qualities, he seemed an odd choice to succeed Gottwald. But he was an efficient bureaucrat, destined to develop into a real master of Party politics and tactics. This was where Novotny's strength lay. Had he had only the Czechoslovak Party to administer, he would have been hailed as one of the most able leaders of the modern era. But the Party was, of course, the self-proclaimed governor and director of every facet of the life of the nation. It was here that Novotny showed his severe limitations. Attaining and maintaining power is one thing, using it constructively is another. In the first, Novotny has been a master; in the second, little short of a disaster.

The first five years of Communist rule in Czechoslovakia were, in a sense, dynamic, in that they witnessed the speedy and wholesale imposition of socialist institutions, the elimination of "public enemies," and the dramatic (if superficial) transformation of society. Many aspects of public activity had, of course, already been socialized before 1948. Still, full socialization in so short a time required great zeal and energy, and, in the five years between 1948 and 1953, the face of the country was completely changed. But on the death of Gottwald, the era of "revolutionist" supremacy ended and that of "bureaucratic" supremacy was ushered in. Conservatism replaced dynamism. To Novotny and the like-minded men whom he steadily introduced into leading positions, all that needed to be done was to administer the structure that had been so hastily erected. The way to do this was simply to follow the basic tenets of Marxism-Leninism as interpreted by Stalin. This was the only known way; there was no other (if one excluded the anathematized Yugoslav system). Within his own frame of reference, Novotny did this well and efficiently; as pointed out earlier, it worked for a time. The nation was so strong that it could stand a great deal of mistreatment.

Thus, for more than seven years, Czechoslovakia functioned as the "model satellite"—economically efficient, politically stable, and loyal to the Soviet Union. The political stability was preserved partly because the economic situation was so good, but partly also because of Novotny's skill. In 1956, he moved promptly and surely to head off the trouble that, after the Twentieth Congress of the CPSU and Khrushchev's secret speech, was sure to come—even in Czechoslovakia. He made one great sacrifice on the altar of de-Stalinization in the person of Alexi Cepicka, Politburo member, Minister of Defense, and brother-in-law of Gottwald. In April, 1956, he called an all-state and Party conference and cut short dissension among the intellectuals. The situation, therefore, was sufficiently shored up to withstand the shocks of the Polish and Hungarian Octobers, and for the regime to be able to continue very much as before. In no satellite country except Romania and possibly Albania did the Twentieth Congress have so little lasting effect as in Czechoslovakia.

Novotny's choice of Cepicka as his victim was a significant one. Aside from the fact that he could not have found a more distasteful person, it was also an opportunity to get rid of one of the old Gottwald revolutionary group with which he had always been out of sympathy. A year later, the most attractive member of this group, Antonin Zapotocky, died, and many expected the vacant presidency of the Republic to be filled by Premier Siroky. But Novotny was elected, thus uniting in himself the posts of head of state and Party leader. Siroky's elevation was probably prevented not by his being a Slovak and hence unacceptable to the great majority of the population, but rather by Novotny's determination, backed by sufficient Party strength, to thwart a rival and assert the supremacy of his own *apparatchik* group in the Party. Two years later, he was to oust Siroky from the Presidency of the National Front organization and to assume that post himself. With the elimination of Cepicka, the death of Zapotocky, and the neutralization of Siroky, any danger to Novotny from the Gottwald group virtually disappeared.

Novotny's success story continued. In 1960 came the new constitution by which Czechoslovakia became a socialist republic. The C.S.R. became the C.S.S.R., and the Red Star replaced the golden crown atop the lion on the national emblem. The model satellite became the second socialist state in the world. But then, in 1961, the disillusionment began. Economic crisis threatened, and, in October of that year, the Twenty-second Congress of the CPSU was held. Novotny seems to have been taken by surprise as much as anyone by Khrushchev's second onslaught on Stalinism. It opened a Pandora's box of problems with which his well-drilled but unimaginative team could not cope.

The most urgent problem was the factionalism it stirred up at the very top of the Party hierarchy. For several years, the man most widely believed to be Novotny's potential successor had been Politburo member and Minister of the Interior Rudolf Barak. A few years younger than Novotny, Barak had risen through the Party ranks after the war, becoming First Secretary of the Brno Party organization. He was very much of the *apparatchik* group and probably owed a great deal of his early prominence to the support and patronage of Novotny. Temperamentally, however, he was very different from the First Party Secretary. He was an extrovert, warm and self-confident in public, with the common touch Novotny so conspicuously lacked—hence, well-liked by the Czechoslovak people, an extraordinary thing for a Minister of the Interior in a Communist state. He was also ambitious, and it was this that produced the collision.

Many of the key aspects of the Barak case are still unknown, but it seems clear that Barak tried to build a base of support for himself from which to challenge Novotny. He had almost certainly been attempting this before the Twenty-second Congress, for in the summer of 1961, he had been relieved of his duties as Minister of the Interior and made a Deputy Premier. (This looked like a promotion but actually meant that Barak was cut off from the base of power from which he had controlled the militia and security apparatus of the country.) Several months later, in February, 1962, it was announced that Barak had been stripped of all his positions and arrested. There was considerable confusion about what charges would be brought against him. It appeared that Novotny wished to have a political trial reminiscent of the Stalin era, but that others—and it was their view that prevailed—wanted only a criminal trial.* In the end, Barak was tried as an embezzler, thief, and conspicuous consumer, and sentenced to fifteen years' imprisonment. His real crime—and this emerged by implication in some of the speeches at the Twelfth Czechoslovak Party Congress held in December of the same year—was his attempt to use the Twenty-second Congress to his own advantage by creating a reform faction within the Party directed against Novotny.

Barak failed because he had no real base of support *inside the Party.* He may have had considerable support inside the state apparatus, but this was not where the real power lay. In any case, he had not been Minister of the Interior since the summer of 1961. His fall was significant in three respects. It showed that Novotny still controlled the Party *apparat,* and it removed from the scene the one man of personality and stature who might have been a popular alternative to him. At the same time, Novotny's forced retreat on the handling of the Barak case was the first sign of confusion and wavering in the Party machine.

The Barak case was only the most dramatic symptom of the strong dissatisfaction within the Party. The further revelations at the Twenty-second Congress about the evils of the Stalinist past had made many Czechoslovak Communists impatient to see their own slate wiped clean. This spelled danger for Novotny. He could

* In a speech in Bratislava on February 22, 1962, Novotny said that Barak had aimed at "seizing political power." This statement was carried by Radios Prague and Bratislava in their reports of the speech but was deleted in the *Rude Pravo* version of February 23. Nothing was subsequently heard of this charge.

plead that he "was not in the highest leadership at the time,"[8] *i.e.*, when such demonstrations of Stalinist justice as the Slansky and Clementis trials took place. But everyone knew that he had been sufficiently senior to have had a hand in much of the dirty work, and many suspected him of having been the main instrument of Slansky's downfall.

Novotny stage-managed the Twelfth Czechoslovak Party Congress, in December, 1962, in fine political style. There was very little change in the composition of the Presidium (Politburo) and Central Committee Secretariat, and the danger seemed to have been averted for a time. But one very important decision was made at the Congress that was to have lasting importance. The newly elected Central Committee, which, unlike the Presidium and Secretariat, contained quite a large number of new names, was entrusted with the task of inquiring into the legality of the political trials that had taken place during the period 1949–54. The extension of the period of review to 1954 was particularly embarrassing for Novotny; he had certainly been in "the highest leadership" since March, 1953, and one of the most notorious miscarriages of justice had taken place one year later. This was the sentencing of the Slovak so-called bourgeois nationalists—Laço Novomesky, Gustav Husak, and others—to long periods of imprisonment.

The Central Committee's findings on these trials were never made public, but they were divulged to a full plenum of the Committee in April, 1963. This led to the first great crack in the solid wall of defense that the Novotny leadership had put up against the forces of change. Novotny was forced to dismiss two of the oldest and most notorious Stalinists in the leadership, Karol Bacilek and Bruno Koehler—Bacilek, a Presidium member of the Czechoslovak Party and First Secretary of the Slovak Communist Party; Koehler, one of the most able members of the Party, an ethnic German whose wife had been Gottwald's secretary.

Bacilek's fall was particularly important because it brought to a head the rising discontent in Slovakia. As leader of the Slovak Party, Bacilek had been particularly disliked among both Communist and non-Communist Slovaks for his association with the centralizing policies of the Prague regime, which were based on the assumption that Slovakia was simply an ordinary region of the country and not a land inhabited by a nation distinct from the Czechs and deserving of a much greater degree of self-government.

The great weakness of the First Czechoslovak Republic had been its failure to solve the vexed nationalities problem. With the rise of Nazism and the constant enmity of an irredentist Hungary, the German and Magyar problems were incapable of solution in the inter-war years. However, the First Republic must take a great deal of the blame for the dissatisfaction in Slovakia, in that it did not grant the Slovaks the necessary autonomy or equality. As a result, the many progressive and far-sighted Slovaks who genuinely believed in the idea of Czechoslovakia, based on equality between the two nations, fought a losing battle in their native land against the clerical-fascist groups of demagogues who preyed on the nationalism and primitive Catholicism of large sections of the population.

The sorry story of the puppet Slovak republic under Msgr. Tiso during the war need not be recounted here. It produced, however, two distinct but not necessarily incompatible effects on the Slovak population as a whole. The first was the realization by most Slovaks that some form of association with the Czech lands was, after all, necessary. The second was that, despite its unfortunate character, the puppet republic had stressed the distinctiveness of the Slovaks as a nation and of Slovakia as a separate entity; hence, any association with the Czechs in the future should be on the basis of full equality—preferably on a federal basis. The Slovak Communist Party, in its own terms, had the same approach. In the underground during the war, it had operated as a unit quite independent of its Czech counterpart. It had spearheaded the Slovak national uprising against the Germans and, though this had failed disastrously, it had given Slovak Communists a feeling of independence and not unjustified pride.

Despite all its pre-putsch promises on this question, the attitude of the Czechoslovak Communist regime after it seized power, in 1948, was a great disappointment to Slovaks—Communist and non-Communist. A centralist policy more rigid than anything known in the First Republic was pursued. The separate Slovak political institutions—like the Board of Commissioners, the National Council, and the Slovak Communist Party itself—impressive though they looked on paper, became little more than rubber-stamps for the central institutions in Prague. There are three probable reasons for this attitude on the part of the Prague regime: first, the traditionally superior attitude of the Czechs toward the Slovaks, an attitude one should not write off as minor; second, the very important tenet of Communist belief that a conflict of nationalities was essentially a bourgeois, imperialist situation, and that once this situation was changed and socialism prevailed, such conflicts would disappear; third, the intelligent yet misguided feeling that bringing Slovakia up to the economic standard of the Czech lands would automatically solve the problem, that the industrialization of Slovakia would break down the separateness, the nationalism, and the religious obscurantism of the population.

The Czechoslovak Communist regime has, indeed, done a great deal for Slovakia in this sense, but without the desired result. Slovak nationalism did not wither away as a result of increased education and industrialism. In some ways, it grew more self-confident and mature with the improvements that took place, more articulate and reasonable in its demands.

After February, 1948, one of the great problems within the Party was what to do about the Slovak Party leaders who were determined to have their say about what should happen in Slovakia. In the Stalin era, of course, there was only one answer to this problem—purge them, frame them, and get rid of them. Vladimir Clementis, universally respected and one of the most attractive political figures in postwar Eastern Europe, was the most eminent of these leaders. He was the first to go, hanged with Slansky in 1952. The other Slovak leaders were purged at about the same time and, in 1954, sentenced to long periods of imprisonment. Through such ruthlessness, the Prague regime had managed to sweep the Slovak problem under the rug. It found Slovaks like Bacilek and Siroky ready to serve its ends—through conviction or opportunism—and steadily proceeded with its policy. The authority of the Slovak governing bodies was gradually diminished, and what was left of it was further and drastically reduced under the socialist constitution of 1960.

The series of misfortunes that befell Novotny in the year following the proclamation of this constitution uncovered the Slovak problem once again. The Twenty-second Congress of the CPSU, with its settling of old accounts, was adopted by a strong group of Slovak intellectuals, almost all of them Communists, as a means of forcing the Prague regime to rehabilitate the dead Clementis and restore full rights to the "bourgeois nationalists" like Novomesky and Husak. Though they had been quietly released from prison, the latter were still under the official Party ban. The ferment in Bratislava was much stronger than in Prague. This was due partly to the greater natural turbulence of the Slovaks and partly to the fact that, on the whole question of rehabilitation and reform, the Slovak Communists had a revered martyr and several living and respected symbols of the humiliation they had suffered. No Czech, after all, could get very indignant about the execution of the odious Slansky.

If the Twenty-second Congress of the CPSU had given the Slovak nationalists and reformists the encouragement they needed, Novotny's dismissal of Bacilek gave them their first important success—more important than the quietly conceded rehabilitation of Clementis and the "bourgeois nationalists." To many, the fall of Bacilek must have indicated that the whole Novotny regime was on the run. It led to a flood of anti-regime criticism against which Novotny's counters were totally ineffectual. The voice of the reformers, the Bratislava cultural weekly *Kulturny Zivot*, throughout 1963 poured out articles calling for a reform of the whole political, economic, and cultural structure. In their reformism (or revisionism, if one wants to use a rather misused word), the Slovak intellectual rebels were later enthusiastically and courageously joined by their like-minded brethren in the Czech lands. The Prague *Literarni Noviny* and *Plamen* joined in the onslaught against Novotny's dogmatist front. The first position to fall was the cultural. As a result of pressure from below, the censors were forced to relax their grip. Books by the outcast Kafka, for example, were restored to their rightful position as literature meriting respect and attention. More important was the publishing of a whole series of books pointing up the injustice and horrors of the "past period." Of these, perhaps Ladislav Mnacko's *Delayed Reportages* was the most notable, with its skillfully drawn picture of official repression and hypocrisy.*

* See below, Chapter 4.

In September, 1963, Novotny made his greatest concession to public pressure by dismissing Viliam Siroky from his post of Premier and removing him from the Party Presidium. A Slovak who had sold himself to Prague centralism, and a dogmatist to boot, Siroky had long been a target of the reformers. He was replaced as Premier by the personable, forty-year-old Jozef Lenart, himself a Slovak and a man with a good deal of popular backing. With Lenart and Alexander Dubcek, who had replaced Bacilek as Slovak First Secretary, the Party in Slovakia assumed a different look, far more congenial to the malcontents than the old one had been.

Siroky was the last piece of personal ballast Novotny had to shed in order to stay afloat. Yet the situation was such that his own position seemed to be in great danger for a time. His inability to stop widespread public criticism of the regime (he himself was never personally criticized, but he was clearly defied on many occasions), and the necessity for him to make personal changes in his entourage, meant a serious diminution in his public authority, not to mention his prestige. Three factors probably enabled him to ride the storm. The first was the slight improvement of the economic situation in 1964, especially with regard to supplies for the population. The food shortages largely disappeared and popular dissatisfaction consequently diminished. If the standard of living had shown a sharp decline, instead of the very small one that actually took place, Novotny might have had to face serious manifestations of discontent on the part of the workers, and the dangerous prospect of the sort of alliance between intellectuals and workers that had been so potent in Hungary and Poland in 1956. This he was able to avert.

Of greater importance was the personal support Novotny received from Khrushchev. The Czechoslovak CP's relations with Moscow are dealt with elsewhere.* Here, it suffices to say that, though there were probably several aspects of Novotny's policy, perhaps even of his person, of which Khrushchev did not approve, the Soviet leader had enough troubles to worry about without adding to them by engineering a change of leadership in Czechoslovakia. The biggest of these problems was the dispute with China,

* See below, Chapter 5.

and it was precisely in this dispute that he had no more loyal ally than Antonin Novotny. Therefore, on the basis of a *quid pro quo* determined more by the political situation than by any personal loyalty, Khrushchev supported Novotny. This must have been a serious blow to the hopes of Novotny's reformist opponents, who had been greatly encouraged by Khrushchev's words and deeds and who may have expected support from him in their endeavors. Khrushchev's visit to Czechoslovakia in August, 1964, to take part in the twentieth-anniversary celebrations of the Slovak Uprising showed clearly where his sympathies lay. This thunderous confirmation of Novotny's revived strength helped Novotny to cross the difficult hurdle of the celebrations of the Slovak Uprising, over the character and significance of which there had been sharp differences between himself and the Slovak nationalist reformers.

Perhaps the most important reason of all for Novotny's survival was that he never lost his grip on the Czechoslovak Communist Party machine or on the greater part of the Slovak Party machine. In bullfighting, there is always a part of the ring to which the bull repairs, where he is strongest and where he feels most at home. It is called the *querencia*. The Party machine was Novotny's *querencia*. Realizing that discretion was the better part of valor in many situations, he was prepared to make a wide range of concessions and was forced to accept defeat in cultural and economic affairs and on the Slovak issue. But he fought skillfully, courageously, and successfully to maintain his hold on the Party. As Party leader for so long, he had gathered around him a great number of *apparatchiks* who were indebted to him and dependent on him. With such powerful support, he could overawe the younger men like Lenart and Kolder whom he was forced to bring into the highest leadership. The new men, for their part, were probably afraid that if Novotny were removed they too might be endangered. After all, they had never been revisionists, and they believed fully in the supremacy of the Communist Party.

It was this basic strength, combined with his great political skill, that enabled Novotny not merely to survive, but to stage an impressive recovery and to reduce the ferment to manageable dimensions. In Czechoslovakia, a considerable area of personal, intellectual, and cultural freedom was carved out, not to be destroyed in the foreseeable future. Freedom of speech in Prague and other Czechoslovak cities surprised most visitors; many Czechs and Slovaks began traveling to the West; the country's film industry recaptured much of its old vitality; the Prague theater became one of the most interesting in Eastern Europe and more interesting than many in the West. The once moribund National Assembly took a new lease on life, albeit in its subordinate role of constructive critic and advisor. By 1964, all these changes could be manifested without defiance of Novotny. Forced by the realities of the situation, he had learned to accept them. The sort of "antagonistic" criticism against which he had so unsuccessfully railed in 1963 decreased noticeably in 1964. The Czechoslovak press continued to be lively and critical, but the criticisms expressed were those the regime permitted as "honest" and "constructive."

Novotny had succeeded in containing the ferment, and by the middle of 1964 he was acting no longer as a repressive, dogmatic leader, but as a middle-of-the-roader, guiding and directing the forces of reform. Far from being defensive, he had now taken the initiative in several directions, most notably in the sphere of economic reform. Such reform had been long overdue in Czechoslovakia, but it was only the economic crisis of 1962–63 that finally forced the regime to consider proposals that were in any way far-reaching or fundamental. Everyone, even Novotny, realized that something had to be done, but opinions differed widely on what that should be. There were, broadly speaking, two schools of thought—one arguing that the present system of economic planning and management was basically sound and that reform was only necessary within the old framework; the other demanding a root-and-branch change of the structure. The first school was initially favored by Novotny and the Party machine; the second was advocated by almost all professional economists. Eventually, however, the gravity of the situation forced Novotny to favor a reform much closer to the ideas of the second, rather than the first, school. The result was the publication in October, 1964, of a comprehensive scheme of reform quite startling in its boldness.[9] Once convinced that there was no alternative to radical reform, Novotny had wisely decided to accept it and "take it over." By doing so, he not only won a certain grudging respect as the flexible exponent of an exciting reform, but also put himself in a much stronger political position to moderate the reform if its implementation showed a tendency to carry the country too far along the road of unorthodoxy. The great danger of the new Czechoslovak economic model, from the Party's point of view, was that it might lead to a serious diminution of political control of the economy. That a diminution would take place seemed more or less certain. Novotny was anxious to make it as small as possible. His efforts in this direction were certain to be among the most intriguing aspects of Czechoslovak internal affairs in the foreseeable future.

Khrushchev's fall, undoubtedly a blow to Novotny, ironically improved his standing within Czechoslovakia. Astonished and affronted by the ouster in Moscow, Novotny refused to make the trip to meet the new Soviet leaders at the celebrations of the anniversary of the October Revolution in November, 1964. It was not until a month later that he consented to lead a delegation to the Soviet Union and restore "normal" relations between the two regimes. Compared with the years under Khrushchev, there is evidently a certain aloofness on Prague's part, and a greater stress on self-reliance. This self-reliance quite possibly will lead Novotny to make further efforts to popularize himself and his regime. Novotny now seems inclined to make concessions—albeit concessions granted from above, and at a pace that he himself sets.

East Germany

The German Democratic Republic, an international problem rather than a nation-state, cannot be analyzed in the same way as other Communist states of Eastern Europe. Its internal political situation has been so inextricably intertwined with the whole range of problems affecting East and West that it would be unrealistic, for the purposes of this book, to discuss more than a few general trends that have affected political life in that artificial unit.

One of the many paradoxes of the G.D.R. is that, while it was obviously intended to be an example of true democracy and progress for the benighted citizens of West Germany, it only succeeded in becoming the most oppressive and crisis-ridden of all the Soviet outposts. One reason for this was the character and training of Walter Ulbricht and the top leadership of the Socialist Unity (Communist) Party. Ulbricht, an able administrator with a good intellect, despite his rather ridiculous appearance, had his predisposition to rigidity and dogmatism strengthened by his stay in Moscow from 1938 until the end of World War II. Returning to power as satrap of a Communist province rather than as head of state, he could not even begin to think about adapting his policy to meet the national needs of the population he governed. Indeed, there was little incentive for him to do so during the Stalinist period, since it was a generally accepted fact of life that the East European states were, first and foremost, appendages of the Soviet Union.

After the Hungarian and Polish upheavals of October, 1956, however, methods of Soviet control shifted. Emphasis was now placed on more political autonomy and the need for the regimes to identify themselves more closely with the peoples they were governing. Prior to 1957, there had also been the important question of what, in fact, was to be done with the G.D.R. The question of some kind of reunification with West Germany was still being considered by the Soviet leaders, probably until the international Communist conference of November, 1957. Until the final decision in favor of separatism, the Ulbricht regime was essentially a holding operation.

But when the decision for separatism was made, Ulbricht was completely unable to do anything to make his regime more acceptable to the population (even had he been disposed to do so). The reason, of course, was the overwhelming desire of the East Germans to be reunited with their brothers in West Germany, and —because of the great prosperity and freedom in the Federal Republic—on the Federal Republic's terms. The escape hatch through Berlin was both the dramatic symbol of this desire and a constant reminder to Ulbricht of his complete inability to approach any sort of identity with the East Germans.

His only policy, therefore, was one of repression—to put out as many fires as he could. At the same time, however, he pressed ahead with building the essentials of socialism in the G.D.R., the most notable example of this being the great spurt toward the full collectivization of agriculture in 1960. Economically, the G.D.R. had become a liability, mainly because of Soviet spoliation in the early years and the steady exodus of skilled manpower through Berlin later. Any question of independent action or of deviation from the Soviet pattern was unthinkable because of the very nature of the regime, the character of the G.D.R., the serious economic weakness, and, last but not least, the presence in East Germany of 300,000 Soviet troops.

The 1957 decision in favor of separatism was only the first step in the attempt to give the G.D.R. some kind of a distinct political and economic profile. It was an important step because it gave Ulbricht the encouragement he needed to press ahead with ruthless socialization. While reunification was still officially a considered proposition, it could not be done, because of the uncertainty that at some time in the fairly near future it might be undone. Once reunification was dropped, the building of socialism became Ulbricht's means of ensuring the growth of two Germanies with distinct political, social, and economic institutions; hence, of making reunification a more difficult proposition than it had been earlier.

But the ease with which G.D.R. citizens could escape through Berlin made the task of building a distinctive state impossible. Not only was it the source of grave economic weakness; its psychological impact was even more serious. The regime was under no illusions about where the East Germans' sympathies lay: it was plain that a population with its heart already in the Federal Republic, with its eyes trained on the checkpoints in Berlin, and with the knowledge that it could pass through these more or less at will—such a population was hardly the stuff of which socialism could be made.

Logically, the Berlin Wall was the necessary and inevitable consequence of the Soviet decision in favor of G.D.R. separatism. One should not, therefore, regard it as the most striking example of Ulbricht's wickedness and tyranny. If a Kadar or a Gomulka had held the reins in Pankow, either might have pressed the Soviet Union to grant permission to build the wall just as persistently as did Ulbricht. The Iron Curtain Kadar built on the Hungarian frontier with Austria after 1956 was, in principle, no different from the wall that Ulbricht was to build in 1961; yet, although his Iron Curtain has ceased to be really necessary, Kadar has been reluctant to take it down.

The Soviet hesitation in granting permission for the wall to be built was prompted by questions of international policy and relations with the West. In 1958, Khrushchev delivered his famous ultimatum that the Berlin question must be solved and a German peace treaty signed, but, in 1959, in one of those sudden switches of policy for which he became famous, the Soviet leader began his strong and partially successful play for a *rapprochement* with the West. The erection of a wall in Berlin would have been thoroughly out of keeping with the "spirit of Camp David," and since the "national" interest of the G.D.R. was something the Soviet Union could always afford to ignore, Ulbricht's requests were continually being shelved.

Yet the more Ulbricht tried to impose socialism on the citizens of East Germany, the stronger became their desire to get away. This became particularly noticeable after the virtual completion of collectivization in 1960. From that time on, the situation snowballed. As popular dissatisfaction increased, more people left; this only increased the demands of the Pankow regime that something be done to stop the outflow; and the people's awareness that the days of free exit might be numbered only further intensified their urge to get out. The Soviet Union, faced with the prospect of a steadily disappearing satellite, finally was forced to accede to Ulbricht's pleadings. Better to risk a temporary deterioration in relations with the West and the severe propaganda defeat the wall involved, that to see its Western bastion wither away. As it turned out, the only serious loss was in the propaganda field.

The Western powers—though they could never admit this openly—may have greeted the building of the Berlin Wall, on August 13, 1961, with a certain relief. The ever-mounting drain through Berlin might have created a serious international situation. The wall now prevented this; at the same time, it gave the West a propaganda advantage. Moreover, if Western troops had intervened to prevent the building of the wall, the danger of an insurrection in East Germany on the style of the workers' revolt in June, 1953, would have been great; and the dilemma posed by Hungary in 1956 might have been recreated in the heart of Europe. In the minds of some

Western officials, the wall was perhaps a practical, if not honorable, way out of their difficulties. This attitude was to have its repercussions. Western passiveness almost certainly encouraged Khrushchev to embark on his Cuban adventure only a little more than a year later. Here, of course, he lost his gamble, but not before the world approached the precipice of nuclear war. As for the peoples of East Germany and of Eastern Europe as a whole—while applauding the prompt action of the American administration over Cuba, they could not help but conclude that the United States had one policy for the Western Hemisphere and another for them.

For the Ulbricht regime on the one hand, and the East German people on the other, the wall created a completely new situation. For the first time, they were in a sealed-off room together. The initial dissatisfaction and anger the act itself had caused in the G.D.R. led to a wave of official repression as severe as anything that had gone before. But after the fury had spent itself, the East German population settled down to accepting the reality of the situation. This did not mean that they became passive—far from it; rather, their opposition took a different form. The avenue of escape cut off, their only recourse was to try to make the G.D.R. a better place in which to live and to force the Ulbricht regime by various pressures into changing its character. No one who knew this regime considered it an easy task, but it was the only alternative. Thus, after the beginning of 1963, there was considerable ferment among the East German writers, scholars, and students; great pressure on the part of the technocratic and managerial classes for a sounder system of economic planning; and discernible rumblings from the thoroughly dissatisfied worker and peasant classes.

After his immediate, almost Pavlovian response of repression, Ulbricht himself came to realize that change was necessary. There is also little doubt that his protector, Khrushchev, applied a good deal of pressure for him to mend his ways. Typically, however, Ulbricht began his reform program in a field he considered the least dangerous and the most pressing—that of economics. In 1964, the regime announced that discussions would begin on a whole new system of economic planning and management. This would involve considerable decentralization and autonomy at the factory level, much greater expertise in management, far more attention to profitability, and a freer play for the laws of supply and demand. This program will be discussed in greater detail in the chapter on economic affairs. Here it is sufficient to say that it was quite startling in its boldness. Of course, in spite of the massive defections, the G.D.R. always had a great deal of economic know-how. It was not surprising that such a program could be conceived; it *was* surprising that it passed the political censors. It was the first great breach in Ulbricht's other and older wall, that of conservative and dogmatic orthodoxy, of Stalinism.

At first, Ulbricht may have believed that this creative program of economic rationalization was all that need be done, that he could still, like King Canute, keep back the waves of greater political and cultural freedom. He certainly tried hard. But in the cultural sphere, despite his fulminations and those of his agit-prop officials—despite, for example, the continued blacklisting of Franz Kafka at a time when that writer was being rehabilitated and honored in neighboring Czechoslovakia—his regime was quietly forced to accept a very definite widening of the area of cultural and educational freedom.

A man like Professor Robert Havemann, who gave "provocative" lectures to his students and a "subversive" interview to a Hamburg newspaper early in 1964, could still lose his post at the Humboldt University and be expelled from the university's Party organization.[10] Yet even Havemann was not imprisoned; and those intellectuals, especially writers, who chose a more circumspect way of expressing their individuality had a certain degree of actual freedom in 1964. Politically, the most important single act of relaxation was the amnesty granted in September, 1964, on the occasion of the fifteenth anniversary of the founding of the German Democratic Republic. *Neues Deutschland,* the mouthpiece of the Socialist Unity Party, revealed that about 10,000 prisoners were released, including a considerable number of political prisoners.[11] The general political atmosphere appeared to have eased; more freedom of discussion was permitted than ever before.

These gestures were partly aimed at improving the G.D.R.'s tawdry image in the world as a whole. The various agreements with the city administration of West Berlin allowing West Berliners to visit their relatives across the Wall during holiday periods, and old-age pensioners (i.e., expendable personnel) to visit West Berlin on similar occasions, were conceived even more directly with this aim in view. Whether such actions would ever achieve their desired end was more than doubtful. One other motive behind the political and cultural relaxation which began in 1964 was the necessity, reluctantly accepted by Ulbricht, of keeping up with, or not remaining too far behind, the other East European Communist regimes in the de-Stalinization process. A regime like that in Romania could afford to become isolated in the bloc; in fact, it eagerly desired it. The East German regime, however, had to fight against isolation and show at least some conformity to a trend it still basically distrusted.

Thus, both internal and external considerations forced the Pankow regime into change. The change was not fundamental. In 1964, probably more people were sent to jail in East Germany on political charges than in the rest of Eastern Europe put together. But at least things had begun to move—faster, indeed, than many had ever thought possible. In 1965, the process continued. Economic reform was carried on, and the standard of living improved slightly. But perhaps the most significant trend was the conscious effort by the Ulbricht regime to win support from the new technical intelligentsia that was coming to the fore in East Germany. This powerful class could, if properly catered to, acquire a strong vested interest in the continuance of the G.D.R. Reunification would seriously jeopardize its privileges, even its position. If its demands were met, therefore, it could become a powerful counterbalance to the sentiments of the mass of the population. Concessions to this class should, of course, alleviate the condition of East German society as a whole and, in this sense, would constitute a favorable development. But they might add yet another obstacle to reunification, which is what the average East German still most passionately desires.

Hungary

So much has been written about the events leading up to the Hungarian Revolution and about the Revolution itself that it is unnecessary to recapitulate them here. I will deal, therefore, mainly with what has become known as Janos Kadar's "new course." It is this policy, its character and its implementation, that became the most striking feature of Hungarian life after 1961.

Many problems faced Janos Kadar when he was installed by Soviet troops in November, 1956. His main task was to complete the work of repression and then to rebuild the socialist state in Hungary. Once the back of the Revolution had been broken, the mopping-up operations were not difficult, although they continued throughout 1957 and 1958. These two years did not witness as grim a reign of terror as had prevailed in the depths of the Rakosi era. Yet, in many ways, they were more tragic for the Hungarian people because they saw the slow grinding down of all the hopes that had been kindled at the beginning of Imre Nagy's "new course," in 1953. Moreover, the events of 1957–58 took place in an atmosphere of anticlimax and embittered disappointment produced by the failure of the 1956 Revolution, and they affected a very large number of people. Once the account had been settled with those who were in any way suspected of aiding and abetting the Revolution, the new and very shaky Kadar regime turned its attention to the two classes that had combined to produce that Revolution: the workers and the intellectuals. The failure of the Revolution had, in itself, broken the link between these two classes; Kadar's job was now to break down the organization of each class separately. Despite Kadar's promises, the form in which the workers' councils had existed during the Revolution was destroyed; the writers' circles were also suppressed and replaced by a new Writers' Association—obviously a tool of the regime. Several of the most prominent writers, like Tibor Dery and Gyula Hay, were put in jail for the part they had played in 1956. The cynical climax of the whole campaign of repression was reached in June, 1958, when Imre Nagy and several of his closest collaborators were sentenced to death as a deterrent to "revisionists" everywhere.

The repression in the two years following the Revolution was easy to carry out. All opposition had been broken; the population was dispirited and disillusioned. What was much more difficult for Kadar was to create something out of the rubble of 1956. He had first to rebuild the Party, the new Hungarian Socialist Workers' Party, as it was called after the Revolution. It was, in the main, the old Hungarian Communist Party with a new label. Its rank and file was overwhelmingly dogmatist or Stalinist; the Imre Nagy wing of the old Party had disappeared. The mass of *apparatchiks* in the new Party looked forward to a return of something resembling the Rakosi era. The Revolution had, after all, been defeated; its lesson, in their eyes, was not that more tolerance was needed, but more control. Kadar and the group around him, however, were certainly not men of this ilk. Several of them, including Kadar himself, had suffered imprisonment and even torture at the hands of the old regime. They fully realized that there could be no going back. They were centrists in their political outlook. Once the necessary repression had been carried out, they had to set about building a Communist society in Hungary. The old Rakosi men and methods had failed, and something new must be tried.

The main prerequisite was to build a bridge to the people. This had always proved a well-nigh impossible task for almost every Communist regime in Eastern Europe. Because of the population's contempt for the Kadar regime, it was even more difficult in Hungary than elsewhere. Kadar had first, therefore, to try to heal the wound of 1956 and then harness the talents and good will of all for the task of socialist construction. It was little use looking for help to the great mass of his Party, which saw no need for a new approach to the people. Moreover, Kadar had always been suspect in the eyes of many in the Hungarian Party. Every dogmatist, no doubt, welcomed the Russian tanks in November, 1956, but they did not welcome the new leader the tanks brought with them. Kadar was known as an old enemy of Rakosi and Gerö; now he was coming back under the auspices of Nikita Khrushchev, the man whose campaign against Stalin and whose antipathy for Stalin's followers in Hungary had been the sole cause, in their minds, for the debacle of 1956.

One can argue, therefore, that what later evolved into the Kadar "new course" was caused by two factors. The first, and most important, was the need to establish some rapport with the people. The second was the very narrow base of Kadar's support within his own Party. His following was probably always smaller than that enjoyed by any other Communist Party leader, with the possible exception of Zhivkov in Bulgaria. If he and his coterie were to achieve anything, they had to appeal to the people over the heads of their numerous opponents. Such a situation, and the policy arising from it, often made Kadar appear very unorthodox from a doctrinaire Communist point of view. He was always a flexible, tolerant, even sentimental, man with a good deal of warmth and human feeling. Yet his flexibility lay in the methods he used to reach the goal; about the goal—socialism and, eventually, Communism—he showed himself to be strictly orthodox. The collectivization of agriculture, effected in three stages between 1959 and 1961, showed that economic and psychological considerations had to take a back seat when one of the basic tenets of Communist belief was involved. Here, he proved less flexible than Gomulka. Kadar's pragmatism, then, should be seen against the background of a basic orthodoxy and simple devotion to Leninist Communism.

Kadar's "new course" began to be discernible as early as 1960, but what gave it its greatest impetus was the Twenty-second Congress of the CPSU. This was the green light from Khrushchev, his friend and protector, that Kadar needed. Throughout 1962, the new course was in full swing, and it received its consecration at the Eighth Hungarian Party Congress in November of that year.[12]

What were the essentials of this program? The first was that, within the Party and government itself, there should be stability, democracy, and an absence of the illegal methods used in the Rakosi era. At the top, there should be collective leadership instead of one-man rule. Kadar was certainly the acknowledged leader of the regime; in 1961 he assumed the Premiership in addition to his post of First Party Secretary. Despite this fact, and although a certain aura, even legend, had grown up around him, there was no personality cult connected with him. There was reason to believe that he always listened to the advice of his colleagues and deferred to the opinions of experts. In this sense, he was a welcome contrast to Gomulka, whose autocratic manner and narrow-mindedness alienated all but a few devoted followers. In his control over the Party, Kadar depended on persuasion rather than on force and terror. Against an intractable old dogmatist like Imre Dogei, he might be forced to use the weapon of expulsion,* but to many a dogmatist opponent, he showed remarkable leniency; to those pre-

* Dogei, a former Minister of Agriculture, was expelled from the Party in April, 1962, for "dogmatism" and "lack of discipline."

pared to support him, he showed considerable generosity. Antal Apro, a prominent member of the old Rakosi clique, was retained as a member of the Politburo and became Hungary's chief delegate to the Council for Mutual Economic Assistance (COMECON). Karoly Kiss, another prominent old Rakosi supporter, was less fortunate, but he was dropped from the Politburo—in a gracious, courteous manner—only when it became obvious that he could not reconcile himself to further changes. Gyorgy Marosan, who was second in the Party only to Kadar before his fall in 1962, evidently had to be dismissed because of his demagogy and uncooperativeness; but, again, he was let down lightly and generously. Nor was such treatment given only to people at the top. Worthy old Party opponents in the provinces were given every chance to adapt themselves to the new order, and a great deal of patience was shown them. The contrast with the Rakosi period could not have been greater. It was this atmosphere that produced a remarkable stability in the Party and state leading bodies, a fact to which the regime press often pointed with pride.

This atmosphere of relaxation and public decency was not reserved for the Party. It spread over the whole population. The secret police changed both its name and its character. A remarkable amount of freedom of speech was permitted, and constructive criticism—the definition of "constructive" was quite broad—was actively encouraged. Class hatred was discouraged, and for the first time since 1948, people could breathe freely. An atmosphere almost of friendliness became noticeable. In March, 1963, a general amnesty was declared which involved the release of many thousands of political prisoners.

Kadar took more tangible steps to try to heal the wounds of 1956 and to mobilize all creative forces for the building of socialism. He was prepared to take men as they were and to proceed from there. He never lost touch with ordinary Hungarian opinion and sentiment, and he also had no illusions about how his countrymen regarded him in the beginning, or what they thought of socialism. He therefore laid stress on what he thought they might respond to: the creation of a strong and viable economy in Hungary (albeit a socialist one) with corresponding rewards of place and privilege for those who contributed most, regardless of whether or not they belonged to the Party or actively sympathized with socialism. Socialism was to be built in the framework of the all-people's state and under the slogan "He who is not against us is with us," which Kadar first used in December, 1961.[13] All men of good will with skills to offer were urged to put them at the service of the state regardless of their social origin or previous political affiliation. In theory, even the highest positions of state were open to non-Party men or women. It has not been possible to ascertain just how far this principle was actually put into practice, but it was beyond doubt that more than lip-service was paid to it. For example, in the new Hungarian Parliament, elected in February, 1963, 40 per cent of the members did not belong to the Party; in the new local councils, elected at the same time, 62 per cent of the members were not in the Party. In 1964, there was also a considerable increase of the non-Party element in the committees of the People's Patriotic Front and certain specifically Party committees; even the Central Committee invited non-Party experts to their sessions. Another proof of the regime's good will was the introduction, in the summer of 1963, of a new ruling regarding admission to the universities. Under this ruling, the "social origin" of the applicants was disregarded.

The introduction of this undoctrinaire and pragmatic emphasis on partnership in economic construction did not mean that ideology was ignored. In fact, the Eighth Party Congress, in November, 1962, proclaimed a so-called Marxist-Leninist offensive. However, the weapons to be used in this offensive were not to be those of terror or "administrative measures," but of persuasion and debate. Actually, when Kadar and his publicists talked about an offensive, what they really meant was a long battle of attrition. There was never any attempt to force socialism down the people's throats; what the regime attempted to do was combat the more overt manifestations of "non-Marxist-Leninist" beliefs.

The need for this became greater when, after 1960, Hungary was exposed to those "non-Marxist-Leninist" beliefs more than ever before. The number of tourists from the West bringing hard currency with them increased year by year, and products of Western "bourgeois" culture steadily streamed into the country. Equally important was the fact that, early in 1964, Western broadcasts to

Hungary were no longer jammed. Conversely, the number of Hungarians allowed to visit the West increased explosively after 1962. In the first nine months of 1963, the number was 73,000; in the same period in the following year, it was 110,000. The increased commercial and cultural relations with the West also contributed significantly to the growing contact.

This "double exposure" led to an upsurge of regime propaganda against the imperialists' "Trojan Horse methods." Hungarians were frequently warned that the imperialists' new "ideological tactic" was to "soften up" the political allegiance, morale, and clear-headedness of the population in socialist countries by using these many closer contacts to smuggle in bourgeois, nationalistic, and anti-Soviet views. It was repeated time and again that "peaceful coexistence," right and necessary though it was, did not imply "ideological coexistence—quite the contrary. The closer the contact between the two worlds, the greater must be the distance between them ideologically.[14]

On still another sector of the ideological front—that of religion—the regime found it necessary to exercise caution. Some 70 per cent of the Hungarian people are Catholic, 21 per cent Presbyterian, 4 per cent Lutheran, and about 1 per cent Jewish. A considerable section of the population is, of course, only nominally Christian, but the regime press often admitted that the majority of Hungarians were still under the influence of religion. This included some Party members, especially in the provinces.

The regime made no bones about its ultimate objective of wiping out all traces of religion, but somehow it had to reconcile the propaganda activities that worked toward that objective with the political desire for some kind of *modus operandi* with the churches in the current stage of socialist development in Hungary. Officially, there was no persecution of religion, although there were, in fact, local instances of this. There was a good deal of "peaceful persuasion," often involving some chicanery, in efforts to dissuade parents from having their children enrolled for religious instruction. Despite this, it was unofficially estimated in 1963 that about half the pupils at elementary schools and about a quarter of the students at higher schools were enrolled for these classes.

For political reasons, the government still continued to grant a yearly subsidy of some 80 million *forint* (approximately $3.2 million at the tourist rate of exchange) to maintain the ministers of the various churches. This was done in the hope that the clergy would exert their still strong influence over large sections of the population to urge them to work for the "construction of socialism." With the Protestant and Jewish clergy, the regime had always had considerable success. After the "neutralization" of Cardinal Mindszenty, it also had success with the Catholic clergy—much more than did the Polish regime. But the Roman Catholic Church continued to be a serious problem for the regime, despite the fact that Mindszenty's successors as chairman of the Bench of Bishops, first Archbishop Grösz and then Archbishop Hamvas, sought to accommodate the Church to its new situation in a much more realistic way than could have been expected of the implacable Cardinal. The regime, for its part, within the limits imposed by its political and ideological objectives, sincerely tried to improve its relations with the Church and was prepared to make concessions to achieve this. This would not only make its task much easier inside Hungary but would also greatly improve the Hungarian image in the West.

There could, of course, never be any real settlement of relations between Church and state in Hungary, or between Budapest and Washington, until the vexed question of Cardinal Mindszenty, a "prisoner" in the American Legation since 1956, was resolved. But a change in attitude on the part of both the Vatican and the Hungarian regime did produce an important, if limited, agreement in September, 1964, whereby a number of long vacant bishoprics were filled. This was hailed by the regime as an important step toward the consolidation of national unity and "socialist democracy" on the basis of a "constructive" dialogue between believers and non-believers. It may also be noted that this was the first agreement the Vatican concluded with a Communist state.

It was precisely this agreement, welcomed though it was by the regime, that caused considerable concern. Just as increasing contacts with the West showed the necessity to fight more strongly against "bourgeois" ideology, so the accord with the Vatican, and the increased confidence the Catholic clergy felt as a result, showed the necessity of fighting more strongly against clerical and religious influence. Under a man like Archbishop Hamvas, the Catholic Church would never be the organized, tightly-knit force it always was under Cardinal Wyszynski in Poland. At the local level, however, there was a danger that the clergy would begin to assert themselves far more than ever before. In July, 1965, a number of Catholic priests were convicted on charges of poisoning the minds of the young against the "people's order," a clear sign of the regime's concern.

The Kadar regime continued to pin its hopes on being able to influence the young, but it was probably the young who showed more cynicism than any other section of the population. It is true that in 1964 the Hungarian Young Communist League had about 800,000 members against a total Party strength of almost 600,000; but among this very large number, few were devoted Communists. The vast majority simply joined for the undoubted advantages which that organization provided. Those young people who had the opportunity to travel to the West often returned cynical or exasperated over the low standard of living in their homeland. It was difficult to see the Hungarian regime getting far with its "ideological offensive" once the Hungarian presence in the West—and the Western presence in Hungary—had been established.

One must draw a distinction, however, between the chronic difficulties the Kadar regime had in molding the Communist man and the attitude of the majority of the population toward the Kadar regime itself. Despite their endless grumbling about conditions, many Hungarians would agree, if challenged, that Kadar was the best leader Hungary could have had under the circumstances. This astonishing metamorphosis of Kadar, from the despised traitor of 1956 to the grudgingly acknowledged leader of 1964, was made possible by two factors. The first concerned the population itself. The events of October–November, 1956, produced a profound disillusionment in Hungary. The collapse of the Revolution and the failure of the Western powers to come to its aid caused many Hungarians drastically to reappraise their country's situation. Stark realism forced them to accept Soviet hegemony of the Communist political system for an indefinite period of time. The task now was to make that reality as comfortable and tolerable as possible. The second factor was Kadar's policy of conciliation; Hungarians compared this policy, with all its limitations, to Rakosi's, and they knew which they preferred.

All benefited, in one form or another, from Kadar's policy. The relaxation of oppression had universal application. But most of the benefits did not go to most of the people. The general standard of living did rise appreciably after 1956, but it was still low in 1964 and caused much dissatisfaction. Moreover, such advantages as the availability of important posts to non-Party members and the disregarding of social origin or previous affiliations did not affect the ordinary man: he would never attain an important post in any case, his social origin had always been impeccable from the Communist point of view, and his previous political affiliations, if any, were probably not right-wing. The main beneficiaries of the new order were the professional classes and the intellectuals, not the workers or peasants.

Of course, Kadar realized this and genuinely tried to meet the just demands of most of the population by well-conceived material incentive schemes in industry and, especially, in agriculture. But, if the first four years of his "new course" were any indication, it was doubtful whether he would ever be able to harness the full energies of the people for the building of socialism even if he could succeed in significantly raising the standard of living. Perhaps no East European Communist regime would ever be able to do this, but, in Hungary, the situation had a particular poignancy, for Kadar had been consciously and deliberately trying to impose a contract on the population that it would not accept. As he saw it, his side of the contract was to carry out his policy of conciliation; this he sincerely did. In return, he expected the people to put their shoulders to the socialist wheel. But the people recognized no contract. They accepted everything that Kadar gave them and expected more. The leniency, the tolerance, and the friendliness of the atmosphere led to absenteeism, slack labor discipline, stealing, and innumerable other "petty bourgeois" manifestations. This is not to say that the Hungarian people did not work hard. Many of them began to work harder than ever before, but not in the "right" kind of way. By 1964, many men in Hungary were holding two or even three jobs and only came to their main place of work to "rest up." Their object was to earn enough money, by hook or by crook, to buy the consumer goods that were coming onto the market in abundance for the first time. A selfish kind of materialism had become the order of the day, against which the regime could rail but which it could do little to counteract.

A similar situation in Poland in 1957 and 1958 was one of the most important factors producing the retrogression that began to be obvious in 1959 and has continued ever since. What happened in Poland could happen in Hungary. If the stagnation in the economy continued, strong voices raised in the Party would probably urge greater discipline and the use of more coercive methods to obtain it. The essential difference between the situations in the two countries was that Poland's Gomulka was never the active proponent of a new course leading to liberalization and subsequent slackness, but was, by nature, a strong disciplinarian who readily introduced the retrogression, while Kadar's name had become inextricably linked with liberalization, the failure of which would involve a great blow to his prestige and authority.

As noted earlier, he was never popular with the rank and file of his own Party. At the very top, he always had a closely knit group of followers in the Politburo and Secretariat, men like Gyula Kallai, Sandor Gaspar, Istvan Szirmai, and Bela Bisku. In recent years, he had also steadily introduced younger "technocrats" into leading positions. But he was still faced by large masses of dogmatically inclined *apparatchiks* who viewed his whole policy with profound mistrust. This opposition was never organized and was without a leader, but it could never be written off. It would only require a real economic crisis for the potential danger to become actual. Then, Kadar's whole policy and perhaps his position would be threatened. While Khrushchev was in power, Kadar could feel safe. There was, between these two men, a particularly close relationship based on gratitude, personal affection, and complicity in the great tragedy of 1956. With the fall of Khrushchev, one of Kadar's main bulwarks collapsed. Now, his strength was not so much the Hungarian Party as the Hungarian people. The irony of the situation was that the people wanted him but would not work for him. He was caught in a dilemma for which there was no easy solution.

In June, 1965, Kadar resigned as Premier and was succeeded by

Gyula Kallai, a Politburo member and Deputy Premier, one of Kadar's most trusted associates. This move had been expected for some time; it had probably been postponed so as not to give the impression that it was a consequence of Khrushchev's fall in the Soviet Union. It did not mean that Kadar had lost any power; he continued as Party leader and as the regime's top man. Nor did it seem that his "new course" would alter. But Kallai is much more efficient and tougher than Kadar; the change was probably thought necessary to bring a more business-like approach into the government and to crack down on the prevailing *Schlamperei*. It remains to be seen whether this can be done without curtailing the freedoms that have been granted the Hungarian people.

Poland

A British journalist, no specialist on East European affairs but shrewd enough politically to know how most lands lie, visited Poland in 1958. The visa application was a mere formality, a much less lengthy process than in the case of, say, the United States. The same journalist applied for a Polish visa in 1963. Until almost the last minute he did not know whether his application would be approved. When he motored into Poland from East Germany, he was subjected to a lengthy and not particularly courteous check on the frontier.

The case of this British journalist was not universal, but it was typical enough to serve as a symbol of what had become known in Poland as the "retreat from October."

For several years after the upheaval of October, 1956, the stereotyped Western image of Wladyslaw Gomulka was that of a man who hardly deserved to be called a Communist at all; rather, a Marxist of the European social democracy and a Polish patriot to boot. The image persisted for a while in certain quarters, but even in the West it began eventually to change; in Poland, it had been wiped out completely by 1962, or even earlier. Gomulka was swept into power in October, 1956, by forces and circumstances over which he had little control. He was not the creator of October but its product; once firmly in power, he began slowly but steadily to disappoint the many hopes the Polish people and all friends of Poland had placed in him.

One could not, however, deny Gomulka his great strength of character and personality, his real political ability in the sphere of Party management and control, and a certain independence in outlook in his dealings with the Soviet Union. This independence—"distinctiveness" would be a better word—began in October, 1956, when he withstood Khrushchev's arrogance with dignity, and continued in a lower key ever afterward under his banner of "the Polish road to socialism." It also showed itself during the Sino-Soviet dispute in his clear unwillingness to go along with Khrushchev to the point of reading China out of the socialist camp. To these different attributes should also be added Gomulka's essential "Polishness," a feature that enabled him, despite self-imposed isolation, to understand how his fellow countrymen responded to given situations. It was probably this Polishness that prevented the "retreat from October" from being more rapid and more serious. In addition to these public qualities were those private virtues of modesty and self-denial which were certainly not found in such Communist leaders as Tito, Hoxha, or Gheorghiu-Dej.

Still, the basic facts about Gomulka, as far as internal Polish politics was concerned, were his strong and orthodox Communist convictions, his authoritarianism, and his mistrust of the spontaneity that brought him back to power in 1956 and had placed Poland's future in his hands. Poland's "own road to socialism" was never, in Gomulka's view, a liberal or a revisionist one. There was very little in it that was constructive or positive. It was essentially a negative or conservative concept, based on a compromise between doctrinaire orthodoxy and a recognition that popular attitudes and prejudices had to be taken into account.

Roughly speaking, the main features of what became known in Poland as the new policy of October, 1956, were: (1) the discontinuance of police terror; (2) a relative freedom of cultural and creative activity; (3) a *modus vivendi* between Church and State; and (4) the guarantee of private ownership in agriculture. To these four might be added a fifth—the improvement of relations with the West, especially with the United States. It may be said that in only one of these did Gomulka genuinely believe, and that was the first. He had, of course, not hesitated to use police terror between 1945 and 1948 when he was rounding up political and class enemies of the new order. Even during this period, however, there was sufficient evidence to show that he disapproved of some of the methods used by the more ferocious of his colleagues.[15] Later, he was himself a victim of Stalinist terror, and when he returned to power in 1956 he was sincerely determined not to resort to such methods himself. The abandonment of "administrative methods" in their worst form, and its guarantee by Gomulka, was one of the very great gains made by the Polish Party and people.

One can argue that point four, the retention of private ownership in agriculture, was also one of the genuinely held tenets of Gomulka's creed; his policy and speeches before he was disgraced in 1948 may be cited as evidence of this. But Gomulka was never *for* private ownership of any sort; he was simply *against* the kind of compulsory collectivization that would alienate the large mass of the Polish people and have ruinous effects on production. The fact that Polish agriculture remained overwhelmingly in peasant hands—recent figures show that 87 per cent of the arable land is privately owned—was due, again, to his political sagacity and his "Polishness."

On point three, the *modus vivendi* between State and Church, neither Gomulka nor the Roman Catholic Primate, Cardinal Wyszynski, had any illusions. Gomulka came to Cardinal Wyszynski in 1956, cap in hand, urging him to accept an unwritten agreement whereby the Primate would urge the faithful to support the First Party Secretary in his efforts to avert chaos in Poland, in return for full freedom of church and religious activities. This was an arrangement of political convenience that suited both sides at a particular time, although the Church gained most of the advantages. Ever since 1957, the state had been trying to whittle away these advantages without coming into a headlong collision that would be disastrous for both sides.

Point two—cultural freedom—was anathema to Gomulka, and this was the area in which the greatest and most abrasive encroachments were subsequently made. As for relations with the

West, Gomulka had been prepared to use these to create an image that would bring him political and economic satisfaction. But he always had a profound distrust for Western society and its values; as the son of a disillusioned immigrant to the United States, he reserved for that country his strongest personal antipathy.

Perhaps more than any other leader in Eastern Europe after 1956, Gomulka set the pattern for the regime he headed. This was due only in part to the strength of his personality. It was also due to his unfortunate inability to delegate responsibility and power and to his dislike of independent judgments on the part of his subordinates. Many people trusted Gomulka; he, on the other hand, trusted very few. He was regularly accessible to only a small handful of old supporters and friends, of whom the most important were the three Politburo members Kliszko, Loga-Sowinski, and Spychalski, all of whom had been disgraced with him in 1948–49. In October, 1956, Zenon Kliszko became Gomulka's chief advisor on Party affairs and on relations with the Church. Ignacy Loga-Sowinski was the regime's trade-union leader; and Marian Spychalski was Minister of Defense. Thus all these men held key positions and kept Gomulka informed on perhaps the most important strata of the Polish state. But none of them would be the sort to offer a constructive proposal, even assuming that their leader would be inclined to listen to one, and such was Gomulka's obstinacy and bad temper that even three such old colleagues would hesitate to challenge him. The result was a conservatism and stagnation emanating from the very top that drove out or underground the large amount of constructive talent that the Polish United Workers' Party possessed in October, 1956.

The best exponents of "creative Marxism-Leninism" in Poland were, in due time, to be removed from their positions. The weeding out began in 1959, but, even earlier, the "liberal disenchantment" with Gomulka had begun. In 1957, the "revisionist" students' journal *Po Prostu* had been closed down and the limits of the newly won cultural freedom sharply defined. Less than a month after his return to power, in November, 1956, Gomulka had taken away the political rights of the workers' councils which had grown up spontaneously in the upheaval of October. The councils were abolished altogether in April, 1959. In May, 1957, a "new economic model" prepared by the recently formed Economic Council was presented. It was approved by the Economic Committee of the Council of Ministers the following July. This was the brainchild of a group of economic reformers headed by Professor Oskar Lange, which, had it been adopted, would have put Poland in the forefront of economic planning and management. It envisaged a thorough decentralization, the autonomy of enterprises, and a much stronger emphasis on the profit motive. But to Gomulka and his advisers, whose knowledge of economics was of the most primitive variety, such proposals smacked of heresy and were quietly shelved.

The negative conservatism of Gomulka's ideas on economic management only became really obvious in October, 1959. As a result of serious economic difficulties in that year, two remnants of the Stalinist era, Eugeniusz Szyr and Julian Tokarski, were brought back into the government as deputy premiers with supervisory powers over the economy. This move was the first in a series of retrograde steps in senior personnel policy. At the same time, Wladyslaw Bienkowski, Minister of Education, lost his post. Bienkowski was one of the most liberal members of the top Polish hierarchy, an old associate for whom Gomulka, despite his politics, had retained a strong personal affection. Though he had never exercised much political influence after 1956, his removal from office was a serious blow to the liberal wing of the Party. In the spring of 1960, a far more influential man disappeared from the scene. It was announced in April that Jerzy Morawski, Politburo member and Secretary of the Central Committee, had resigned. Morawski had been one of three young Central Committee secretaries who played a considerable part in inspiring and engineering the October rising, and his reputation was such that he was considered by many to be a possible successor to Gomulka.* The two others were Wladyslaw Matwin and Jerzy Albrecht. They too had gradually lost their influence. Matwin, perhaps the most liberal of all the prominent Party officials, also had committed the serious political mistake of making himself utterly distasteful to Gomulka

* In September, 1964, Morawski was appointed Ambassador to Great Britain.

personally. As early as February, 1957, he had been sent back by Gomulka to his former post as First Party Secretary of the Wroclaw administrative region (voivodship), and, though he retained his post as a Central Committee Secretary, his influence steadily dwindled. It was no surprise when, in 1963, he was finally dismissed from his provincial post and also lost his place in the Secretariat. Albrecht was treated more ceremoniously. Though he was removed from the Secretariat in 1960, he was transferred to the government post of Minister of Finance and, at the Fourth Party Congress, in June, 1964, retained his full membership in the Central Committee.

The elimination of these three liberals roughly coincided with the emergence of a new, "hard-line" group in Polish politics commonly known as the Partisans. This group was comprised of a number of men whose common denominator was their service in the Polish Communist underground during the war. They were essentially "native" Communists, as opposed to "Muscovites," and they highly resented the stranglehold the latter had taken on the Party after 1948. Some had been persecuted by Bierut's regime during the Stalinist period, and most had lost whatever positions of influence they had ever held. The group had no real ideology; it was interested in power. It basically approved of the internal policy of the Stalinist era but disapproved of the men who carried it out. Many of these men (Minc, Berman, Zambrowski) had been Jews, and the Partisans were strongly anti-Semitic. As nationalists, they also disapproved of the excessive dependence on Moscow that was, of course, inherent in the Stalinist system. At first, they probably saw some hope in Gomulka's return in October, 1956. Like them, he was a "home" Communist and a resistance fighter, whose fall in 1948 had also been the beginning of their own slide into oblivion. But, in their eyes, October, 1956, was soon revealed as a great fraud, organized by a predominantly Jewish group within the Party in order to stay in power, with Gomulka merely being used as a façade. To make matters worse, to their mind, the October bandwagon had been joined by a host of "liberals" and revisionist intellectuals for whom they had the greatest contempt.

Thus, October, 1956, far from giving the Partisans the opportunities they considered their due, seemed only to have blocked their path still more firmly. As a small minority in the Party, they could not hope to assert themselves directly. The tactics they chose, therefore, were those of subterfuge and conspiracy—to remove "Jews, liberals, and revisionists" from as many positions as possible, high or low, by any method possible, and to get them replaced by men of their own group or at least by men of a conservative, dogmatic mold. They never had in mind the removal of Gomulka; this would have been impossible, and any attempts at it would have led to their complete destruction. But they—and not only they; other conservative elements were doing the same—cleverly played on Gomulka's predilections. He had many prejudices in common with them: he disliked intellectuals and theorists, he believed in primitive Communism and discipline and raved against the deplorable slackness in so many walks of public life. All this could be skillfully exploited by the Partisans. At the same time, they had to be careful: for all his faults, Gomulka had a broad streak of decency about him; he deplored anti-Semitism and would not condone the frame-up, police terror tactics, and smears the Partisans were ready to use. This side of their activity had to be kept hidden from Gomulka as far as was possible, and here, the Partisans were aided by the fact that Gomulka chose to cut himself off from much of the activities of his subordinates.

The man who, by 1962, had emerged as the undisputed leader of the Partisans was Mieczyslaw Moczar. Born in 1913, Moczar was a professional noncommissioned officer in the Polish Army before the war, and it was then that he joined the illegal Communist Party. During the war, he fought bravely in the Communist underground. After the war, he became a stanch follower of Gomulka and seemed to be heading for a promising career. But when Gomulka fell, he also went into shadow, having been personally accused by one of the most prominent "Muscovites," the Jewish Roman Zambrowski, of a "conciliatory attitude toward the rightist and nationalist deviation."[16] (Thus began the very strong enmity between these two men which was to have its triumphant climax for Moczar fifteen years later.) Moczar only returned to real favor in July, 1956, when he was re-elected to the Central Committee. In December, 1956, he was appointed Deputy Minister of the Interior, thus returning to the kind of police and security work in which he had gained unenviable notoriety immediately after the war. As an old and loyal supporter of Gomulka, Moczar most probably expected that, after October, 1956, his turn had come. The fact that it did not come was probably the main reason he chose the conspiratorial road to power that characterized the activities of the Partisans. Personally, Moczar (considered to be a man of real ability and considerable charm) was perhaps not the best of conspirators because of a tendency toward boastfulness when under the influence of rather copious drafts of vodka, which he frequently imbibed.

The Partisans succeeded in acquiring a strong ally at a higher level in the Party—one who, for a period after 1960, was gloomily being predicted a future Party leader. Ryszard Strzelecki had also been a Communist underground fighter in World War II and was close to Gomulka from those early days. The strong personal tie between them had been cemented in the days of Gomulka's disgrace, when Strzelecki adopted Gomulka's son and gave him his own name. An ally of Gomulka, he did not, however, suffer the same fate as his leader, although his position in the Party was "frozen" after 1948. In 1951, Strzelecki became Minister of State Railways and held this post for the next nine years; then, in early 1960, he became a Central Committee Secretary, replacing Morawski. His emergence in 1960 was probably mainly due to Gomulka's opinion of him as an efficient, strong-handed *apparatchik.* There was no reason to believe that he came to prominence as a result of Partisan pressure. Indeed, his association with this group began after, not before, his elevation to the Secretariat. Once in the Secretariat, Strzelecki evidently saw the group as a ready-made faction on which he could base a drive for more power.

The combination of Strzelecki at the top level and Moczar at a lower level proved very effective. Strzelecki, with his influence over Gomulka, could persuade the Party leader on the higher decisions affecting either personnel or policy, while Moczar, probably shielded by Strzelecki, could carry on the dirtier work lower down. Indeed, between 1961 and 1963, the Partisans achieved striking success in getting their men appointed to key positions in the Ministry of the Interior, the whole security apparatus, and certain branches of the armed forces. They scored their greatest success in

June, 1963, when Roman Zambrowski, Moczar's enemy and one of the most prominent Jews remaining in the Party, a former Stalinist who had been made to look relatively liberal in his later years, was removed from the Politburo and Central Committee Secretariat. At a Central Committee plenum the following month, Gomulka himself delivered a blistering attack on the intellectuals and came out heavily for the most dogmatic kind of "Partynost" in the arts.[17] It was the kind of speech that could have been written by any of the Partisans or neo-Stalinists who had thrown in their lot with them.

At that very same plenum, however, when the Partisans seemed to have reached the peak of their success, they received two setbacks that showed that Gomulka had at last become aware of the serious danger they presented to the delicate balance of forces and opinion within the Party. In the first place, Strzelecki was not promoted to the Politburo in place of Zambrowski, as had been expected. In the second, the Jewish Artur Starewicz, long a target of the Partisans, was promoted to the Central Committee Secretariat and put in charge of the cultural and journalistic fields, a province that had formerly been Strzelecki's. Starewicz was not a "liberal," but a reasonable man and one with whom it was possible to argue. His appointment gave the beleaguered intellectuals some reason to believe that Gomulka's bark was worse than his bite, and that the cultural policy announced at the plenum would not be imposed in its full severity.

All this was Gomulka's way of telling the Partisans they had gone too far and of placating other sections of the Party who were concerned at their advance. In the following months, it became clear that other notable objects of Partisan attention, chiefly Premier Joszef Cyrankiewicz, were not only out of danger but increasing their prominence and consolidating their positions. At the Fourth Party Congress, Gomulka once again showed himself to be a political master. He arranged the Central Committee elections so that the Partisans made several gains but received another check to their hopes and expectations. Moczar was not allowed to speak at the Congress, and Strzelecki only advanced to candidate-membership in the Politburo, a half-promotion which, according to reliable reports, considerably humiliated him. It is true that, a few months later, Strzelecki was promoted to full Politburo status, taking the place of the dead Aleksander Zawadzki, and that Moczar became Minister of the Interior. But it appears that Strzelecki was promoted on condition that he cease his factional activity, and Moczar's promotion was to some extent neutralized by the transfer of former Minister Wladyslaw Wicha, by no means a Partisan, to the Central Committee Secretariat in charge of internal-security matters. The Partisans' bandwagon had been checked, and they now had to revert to their burrowing.

But opponents and observers who tended now to write the Partisans off seriously underestimated the resiliency of Moczar and his associates. Their tactics now took a different course: Moczar strove to build up a large following in lower Party ranks and among the people. He became president of the Polish veterans' association (Zbowid) and from this platform sought to become the champion of all who had served Poland in battle, regardless of political affiliation. His appeal went out also to the young technocrats, who saw him as a hope for more rapid advancement and a leader who, by strong-arm efficiency, could pull Poland out of the stagnation into which she had sunk. His anti-Semitism also brought him considerable sympathy. As a result of his clever tactics and the exploitation of his compatriots' dissatisfaction and prejudices, Moczar gained a reputation as the man of the future. In July, 1965, Gomulka once again tried to cut him down to size, by withdrawing the corps of internal-security troops from the control of the Ministry of the Interior and placing it under the Armed Forces Ministry. But Moczar had survived such checks before, and, unless the situation in Poland markedly improves, he would go on profiting from the existing dissatisfaction.

The new Central Committee which emerged after the Fourth Party Congress had shown that Gomulka still mastered the scene. He checked the Partisans and struck down several "liberals" whom he had always disliked. The Central Committee was packed with his supporters, many of whom had no real political profile. Some of these were younger men of technocratic bent and training, but the predominant features of the Central Committee members were conservatism and lack of personality. This group would give little trouble—and contribute few ideas. Its composition reflected the regime's preoccupation with economic problems, but it gave no real assurances that these would be tackled with the requisite imagination and right resources. In particular, the appointments to the Politburo of Eugeniusz Szyr and Frantisek Waniolka, two orthodox, conservative economic stalwarts, gave little hope that Gomulka was genuinely convinced that basic economic reform was necessary.

Yet, Poland's serious economic difficulties in 1963 and 1964 brought up, once again, the question of the new economic model that had been shelved in 1957. In the Theses of the Fourth Party Congress, there were signs that the economic reformers had at last succeeded in reasserting some influence. This was confirmed by government decrees in July, 1964, calling for groundwork to be prepared for a new reform. Exactly one year later, a new reform was outlined;[18] it was a cautious one, showing no real inclination to tackle the basic causes of Poland's economic ills.

But however timid, it was still a step in the right direction. In other fields, either the *status quo* has been maintained or there has been actual retreat. The five planks of the Polish October have already been enumerated, and I have said that in only one of these did Gomulka genuinely believe—the sense of police terror. In the following eight years, this provision was generally adhered to, but the difficulty the British journalist had in obtaining his Polish visa was typical of a general tightening up of many areas in which the Polish citizen or foreign visitors came into contact with the state. The power of the militia and the security apparatus definitely increased in Poland after 1960. A much closer watch was kept on the public—especially on those sections that had dealings with Westerners—than in the very free period following 1956. One cannot call this a return to the police terror of the Stalinist period; there probably still was more liberty in Poland in 1964 than in any other East European Communist state except Yugoslavia. But this liberty was diminishing. In contrast with Hungary, where the situation was going from bad to better, in Poland it was going from good to worse. On the lower level, the Partisans had been largely instrumental in creating a climate of restriction. This had been facilitated by Gomulka's predisposition to authoritarianism.

That cultural freedom had become, in relative Polish terms, severely restricted by 1964 was shown by the famous protest of the thirty-four intellectuals in March of that year. (This incident will be discussed at length in the chapter on cultural developments.) It is sufficient to say here that the protest, sent to Premier Cyrankiewicz, was a *cri de coeur* against the encroachment on the great amount of cultural freedom that had been gained in 1956 and 1957. In 1963, there had been severe restrictions on the amount of newsprint supplied for books and cultural magazines; two very prominent reviews, *Nowa Kultura* and *Przeglad Kulturalny,* had been discontinued and replaced by a conservative Party organ entitled *Kultura;* and in July of that year, Gomulka set the tone by speaking of socialist culture in almost Zhdanovite terms.

Again, one should not lose sight of the fact that, in comparison with the rest of the bloc, a great degree of cultural freedom still obtained in Poland. What alarmed the intellectuals was the very clear indication that the regime was trying to turn back the clock. The signatories of the March, 1964, letter acted because they realized that time was running out. The publication of this letter in the West and the ensuing stir caused the regime great embarrassment. Its first reaction was one of repression. Later, however, a number of concessions were granted, including the appointment of a new Minister of Culture, Lucian Motyka—obviously a placatory gesture. There followed an uneasy truce; the intellectuals won certain concessions, but, at the same time, several trials were held in 1965 of writers accused of "slandering" the Polish People's Republic in works that they had published in the West under pseudonyms. Repression was, therefore, continuing.

Similarly, if anyone were to compare Church-state relations in 1957 and the present, he would see two very different situations. The *modus vivendi* of 1956 could not last, of course. In a sense, neither the state nor the Church respected the spirit of the agreement. Once the Polish Party had recovered from the shock of the October upheaval, it set about trying to reduce the Church's influence and power. The Church, for its part, regarded the *modus vivendi* simply as a springboard, a fact of which it made no secret, and forcefully presented itself as the sole repository of all that was patriotic and fine in the Polish tradition. It challenged the regime to a power struggle for the mind of Poland, and, in the Polish countryside, it soon became obvious that the village priest and not the local Party secretary was the real master.

In Poland, therefore, there existed something unique in all of Eastern Europe—a strong and dynamic alternative center of power. In meeting this challenge, the Communist regime had to tread warily. It could not carry out a direct frontal attack on the Church without risking another upheaval or, more probably, a nationwide reaction of passive resistance that would have disastrous economic effects. It chose, instead, a series of administrative pinpricks and chicaneries. Though these were legally defensible in some cases, they ran counter to the whole spirit of the *modus vivendi*. Such measures included various forms of taxation on the clergy, military conscription of theological students, forbidding of religious instruction in the state schools, refusal to allow the building of new churches, harrassment of pilgrimages, etc. These were measures against which the Church hierarchy protested bitterly, but they did not constitute the kind of mass assault that would stir up the wrath of the faithful. In any case, the Polish peasantry, in which the Church's great strength lay, was probably better off than it had ever been in its history. It was, therefore, not likely to get excited over such piecemeal attacks on the Church.

By 1962, the regime accompanied these small harrassments with greatly increased propaganda attacks in the press and radio against the Church. Much more important, however, were its attempts to divide the hierarchy and to discredit Cardinal Wyszynski. These attempts became particularly dangerous during the reigns of Pope John XXIII and Pope Paul VI. Having completely failed to draw support away from the Polish Church by the use of such organizations as the progressive Catholic Pax movement, it took up the approach proclaimed by Pope John—in an attempt to show how out of touch the "reactionary" Cardinal Wyszynski was with the Vatican's new outlook. It used Pope John, that is, as an instrument of propaganda against the Polish ecclesiastical hierarchy. In its very difficult situation, the Polish episcopate, composed of more than seventy bishops, showed remarkable solidarity, although in a body so large there must have been a faction that did, indeed, consider the Cardinal's position too inflexible.

Among the Polish laity, especially among Catholic intellectuals, of which the so-called *Znak* (Link) group was the most articulate, a strong opinion developed in 1963 and 1964 that a new attempt for understanding between Church and state should be made, involving compromises on both sides. The conclusion of an agreement between the Vatican and the Hungarian state in September, 1964, only increased these desires. But it also encouraged the regime to press for some kind of concordat between the Vatican and the Polish government; such a concordat, it was thought, would serve to undermine Cardinal Wyszynski's authority in his own Church by enabling the Polish Government to negotiate directly with Rome or its representatives on matters affecting Polish church-state relations. The regime's overtures were rebuffed by the Vatican, but its efforts continued. In view of the Cardinal's unbending attitude, it seemed probable that more and more members of the Polish laity would approve of them.

It would be a mistake to think that all these developments gravely weakened the Church in Poland. It still had wealth, a vast body of priests, and an organization that, in size and strength, was phenomenal in a Communist country. But, in contrast to the years between 1956 and 1960, it had gone very much on the defensive. It was not so much leading the faithful into battle as warding off the attacks from many sides and even from within. Most of Cardinal Wyszynski's sermons in 1964 and in 1965 read like a catalog of grievances; they were defiant and courageous, but hardly confident or optimistic. This represented, if not a victory, then an undoubted gain for the Communist state—a sign that it, rather than the Church, held the initiative.

In his maneuvering against the Church, Gomulka showed the same political skill he demonstrated in managing the Party. In his handling of the peasantry, he also displayed his sagacity—by leaving well enough alone. The system of free peasantry is the one October freedom that remains completely unscathed. By permitting this, Gomulka secured three advantages: he gained the political support, or at least the acquiescence, of the countryside—something that, because of collectivization, no other Communist leader except Tito has achieved; he neutralized the adverse effects that his policy toward the Church might have caused in the countryside if the peasants had not had a relatively high standard of living; finally, he avoided the economic ill effects that collectivization usually brings in its wake. Indeed, in years when the rest of Eastern Europe gave deplorable harvest results, the uncollectivized Polish agriculture showed vitality and resilience and produced enviably good crops.

Gomulka's policy of leaving well enough alone in agriculture did, therefore, pay political and economic dividends. But agriculture was probably the only area of public life in which he achieved a positive success. In the rest, there was stagnation or retrogression. By the mid-1960's, the Party had lost most of the inspiration that had fired it in 1956 and 1957; Gomulka, once the symbol of leadership and hope, had become the skilled political manager whose authority was used to keep the Party together rather than to lead it. The whole of Polish industry had become seriously run down. Gomulka had shown himself pathetically unable to adapt to the realities of a technocratic age. Worst of all, the Polish population, whose vivacity and courage no one has ever doubted, had relapsed into apathy, shiftlessness, and disillusionment. This was because the Polish October had been killed, and the man mainly responsible for its death had been Gomulka.

The situation was such, indeed, that many people were beginning to wonder who might be qualified to take Gomulka's place, and the Party leader's illness added urgency to the speculation. The name of Edward Gierek, the highly successful Party leader in Silesia, was widely mentioned, especially by those who could not bear the thought of either Strzelecki or Moczar. But it was feared that, if Gomulka went, the only organized force capable of taking over would be the Partisans and their hard-line colleagues, since the rest of the Party was too divided to present any real opposition to them. It appeared, therefore, that Poland had worked into a position where it could not afford the man whom it could not do without.

Romania

By the mid-1960's, Romania was well established as a factor of importance in the Communist world and in East-West negotiations. Her new-found stature was due to a successful defiance of the Soviet Union over the issue of East European economic integration, neutrality in the Sino-Soviet dispute, and the solid improvement in her relations with Western powers. But she had still not achieved much distinction by virtue of any great "liberalism" in her domestic policies. Internal reforms had been introduced, but they were slow in coming; the regime seemed happy to evade them for as long as it could.

At a Central Committee plenum of the Romanian Workers' Party, held in November–December, 1961, in the wake of the Twenty-second Congress of the CPSU, First Party Secretary Gheorghe Gheorghiu-Dej blandly informed his audience that the question of Stalinism and the oppression that went with it had been irrelevant in Romania since 1952, when the Pauker-Luca-Georgescu trio had been removed from office. Any other remnants of the black past, said Gheorghiu-Dej, had been erased by the dismissals of Iosif Chisinevschi and Miron Constantinescu in 1957, immediately after the purge of the anti-Party group in Moscow. There was now, therefore, no reckoning to be made with the past and no slate to be wiped clean.[19]

Gheorghiu-Dej's performance at this plenum was a masterly exercise in diversion. The Twenty-second Congress posed a very difficult problem for him, since he, Hoxha, and Ulbricht were the only dictators in Eastern Europe who had held power uninterruptedly since 1945. Therefore, any indictment of the crimes perpetrated in Romania during the Stalin era obviously indicted him. To extricate himself from this delicate position, Gheorghiu-Dej chose to rest his whole case on certain half-truths and on his ability to ignore much of what had happened in Romania after Stalin's death. It was true, of course, that in the first few years after World War II the most powerful figure in the Romanian Party was not he, the nominal leader, but Ana Pauker, who headed a hard core of Soviet-trained Romanian Communists, several of whom, like Pauker herself, were Jewish. Gheorghiu-Dej tried to make capital of this undeniable fact by arguing that he had been virtually helpless in the face of this group, and that he had not even been privy to the "illegal" actions perpetrated against both people and Party members at that time.

His trump card was, of course, that he purged the Pauker group in early 1952, almost a year before Stalin died. This was true, but just what circumstances prevailed when the Pauker group was purged remained unknown. It was a point of crucial importance if, as Gheorghiu-Dej now implied, this purge had been carried out independently of the Soviet Union and even in defiance of it. (Then there would be some justice in placing the beginning of the Romanian defiance of the Soviet Union as far back as 1952.) It was more probable, however, that Gheorghiu-Dej and his "native" Communist group carried out their action with Soviet support and were able to take advantage of the morbid bout of anti-Semitism in which Stalin engaged shortly before he died. (This period also saw the fall of the Jewish Rudolf Slansky in Czechoslovakia.) Even if this second interpretation was closer to the truth, it was nevertheless convenient and not altogether implausible for Gheorghiu-Dej to claim that he had been a nationalist even before Stalin's death.

The assumption of real power by the "home" Communist group in the Party—of which Gheorghiu-Dej, Gheorghe Apostol, and Chivu Stoica were the most prominent—certainly did not mean that Soviet influence and presence in the country diminished. Soviet-trained leaders—like Emil Bodnaras, who controlled the armed forces, Petre Borila, and, until 1957, Iosif Chisinevschi—retained their seats in the Politburo; the secret police and the entire security apparatus continued for several years to be in the hands of Soviet or Soviet-trained officials; finally, Soviet troops continued to be stationed in the country until 1958. Nor did any evidence suggest that the post-Stalin relaxation throughout Eastern Europe was particularly striking in Romania. Indeed, Lucretiu Patrascanu, the Romanian Communist leader imprisoned in 1948 on charges of nationalism, was executed in 1954 as a grim deterrent to those who might wish to push relaxation too far.

In 1954, Gheorghiu-Dej, who had previously been Premier as well as Party leader, relinquished his Party post. Thus, like the other East European leaders, he followed a pattern set in Moscow after Stalin's death. In contrast with the other leaders, with the exception of Chervenkov in Bulgaria, he retained his government post, making Gheorghe Apostol First Party Secretary. The transfer was, of course, only nominal, and the game of musical chairs continued in 1955 when Gheorghiu-Dej took back the Party leadership and gave the Premiership to another of his faithful followers, Chivu Stoica.

That such manipulation was possible showed Gheorghiu-Dej's mastery of his own Party. But he evidently was not completely satisfied that his mastery was total; he believed that there was still danger from both the right and the left. In the summer of 1957, taking his cue from the purges in Moscow, he dismissed Chisinevschi and Constantinescu from the Politburo. Despite the specious similarity of the charges against them, these two men were entirely dissimilar. Chisinevschi was a Bessarabian Jew trained in the Soviet Union; he was a protégé of Pauker, one of the "cosmopolitan" hard-liners of the immediate postwar period, perhaps the last dangerous representative of that group. Miron Constantinescu bore striking similarities to Patrascanu: He was a "home" Communist who had been prominent in the Communist youth organization before World War II, and one of the few intellectuals among the "home" Communists' group. (Another was Ion Gheorghe Maurer, with whom Constantinescu also had much in common.) Constantinescu's sin, though this was not publicly divulged, was that he strayed too far toward reform and "revisionism" and wished to see a much fuller implementation in Romania of the message of the Twentieth CPSU Congress.

By eliminating Chisinevschi and Constantinescu at the same time, therefore, Gheorghiu-Dej killed two birds with one stone, striking down the last powerful exponent of the left and eliminating the one man (after Patrascanu) capable of rallying the reformist tendencies around himself. After this purge, there was no serious opposition to Gheorghiu-Dej in the Romanian Workers' Party.

Had the Party not been so ruthlessly united around the leadership, the Romanian regime could not have carried through its successful defiance of the Soviet Union in 1963 and 1964. (Romania's "nationalist deviation" is dealt with elsewhere in this book. See Chapter 6, pp. 202 ff.) According to reliable reports, Khrushchev tried to suborn certain Party leaders in order to overthrow Gheorghiu-Dej in 1963. The main target of Soviet efforts was unofficially reported to be Emil Bodnaras. Soviet-trained and formerly a Soviet citizen, an ethnic Ukrainian rather than a Romanian, Bodnaras was the most likely man for the Soviets to approach. He was also a man who enjoyed considerable respect in the Party and in the armed forces. But Bodnaras refused to be subverted, either because he had made his peace with the "home" Communists and had become a loyal supporter, or because he realized that to attempt anything was hopeless. In any case, he was amply rewarded. Gheorghiu-Dej, with all the skill of the wise leader, used Bodnaras on important missions to China and Yugoslavia and, in doing so, thoroughly implicated him in the whole anti-Soviet maneuver.

Whether the Soviets approached the other most prominent "Muscovite" in the leadership, Petre Borila, is not known. Borila was probably the last important member of the old Bessarabian wing of the Romanian Communist Party and had spent twenty years, from 1924 to 1944, in the Soviet Union. He may well have had misgivings about Romania's policy of independence, and it was very noticeable that he dropped almost completely from the public eye after early 1962. At the Ninth Party Congress in July, 1965, he was removed from the Presidium. If Borila was opposed to Gheorghiu-Dej's policy, then it was a wise and characteristic tactic on the latter's part not to dismiss him immediately. Such a step would have created wavering throughout the entire Party and, on the other hand, might have been considered by the Soviet Union as close to open provocation. It was better to keep him in office until the moment came when it was convenient to drop him quietly.

Gheorghiu-Dej's skillful handling of men may also be seen in the very different case of Ion Gheorghe Maurer, who was appointed Premier in 1961 and later became perhaps even better known in the West than Gheorghiu-Dej himself. Outwardly, the two men had little in common. Maurer is a "home" Communist but definitely not of worker origin (like the group clustered around the Party leader). Born in a middle-class, professional family, Maurer started life with most of the advantages that the vast majority of the population lacked. He was soon attracted to Communism and, as a successful lawyer, achieved considerable notoriety in the 1930's by acting as defense counsel for several prominent Communists, among them Ana Pauker. In 1944, he established a close bond between himself and his future leader by rescuing Gheorghiu-Dej from a detention camp (where he had been imprisoned since 1933).

After a period of eclipse during the Pauker supremacy, Maurer slowly began to climb the ladder, but it was only after 1956 that he became well known. Once established, however, his rise was meteoric. He first became Foreign Minister; then, on the death of Petru Groza in 1958, he was made titular head of state (more correctly, Chairman of the Presidium of the Grand National Assembly). At the Third Party Congress, in June, 1960, he achieved full Politburo status. In March of the following year, he replaced Chivu Stoica as Premier. This move also saw the establishment of a State Council with Gheorghiu-Dej at its head, who thereby combined the offices of chief of state and Party leader. Gheorghiu-Dej evidently saw the value of a man like Maurer in a period when intra-bloc and international diplomacy was becoming so important. Maurer was cultivated, polished, a good representative. He was ideal for the post and certainly repaid all the trust and confidence that his leader placed in him. Moreover, he was no threat to Gheorghiu-Dej. He had very little organizational following in the Party and seemed to have very little ambition to build one.

In the course of the early 1960's, it became increasingly clear that the man becoming the most powerful in the Party after Gheorghiu-Dej was Nicolae Ceausescu. Still in his forties and the youngest man in the Politburo, Ceausescu nevertheless had considerable experience behind him, and, as Party leader responsible for cadres and organization, he had had ample opportunity to build up a following. It was no surprise, therefore, that, when Gheorghiu-Dej died in March, 1965, Ceausescu succeeded him as the Party leader. He did not, however, succeed to the position of head of state, a post that went to Chivu Stoica, a veteran Party leader who had been Premier from 1955 to 1961. Stoica was an old colleague of Gheorghiu-Dej's, and his appointment was probably a conciliatory gesture to the older Party members who looked askance at Ceausescu's promotion.

The immediate task of the new Party leader was to strengthen his control over the high Party agencies, a task he was able to accomplish at the Ninth Party Congress in July, 1965.* The new Central Committee elected at that congress showed a heavy sprinkling of "Ceausescu men."

After Gheorghiu's death, Ceausescu moved promptly, in fact, to make his presence felt within the Party and in the country generally. Always a forceful and energetic man, he made it clear that he would not allow himself to be dominated by the shadow of Romania's dead leader. At many public appearances between March and the Ninth Congress in July, he did not hesitate to criticize certain aspects of national policies under Gheorghiu-Dej, especially in economic planning and in agriculture. He also introduced quite revolutionary changes within the Party. Candidate-membership, a probationary period before full acceptance as a member, was abolished, and the title of Party leader was changed back to Secretary General, the old title that had gone out of favor throughout Eastern Europe in 1953 because it smacked too much of the personality cult. The Romanian Workers' Party became the Romanian Communist Party, and Romania became a Socialist State, instead of a People's Republic. By steps such as these, Ceausescu sought to begin a new era. He was relatively young, and the new era might last a long time.

Ceausescu is considered a militant nationalist, and there is no reason to believe that, under him, Romania will retract her independent stand in relations with the Soviet Union. In domestic affairs, it is still too early to tell how quickly Ceausescu will proceed with reform. Gheorghiu-Dej had slowly initiated a policy of concessions that were intended to bring Romania out of the Stalinist trough in which she had languished for almost twenty years. The standard of living had begun to improve perceptibly by 1963. The all-pervasive presence of the secret police began to recede, and, by the summer of 1964, all political prisoners had been released. A slight but noticeable relaxation in cultural affairs also began. Efforts were made, in addition, to bring the regime closer to the people by enlarging the Party: by the summer of 1965, membership

* It was decided to consider this congress the Ninth rather than the Fourth because the Party, having changed its name back to the Romanian Communist Party, now included in its calendar *all* eight previous congresses, whether before or after the date when the Communists came to national power.

had grown to 1.4 million. All these efforts to bring the Romanian people into closer contact with the regime were part of a policy initiated by Gheorghiu-Dej, to project the Party as the continuance of all that was finest in the national tradition.

Ceausescu has continued this policy and in some respects even accelerated it. Relaxation in the cultural and academic fields became more pronounced, and in June, 1965, the new "socialist" constitution introduced more safeguards for the liberty of the individual. But Romania still lagged far behind Poland, Hungary, and even Czechoslovakia in internal "thaw." Ceausescu seemed always at pains to stress that no abuses of the concessions granted would be tolerated. When he gathers confidence and strength, it is possible that reform will be pressed more quickly. A comprehensive reform program would immeasurably strengthen the popular support the regime had already gained by its nationalist policy.

Conclusion

If one looks at the whole decade during which Khrushchev was Party leader in the Soviet Union, it becomes clear that all the countries whose internal affairs have been reviewed in this chapter saw varying degrees of relaxation and liberalization during that time. The East European countries were better places to live in by 1964 than they had been in 1953.

The progress had not, however, been smooth in every country, and 1964 was not, in every case, the peak year for liberalization. This was most notably so in the case of Poland, where there had been a steady decline after 1958. Nor was it the peak year for either Bulgaria or Czechoslovakia. Bulgaria had two peak periods within the decade. The first lasted for about fifteen months after the April plenum in 1956; the second, for about the same length of time after the Twenty-second Congress of the CPSU, in October, 1961. Following both these periods, an alarmed regime succeeded in pushing the stakes back within more tolerable confines. In Czechoslovakia, the liberalizing ferment was probably the greatest in 1963, when the Novotny regime was reeling under blows delivered from many quarters. In 1964, however, the regime came back quite strongly and put itself more firmly in control of the situation.

In the other three countries, however, 1964 could be considered the peak year, if one overlooks the fleeting freedom of Hungary in 1956. In the G.D.R. and Romania, the peaks were still all too low, but modest beginnings had been made that were continued after Khrushchev's fall. In Hungary, the level was very much higher and would continue to rise if the pronouncements by Kadar were anything to go by. However, as we have seen, the possibilities of a reversal were not to be ruled out, and, in fact, 1965 did see a certain retrenchment and tightening up in some parts of public life.

It is practically impossible to make generalizations from such varied situations. Still one can say that, during the Khrushchev decade, the original impetus toward liberalization came from the Soviet Union, and from Khrushchev personally, in four of the six countries—Poland, Hungary, Bulgaria, and Czechoslovakia. (It is significant that the other two countries were Romania and the G.D.R., where liberalization was least noticeable.) It was the Twentieth Congress of the CPSU that prompted the first reforming wave, in 1956. In Poland, this wave had results, many of which were still in evidence by 1964 despite the subsequent retrogression. In Hungary, it led to the Revolution and the subsequent repression; but the memory of the Revolution was one of the principal reasons for the relaxation that came later. In Czechoslovakia, it was immediately checked by a confident Novotny, but in Bulgaria, it led to the April plenum and the subsequent reforms. The Twenty-second CPSU Congress, in 1961, which dispatched the second punitive expedition against Stalin's ghost, was received coldly by a Polish regime bent on repairing the "damage" of 1956. In Hungary, however, it confirmed Kadar in a policy he had already begun. In Czechoslovakia, it caught Novotny already in a state of disarray and forced him to bow to pressure he had been able to resist earlier. In Bulgaria, it caused a second burst of reform, initiated by Zhivkov himself but later almost completely halted because of the dangers involved.

In the G.D.R. and Romania, the influence of the Twentieth and Twenty-second Congress was much less marked. When the first real signs of reform did come to East Germany, they were a result of the new situation caused by the building of the Berlin Wall and a desire on the part of Ulbricht to recast his image. In Romania, Gheorghiu-Dej neatly sidestepped the issues of both Congresses, and when reform finally came, it was at a measured pace and at the time that Gheorghiu-Dej, not Khrushchev, thought fit. This is not to say that the Romanian and East German populations were not affected by the Soviet de-Stalinization campaigns. They caused rumblings of discontent in both countries, but these did not result in any real change of course by the regimes.

Liberalization in the G.D.R. and Romania began so late and was, especially in the G.D.R., on such a small scale that it was difficult to view it in any sort of perspective. It was an encouraging sign, however, that it continued after Khrushchev's fall. In Romania, once Ceausescu had thoroughly established himself, there was no reason for the pace to slacken. The regime was enjoying a good deal of popular support because of its defiance of the Soviet Union and its nationalist posture. It could, therefore, carry out its reform confident that it would not be hoist with its own petard. The Pankow regime, however, could have no such assurance, and there was always the danger that it might attempt to clamp down again before it was too late.

The four other countries under review experienced both the benefits and the disadvantages of Khrushchev's methods. It probably required a political earthquake like the Twentieth Congress to shake the Communist world out of its Stalinist mold, but, while the system in the Soviet Union was able to stand the shock, in most parts of Eastern Europe it proved almost too severe a remedy. The Communist system had survived many rigors in the Soviet Union and was accepted by most of the population. In Eastern Europe, it was new, rickety, and generally disliked. The quite sudden furors that the Twentieth and Twenty-second Congresses caused, while strengthening the regime in the Soviet Union, endangered its counterparts in Eastern Europe. Relaxation, therefore, was followed by repression. In Hungary, the relaxation led to revolution quelled by blood. After two or three years of repression, it resumed again, but this time it was directed from above and was not pushed from below onto an unwilling regime. In Poland, it led to a quieter and more successful revolution, but then to a continuing period of steady retrogression. Twice in Bulgaria and once in Czechoslovakia, the relaxation led to situations which, for different reasons, the regimes considered dangerous and tried to change before they got out of hand.

In the next chapter, we shall deal with a theory developed by a Czechoslovak professor on cycles in the development of socialist economies. During the Khrushchev era, there were also political cycles in most of Eastern Europe, prompted mainly by Khrushchev's political manner. They caused booms of various dimensions, followed by recessions of various dimensions. It was doubtful, however, whether these would occur again in quite the same form or for the same reasons. Even before Khrushchev's fall, the influence of Soviet internal events on Eastern Europe had lessened considerably, and in all countries (excluding Albania), the worst excesses of Stalinism had largely disappeared. The stage seemed set for a more ordered course, with the main vehicles of reform no longer political but economic and technological. The economic reforms that began at the end of the Khrushchev era have been called the "second stage of de-Stalinization." If these succeed, they will be the best guarantee that the political gains already made will be not only maintained but enlarged.

TWO

Industry and the National Economy: Development and Reform

IN 1964, ECONOMIC reform was in the air in Eastern Europe; in 1965, it was actually being applied in many places. In every country, though not so dramatically in some as in others, the accent was laid not so much on quantitative production as on revamping the system of economic planning and management so as to give better results in terms of productivity, costs, quality of the product, and the right kind of commodity for the market. It was this kind of thinking that led to the drafting of complete new schemes of economic management in some countries, and in others, to piecemeal reforms that would have far-reaching effect if allowed to operate as planned.

The most important of these reforms will be dealt with individually in the following pages. First, however, it is necessary to deal generally with the situation that made reform not merely desirable but in some cases a pressing necessity.

In the early years after World War II, the first essential throughout Eastern Europe was to repair the damages to the economies that the war had wrought. In certain countries, this was not so urgent as in others, since war damage and spoliation had been uneven. Thus, Bulgaria and the Czech lands of Czechoslovakia had escaped with relatively little damage, while the Polish and Yugoslav economies had been almost completely destroyed; toward the end of the war, the fighting in Romania and some parts of Hungary had also brought great destruction. But the generalization that the first economic aim of the individual states in Eastern Europe was to reach the immediate prewar production levels holds true. The difficulties were immense, and the situation was not helped by the Soviet policy of plunder and exploitation to which Eastern Europe was subjected—whether directly, through plain looting, or "legitimately," through various war reparations extorted from those countries that had fought against the Soviet Union. Yet the recovery was astonishingly rapid; by 1949, most countries had reached prewar industrial levels. One can argue, of course, that, in the cases of countries like Bulgaria, Romania, and even Hungary, the prewar levels were so low that to re-attain them was no great accomplishment in itself. But in view of the difficulties, to have attained anything in those four years was an achievement not to be underestimated.

The credit for this should not by any means go to the Communists alone. Until 1948, most countries of the area were ruled by precarious coalitions in which the Communists shared power with members of the prewar "bourgeois" parties. It is true that Communists were often the driving force in reconstruction—one striking example was in Hungary, where Erno Gerö, later to destroy his reputation by the worst excesses of Stalinism, won great respect for his unbounded energy and fine organizational ability—but if they succeeded in capturing most of the limelight, it was at least partly because the politicians of the other parties were preoccupied with trying to ward off Communist attempts to undermine their positions. And one should not overlook the great contributions made during this period by many patriotic "bourgeois" experts, managers, officials, and technicians, who supplied the expertise most of the Communists palpably lacked. Most of these men were to be thrown on "the rubbish heap of history" when the Communists completed their triumph.

The completion of this triumph roughly coincided with the attainment of prewar industrial levels. There was an obvious need to continue economic development at a sustained pace, and this would almost certainly have been done no matter what type of government had been in power. But a heavy industrial base was regarded as the essential prerequisite for a socialist society, and everything was neglected in favor of building it. The orthodox Communist regimes, their enthusiasm for this theory gaining megalomaniacal dimensions, entered an epic race to build up heavy industry, disregarding all rational economic considerations. The pattern was the same everywhere; even the German Democratic Republic and Czechoslovakia, with already highly industrialized economies, seemed to act on the assumption that they were as underdeveloped as Bulgaria or Romania.

Thus, the five years between 1948 and the death of Stalin saw generally similar economic development everywhere. Ever-increasing annual rates of investment were drawn from the nations' incomes, ever-increasing shares were allocated to heavy industry and construction—the highest shares, of course, in the backward countries like Bulgaria and Romania, but excessively high ones even in more developed countries. Stress was laid on heavy manufacturing such as in the metallurgical industries and machine building. It was autarky run wild: every country concentrated on producing the same kinds of heavy industrial goods, every country sought to become a little Soviet Union. Despite the founding of the Council for Mutual Economic Assistance (COMECON) in 1949, there was no genuine attempt at international coordination or correlation. The emphasis was solely on quantitative expansion.

The whole mad scramble certainly achieved something. Very impressive rises in industrial production were registered. The combined industrial production of the G.D.R., Czechoslovakia, Poland, Hungary, Romania, and Bulgaria was 114 per cent higher in 1953 than in 1949, with phenomenally high quantitative progress in the last two countries.

This period also saw a tremendous expansion in the industrial labor force throughout the whole area, and for the first time (not counting periods of war), women appeared in large numbers in the labor force. Their appearance was due mainly to the policy of deliberately lowering real wages and living standards. Most of the men came from the countryside, which was experiencing the effects of the first great agricultural collectivization drive. All this labor, except for the private craftsmen who were being squeezed out of their own businesses, was relatively unskilled. But as long as labor was plentiful, productivity did not become an issue.

Considering that everything was subordinated to increased production of heavy industrial goods, it is not difficult to imagine what happened to the standard of living during this period. Agriculture, in every case in the throes of the collectivization drive, was starved of investments. Wage levels were deliberately depressed. It has been estimated that living standards fell by an average of 20 per cent between 1948 and 1953, and this in an area where living standards had in many places always been notoriously low.

From a long-term economic point of view, perhaps the greatest mistake made during this period was the relative failure to develop a raw-material and power base. In generalizing, one can say that Eastern Europe is not particularly well endowed with industrial raw materials when compared with North America, Western Europe, or, of course, the Soviet Union. An industrialized Eastern Europe will always be to a large extent dependent on raw materials from elsewhere. But it is not as poverty-stricken in this regard as was earlier believed. In addition to her internationally famous oil deposits, Romania has great quantities of natural gas and timber and is the richest country in the whole area in natural resources. Bulgaria has some iron-ore deposits (not enough, it is true) and some oil and coal; it also has enough rivers to provide a good source of electrical energy. Poland has good coal, natural-gas and sulphur deposits, and salt. Even Hungary, perhaps the most poorly endowed country in the area in this respect, has large quantities of bauxite. Hungary, Romania and Czechoslovakia have (or had) considerable quantities of uranium.

The right course in the beginning would have been to place greater emphasis on exploiting these raw materials and less emphasis on the manufacturing industries. The policy actually pursued led to two serious consequences. First, the whole area became overwhelmingly dependent on the Soviet Union for its industrial and, in most cases, its agricultural raw materials. This was no great sacrifice for the Soviet Union; on the contrary, it fitted in with her early postwar economic policy in Eastern Europe. She was able to get rid of her surpluses of (often low-quality) coal, iron ore, oil, etc., for quite high prices and receive certain manufactured goods from her satellites at low prices. In the rare instances where Eastern Europe possessed something of which she was short—for example, Czechoslovak or Romanian uranium—the Soviet Union took a direct hand in exploiting it and later imported all of it at prices that were hardly, one assumes (although exact figures are unknown), disadvantageous to her.

The second consequence was, in its way, just as serious. The neglect of domestic industrial resources led increasingly to a disparity between the volume planned for the manufacturing heavy industries and the volume of raw material available. Initially, the Soviet Union had been able to provide all that was required and more, but the titanic targets of some East European industries meant that later it became not so easy. These shortages, combined with irregularities of delivery, brought occasional chaos to an already unsophisticated planning system and was one of many reasons why targets became increasingly harder to attain. The time was coming for something Marxists never believed could happen in a planned economy—a recession.

When Stalin died, it became obvious that the system associated with his name could not continue. Nowhere was this more obvious than in the economic sphere. Change naturally began in the Soviet Union but was quickly adopted in the satellite countries. From a purely economic point of view, it was clear that previous practice had created dangerous imbalances that would have to be rectified. The regimes also had to take into account the open outbreaks of dissatisfaction and the less dramatic manifestations of discontent in Eastern Europe, of which economic considerations, especially the very low standard of living, were a main cause.

The result was that, throughout Eastern Europe, the megalomaniacal targets in heavy industry were scaled down. Agriculture and the consumer-goods industries began to receive a greater share of investments, wages were slightly increased, and the prices of some consumer goods were lowered. The "new course" determined by Premier Malenkov in the Soviet Union was adopted in varying degrees throughout the area. The Homeric period in Eastern Europe's economic development was largely over.

This did not mean that a basic change in economic outlook was forthcoming. Scaling the targets down from the gigantic to the merely ambitious was no real solution, especially in the more developed countries, where disproportions and imbalances had their most serious consequences. In the less developed countries like Romania and Bulgaria, where heavy industry was still largely in its infancy, such disproportions were not so grave, because the economic network was not so complex. But in more advanced economies, it was simply postponing the not-too-distant day when an overhaul of the whole structure would become necessary. As it was, there was no real disposition for basic change anywhere in Eastern Europe. That was why Khrushchev's 1955 decision to scrap Malenkov's new course and return to the primacy of heavy industry was welcomed. The less advanced countries certainly considered Malenkov's initiative had been much too premature for them, regardless of whether or not it was good for the Soviet Union. Until they had built their heavy industrial base, any talk about playing down the primacy of heavy industry was "unrealistic" and self-defeating.

The more realistic planning cycle that began in 1956, therefore, still involved changes in degree rather than in principle. Heavy industry was still the key, and the targets were still ambitious. But over the area as a whole, planned investments were fewer and industrial targets lower than in the Stalinist years. In general, greater stress was laid on completing industrial projects already begun than on beginning new ones, and provisions for limited increases in consumption were included in the investment allocations.

These concessions proved inadequate to eliminate the economic tensions in some countries. In 1956, economic grievances, combined with a whole spectrum of national, political, and psychological factors, produced the upheavals in Poland and Hungary as well as discontent in other countries. It was a classic case of the population rebelling not because they were more downtrodden than they had ever been before, but because conditions, in many respects, had improved and because the possibilities lay open to make further improvements.

The main economic consequence of the Polish and Hungarian

upheavals in 1956 was that they further shook the regimes' complacency; every government in Eastern Europe was forced, in varying degrees, to take steps to head off serious economic disruption. First of all, a thoroughly alarmed Soviet Union had to step in with economic transfusions. In 1956 and 1957, the U.S.S.R. extended some $1.2 billion in loans and credit to Eastern Europe. (About two-thirds of this went to the G.D.R., Poland, and Hungary, much of it in industrial or agricultural raw materials.) This Soviet help, combined with further steps toward moderation taken by the regimes themselves in 1957, enabled the East European economies to ride the storm. By 1958, the more serious dangers had been averted; the economies of the different countries again began to move forward impressively, and in a much less frenzied manner than in the first gigantic lunge. The single exception was Bulgaria: in 1959, she suddenly revamped her whole economic plan with a tremendous upward surge, evidently feeling that since hers was the most backward economy (excepting Albania's), another short Homeric period was both ideologically sound and economically feasible.

The First Reforms

We have seen how, until 1957–58, the improvements made in economic planning were essentially ameliorative. They involved mainly an *ad hoc* scaling down of targets and re-allocation of investments. They did not touch the basic features of economic organization, planning, or management. But by 1957, the Soviet Union, much more experienced in the socialist economic system than any other country, had realized that more important organizational reforms were necessary. The results of this change in outlook were quick to show themselves. In 1957, the first major Soviet industrial reorganization began, and in 1959, a new seven-year planning cycle was rather abruptly introduced.

The need for economic reform was even more pressing in the satellite countries than in the Soviet Union, as the events of 1956 had clearly shown. Better planning coordination, more efficiency, and more material incentives were needed; since the Soviet Union had already given the go-ahead signal, there was nothing to inhibit the still-obedient East European regimes from following suit.

It is fair to say that the limited reforms embarked upon from 1957 to 1959 in satellite Eastern Europe had already been in operation for several years in Yugoslavia. One may argue, therefore, that one should attribute the reforms to the continuance of Yugoslavia's influence in the whole area. The argument is true, however, only insofar as the Yugoslav example influenced Soviet practice, since the reforms carried out in Eastern Europe were *directly* influenced by what was happening in the Soviet Union. The reforms referred to here are the post-revolutionary ones initiated by the governments of these countries, not the spontaneous reforms instituted from below. The workers' councils that sprang up during the revolutions in Poland and Hungary certainly drew their inspiration from Yugoslavia; but the power of these councils was drastically reduced in both these countries once the new regimes were safely installed and felt sufficiently confident. Any Yugoslav influence on regime-sponsored reforms was, therefore, of an extremely indirect nature. (Later, in 1963 and 1964, the situation was rather different. The new and really basic reforms that were to be introduced in most countries in Eastern Europe in this period were clearly similar to those carried out earlier in Yugoslavia [some, in part, went a good deal further than the Yugoslav reforms]. Here, the Yugoslav influence was much more direct, and this time it was officially, rather than unofficially, embraced. But this was after the Soviet bloc's *rapprochement* with Yugoslavia, after Tito's proselytizing proclivities had greatly diminished, and after he had ceased to be the forbidden fruit he had been in the past. Finally, it was not the Yugoslav reforms that gave the spur to the renewed changes in East European economic thinking, but the discussions and pilot projects in the Soviet Union that began in 1962. Without these, the schemes of the satellite countries would never have been implemented so quickly.)

In conception, however, as opposed to implementation, the cradle of real economic reform was not the Soviet Union but Poland. In 1957, the Warsaw government was presented with a blueprint for a new economic model that contained all the basic tenets of the schemes to be approved six or seven years later—

decentralization, factory autonomy, accent on the profit motive, and a freer play of market forces. This model will be dealt with later. Suffice it to say that, though it was officially approved by the Polish Government, it was immediately shelved as being too radical.

In terms of the political and economic thinking of the satellite rulers at the time, the new Polish economic model was certainly premature. They were ready for a modification of the old system, not the introduction of what would amount to a new system. In the few years after 1957, this modification mainly consisted of a change in the functions of the central planning apparatus through the introduction of varying degrees of decentralization. They were ready for only the first step of the comprehensive reforms of the 1960's. In the late 1950's, decentralization meant making a clearer distinction between the planning and operational sectors of economic control, a cutting down of the managerial prerogatives of the central planning authorities. Previously, these authorities had fixed individual plans of different factories in the greatest detail. Now, they set more general indexes and left it to local initiative to fix the details. Similarly, planning periods were extended over fifteen and, later, twenty years and were also less rigorously paced. Henceforth, it was possible to adjust annual plan targets—upward or downward—within these longer target periods, according to conditions in any given period.

Decentralization was the main theme of all the reorganization programs carried out in Eastern Europe during the late 1950's. It was, in most cases, accompanied by a greater stress on economic accounting, more careful and sophisticated planning to try to cure the chronic ailment of imbalances, a number of price reforms, and the introduction of management and workers' premium systems, with the factory director being given more leeway to dispose of his wage fund than before. Reforms along these lines were carried out—in varying degrees—in each country. In Czechoslovakia, for example, a broad decentralization measure was approved in 1958. In Romania, on the other hand, very few really noticeable changes were made, although even here much stricter methods of economic accounting were introduced and the number of centrally planned production indexes began to drop sharply year by year.

The main trouble with these measures was that they usually did not go far enough. When they did, as in the case of Czechoslovak decentralization, their effects tended to alarm the central authorities and cause a reversion to tighter control. Some of the fear of decentralization was political, but some of it was also caused by a legitimate economic fear that local authorities would not use the share of investments allotted to them wisely. In Yugoslavia, where decentralization had gone very far by 1959–60, these fears certainly proved justified. Many uneconomical projects (the so-called political factories) were built, not to mention many civic constructions like extravagant rest homes and sports stadiums.

The same sort of thing happened on a smaller scale in Czechoslovakia, with the inevitable result that in two years the whole decentralization scheme was virtually scrapped. A further reason for the discontinuance of the reform, however, was that, in 1958 and 1959, when it had just begun, industrial development in Czechoslovakia and in Eastern Europe generally began to quicken its pace. This was not because of the reforms but mainly because big industrial projects, started earlier in the 1950's, had been completed and had begun to pay off. Hence there was no real incentive to press ahead with a reform born of difficulties that seemed to have been righted.

At the beginning of the 1960's, therefore, some of the earlier reforms had apparently either been forgotten or shelved and the question of really basic change postponed indefinitely. Even in Yugoslavia, the pace-setting country, a period of retrenchment and recentralization began in 1961. But far-reaching reform was just around the corner. What brought it so close was the fact that, unexpectedly, the old, basic weaknesses of the East European economies, especially the more advanced ones, were exposed again —in other words, recession set in again. This was true in Poland and Hungary, but especially in the G.D.R. and Czechoslovakia. The problem of an overly narrow raw-material base began to have a serious effect on production possibilities. The central governments were finding that they did not have the means to carry the investment load with which they had burdened themselves and were forced to decentralize by making the local councils and factories, as well as the population (through individually owned housing), assume more responsibilities. So many new investment projects were unfinished that it became necessary to find ways to finish these projects before new ones were begun.

In all countries, the whole industrial infrastructure (especially communications) had been allowed to fall into a state of antiquated disrepair; labor productivity was increasing more slowly than were individual wages and salaries; manpower, at least in the G.D.R. and Czechoslovakia, was getting impossibly scarce; industrial machinery was becoming obsolete or was not being used to full capacity; stocks of unsalable goods were growing; and the waste of materials was enormous. In an era of increasing world trade, it was realized that East European goods were pitifully below the accepted world standard, and the Soviet Union was getting tired of being the garbage-can for satellite produce. The old Party stalwarts who had mismanaged the economy for years were clearly unsuited to the technocratic age. These were probably the main ills of the East European economies. They had always been present, but, by 1962–63, their ravages showed clearly. This was not so evident in the less developed economies of Romania and Bulgaria, which continued to register good quantitative progress; but, in the G.D.R., Czechoslovakia, and Poland, a stagnation of crisis proportions became evident.

In this context, it is worth noting a sensational article by a Czechoslovak economist, Professor Josef Goldmann, which appeared in the September, 1964, issue of *Planovane Hospodarstvi,* one of Czechoslovakia's most important economic journals. Professor Goldmann, who had been imprisoned after the Slansky trial and had spent many years in enforced obscurity, made a dramatic comeback in this article. What he said, in effect, was that the East European economies, especially the smaller, relatively advanced industrial ones, had shown themselves as susceptible to "boom-and-bust" cycles as Western capitalist economies. By taking the examples of Czechoslovakia, the G.D.R., Hungary, and Poland, in the immediate post-Stalin era and in the period beginning in 1962, he showed that recessions (he did not actually use the word) had been caused by overinvestment in the manufacturing industries to the neglect of the raw-material base. This had led initially to a growth rate in excess of the optimum and to the development of the "raw-material barrier," to which the slow progress made in agriculture also contributed. The economies only started to pick up again, as they did in 1958, when big investments made in the earlier period started to pay off in the form of completed, operating projects.

Professor Goldmann was a little too dogmatic in some of his convictions, most notably when he flatly stated that the scaling-down of targets after Stalin's death was due solely to the workings of the economic cycle and was not prompted at all by political considerations of mass discontent. But the burden of his argument held true, and, in orthodox Communist circles, it must have been a bombshell. Professor Goldmann's prescription for the recurring ills he had diagnosed was not only to stop doing the things that had caused the illness but also to switch over to the kind of reformed system that his government was introducing at the time. Under the "traditional" system, as he called it, the illness would inevitably recur.

Goldmann wrote his article two years after the first suggestions for reform were aired. In the serious situation that again began to develop, all that was needed to crack the shell and hatch the constructive imagination of East European economists was some initiative from the Soviet Union. This came on September 9, 1962, with Professor Y. G. Liberman's *Pravda* article entitled "The Plan, Profits and Premiums." The essence of Liberman's ideas was that profit should be regarded as the motor of economic activity. What he suggested was actually not very startling. He simply wanted to encourage enterprises to correlate their output with consumer demand; he was eager to stimulate the use of better technology and to improve quality. It was his description of the existing system—its waste, rigidity, and incongruities—and the unstated implications of his ideas that were the real bombshells. "Libermanism" (despite the Professor's own, perhaps diplomatic, protestations) would, if carried to its logical conclusion, imply the scrapping of the whole centralized system of planning, the adoption of profit and not volume as the yardstick for economic efficiency, and the introduction of some rudiments of the market mechanism.

Liberman's article provoked wide discussion among Soviet economists. Two months later, Khrushchev himself stepped in, endorsing some of Liberman's ideas and encouraging discussion of them. The stage was set for the discussion to begin in Eastern Europe.

The following is a country-by-country review of the proposals for economic reform in Eastern Europe and their implementation.

Bulgaria

From one point of view, it was odd that Bulgaria should have embarked on any economic reform at all. This was not so much because of the conservatism of the Bulgarian leaders as because the Bulgarian economy, in 1963, when the relevant discussions started, was still in a relatively underdeveloped stage and maintained a fairly impressive rate of growth.

Rapid quantitative progress, however, does not necessarily betoken efficiency, and even the most rabid defender of the Bulgarian regime never claimed that its economy was efficient. The Bulgarian press itself had always been the first to admit the contrary. In fact, economic weakness had been a notable Bulgarian characteristic for several years; it was realization of this that prompted the interesting series of discussions that opened in May, 1963, in the pages of *Novo Vreme*, the theoretical monthly review of the Party Central Committee. The debate only warmed up, however, in November, with an article by Professor Angel Miloshevski on material incentives and worker participation. What Miloshevski proposed was nothing less than the adoption of the Yugoslav workers council system:

> We find that, in order to reach a more complete solution to the question of increasing the interest and the activity of the workers in the state enterprises, a form of management must be established which ensures the workers' more immediate participation in the management of enterprises, in the disposal of the means of production. Parallel with the rights of the directors, the rights of working people—of the individual plant—must be increased. It can be considered that the conditions are already ripe for the creation of such an organ in our state enterprises through which the workers shall participate in the solution of many questions of production, connected with the organization of labor, with labor remuneration, with

> the distribution of profit; that they shall have a word to say even in the appointment of the director of the enterprise, etc.[1]

Miloshevski's proposals were not subsequently adopted by the regime, but it was significant that they could have been voiced at all.

Even more important was an article published in the December issue of *Novo Vreme* by Professor Petko Kunin. A rehabilitated follower of the executed Traicho Kostov, Kunin had always been considered one of Bulgaria's most able economists. His article was more comprehensive than Miloshevski's. He argued that all factories should be self-supporting, that they should operate "without being 'financed by the state.' " He called for a new system of planning and accounting that would give full scope to real economic competition among the factories, the "most rational and economic use of basic and working capital funds and of the labor force, for profits and profit-sharing to be used as 'stimulating device.' " Profits, he argued, should determine the remuneration of managers and be the main source of increases of wage payments. (In connection with profits, it should be noted that, in Bulgaria as in all of Eastern Europe, these were defined differently than in the West. In the East, profits were gross revenue minus all costs except labor costs. In the West, they were gross revenues minus *all* costs, including labor costs.)

Those who expected the regime to put up orthodox economists to counter Miloshevski and Kunin were agreeably disappointed. In fact, early in 1964, the regime itself introduced some clearly reformist measures.

At the beginning of the year, an experiment along the lines suggested by Kunin was begun at the Liliana Dimitrova textile plant in Sofia. It involved "non-state financing" and a system of remuneration and premiums based on profit. The first results on the operation of the system were very encouraging.

In February, 1964, a national conference of industrial accountants was held in Sofia at which it was disclosed that a completely new system of planning and management was being prepared. According to a speech made by the Minister of Finance, Dimitar Popov, experiments in the new system were to begin the following June and would be continued into 1965; by the end of 1966, it was hoped, the new system would be applied throughout the country.[2] The regime did not come out with an official blueprint for reform, but from various articles, it was possible to see the course the reforms would take.

The first really specific article on economic reform, written by Ivan Mironov, was published in the May, 1964, issue of *Ikonomicheska Misal.* Mironov began by advocating that wages and capital accumulation be tied to the profit level of individual plants. He also proposed that each enterprise be subjected to a property tax and interest rate on capital; there should also be depreciation rates reflecting true wear-and-tear and obsolescence. This idea carried Kunin's idea of enterprise self-sufficiency one stage further, since it would enable the factory to replace its own capital without having to avail itself of "free capital" from public funds. As a consequence of these measures, capital would become more expensive and would be more intensively used. Tax and interest rates would not be the same for all branches but would be varied by the regime according to whether it wanted to encourage or discourage certain industries. Furthermore, since factories would now be charged for the capital in their possession, it would be necessary to have free sales of capital among enterprises and to permit one enterprise to lease capital—e.g., a building or a large machine—to another.

Mironov believed that, when the accumulations of each plant (and a considerable part of the wages) depended on the rise of the profit, the workers could not be indifferent to the problems of management and the result of the work of their enterprise. He was also specific in saying that, in effect, every socialist enterprise should follow the path of its capitalist counterpart by trying to maximize its own profits.

Articles like Mironov's, helpful though they were as pointers, gave no indication of which proposals were actually being implemented in the fifty or so pilot experiments being conducted at the time. Later, however, two articles written by a Yugoslav reporter accredited in Bulgaria, Frane Barbieri, gave some idea of the nature of these experiments. (These articles appeared in the Belgrade *Politika* of October 15 and 18, 1964.) The first was particularly valuable because it described the reforms at the "Druzhba"

("Friendship") bottle- and jar-making plant near Sofia. If one used this description as a corrective to some of the more radical proposals of the Bulgarian economists, one could arrive at a reasonably accurate picture of the nature and scope of the experiments.

Since the way prices were determined would greatly affect the degree of over-all freedom granted to each plant or factory, it was not surprising that this question loomed large in the discussions on the reforms. In 1964, the Bulgarians seemed rather conservative in this respect. D. Nachev, in an article in the September issue of *Partien Zhivot*, another monthly journal of the Party Central Committee, revealed the dilemma of the planning authorities when he urged that prices be "realistically fixed" to "reflect the relationship between producer and consumer." But he added the ominous proviso that they should "not diverge from the interests of the state," at the same time taking comfort from the fact that instructions had been given to the price-fixing bodies to fix prices which would more accurately reflect market forces.

It was clear, therefore, that prices would continue to be centrally fixed, and it was simply hoped that the planning organs would be flexible and realistic in their decisions. This was strongly confirmed by Barbieri, who quoted Grisha Filipov, a Vice-Chairman of the Bulgarian State Planning Commission, as stating that the "market can establish neither prices nor production, for this leads to disorganization. They would remain established strictly according to plan." Nor could there be any question of the factories' freedom to contract. At the "Druzhba" plant, Barbieri found, the management had to try to maximize its profits within the framework of price, production, and distribution plans all still fixed by the state. Only on these preconditions was the profit motive allowed free rein. Obviously, as far as the determination of commodity prices was concerned, the Bulgarians had scarcely dared to dip more than their big toe in the water.

On the pricing of capital, however, the steps taken were already far greater. Here, Mironov's and Kunin's ideas of abandoning the system of providing state funds or free capital to enterprises were being put into practice. The enterprises themselves were now required to supply most of their own new capital—which would originate either out of the capital funds already in their control or from funds obtained from banks as repayable credit. The internal capital funds, the two components of which were depreciation and the firm's share of profit, were lumped together in "Development and Technical Improvements Funds." These funds were deposited in banks which were required to pay the enterprises interest on the deposits. Although the depreciation rates had not been announced, a small percentage of the depreciation allowance reverted to the state. The rest, amounting to well over half, went to the banks in the name of the factory concerned.

Factories were also allowed to sell unneeded capital, once permission from higher authority had been obtained. To encourage such sales, the regime began to levy a 6 per cent charge on both fixed and circulating capital. It was not clear, however, whether this rate was on the gross value of capital, as in Hungary, or on the net value, as in Poland. The purpose behind the introduction of a capital interest rate will be dealt with more fully in the section devoted to economic reform in Hungary; one might simply say here that it was an important instrument in promoting the more efficient and intensive use of capital and in facilitating a better evaluation of it; it was also useful in unearthing new sources of investment funds. The levying of the charge meant that if an enterprise manager held on to capital equipment he did not need (a common practice in all Communist states), the enterprise's wage fund would be affected. Thus, it paid the manager and the workers to get rid of surplus capital.

The factories' freedom to use their investment funds as they wished was still restricted in Bulgaria. Filipov, in his conversation with Barbieri, said quite openly that it was still essential to accumulate and distribute investments centrally, since the state still had "too many obligations" and needed "too great an amount of funds." To illustrate what he meant, he pointed to huge investments that the state had to find for the giant metallurgical complex at Kremikovtsi, near Sofia, the first part of which was commissioned in 1963. In a way, this official position was understandable. As long as there was an "investment boom"—and in 1965 Bulgaria still seemed in the middle of one—controls on investment expenditures could be reduced only very slowly. The need to meet investment plans and, perhaps later, to pay off the massive debt to the Soviet Union, made genuine decentralization of investments a future rather than a current proposition. Such decentralization would only become easier after a reduction in the proportion of income devoted to investment.

Under the Bulgarian reform, as in all the others, the turnover tax, an old Communist favorite, continued to be used to adjust sales prices so that they would more closely approach the market value. Another tax designed to play an important part was the so-called progressive-profits tax, which replaced the previous "deduction from profit." This apparently was not a real profits tax but rather a tax on what one Bulgarian writer called "the earnings of the enterprise." The "adjusted" earnings were considered to be equal to the gross receipts of the enterprise minus the turnover tax and the non-labor operating costs. Expenditures that were not considered economically justified were not counted as costs until after the progressive-profits tax had been levied. This was a state device for having these economically unjustified expenditures taken out of the wages fund rather than out of the sum that would go to the state in the form of the progressive-profits tax. It was another attempt to cut down the wastefulness that characterized the Bulgarian and other East European economies.

The wages themselves were to be very closely tied to the earnings of the enterprise. The wage fund was to consist of whatever was left after deducting from the achieved output all the taxes, contributions, interest rates, economically unjustified costs, assessments for various material funds, and ordinary non-labor operating costs. The fund was then assessed for social-security contributions, which went directly to the state. The money remaining for individual distribution was divided into two categories: "guaranteed" wage payments and "variable" wage payments.

"Guaranteed" wages were to be paid to the employees regardless of the total performance of the enterprise. For the ordinary worker, this part of his wages amounted to about 90 per cent of his basic wage; for the management staff, it was considerably less, some 70 to 75 per cent. The "variable" wage was to consist of bonuses or awards; as far as the worker was concerned, its amount would depend on individual or group performance. It was obviously the "variable" wage that the regime hoped would be the main source of material incentive.

In the sphere of worker participation, the 1964 Bulgarian experiments did not go nearly so far as, for example, Professor Miloshevski had hoped in his *Novo Vreme* article of November, 1963. The Yugoslav example still remained safely over the Serbian border. But while the system of "one-man management" was essentially preserved, the director, "the representative of the state," had to consult with the enterprise's "production committee." This committee generally included five or six members for every 100 employees, with a number of officials serving *ex officio*. This was to help the management in promoting the increase of labor productivity and the profitability of production. It was also supposed "actively to influence" all questions relating to the organization of labor and production. It would have the main say in the distribution of the variable wages and—what could be really important—"an active say in all questions of management." Of course, it remained to be seen what this last privilege would really amount to. In the meantime, it seemed that any decision of the production committee was not effective until signed by the director. In case of a dispute between the two sides, there was no arbitration court that could decide the issue; the manager, in effect, was always right.

These, then, were the general outlines of the kind of economic reforms that were proposed in Bulgaria and, in 1964 and 1965, were actually being initiated on an experimental basis. Though the schemes were not so radical as those being proposed in Czechoslovakia, for example, they were important enough, and they involved the first real assault in Bulgaria on the orthodox notion of a command economy. It was certain that they met with considerable resistance and doubt from several sections of the population, not only from the officials who would be adversely affected by them, but also from a suspicious working class. This adverse reaction, plus the technical and administrative difficulties involved, necessitated postponing the general application of the reform. It seemed quite likely that the program would not be fully under way before 1967, and changes would certainly occur before it was perfected. A lot could happen before 1967. But if economic reform continued to proceed steadily in the Soviet Union, it was difficult to see how the Bulgarian program could be in real danger. The more Bulgaria inched away from the old system, the more difficult it became to return to it.

Czechoslovakia

Nowhere did the endemic ills of the Communist economic system strike harder than in Czechoslovakia, the most advanced country in the East European alliance. It was the very severe winter of 1962–63 that laid bare the holes in what had seemed a most impressive fabric. During 1963, the annual plan for industry had to be lowered twice, especially in the foundry, power-engineering, and construction industries, and in transport. In the end, total industrial production in 1963 was 0.4 per cent lower than in 1962. The deficit was even higher in some sectors, reaching a full 10 per cent in the construction industry. In the same year, the value of industrial rejects came to the astonishing figure of 1.5 billion crowns (more than $200 million at the official exchange rate). Later, it was admitted that the general standard of living had also dropped slightly in 1963.

The only redeeming feature of the whole economic performance in 1963 was a good showing in agriculture, in which an increase of some 7 per cent was registered. But this had to be measured against a disastrous year of 1962, when agricultural production had fallen by 7.6 per cent. Thus, the good record in 1963 did not even attain the level reached in 1961.

It was not surprising, therefore, that 1963 saw the opening of a series of debates among Czechoslovak economists on changes in the economic system. The first notable contribution came as early as February of that year, when Radoslav Selucky, a young Leningrad-trained economist, in an article for one of the Prague cultural weeklies, criticized what he called the "cult of the plan"; this, he said, was a manifestation of Stalinism just as dangerous as the now proscribed personality cult.[3] Selucky soon established himself as the boldest exponent of reform and was personally criticized for his pains by First Party Secretary Novotny himself. But the issue was soon taken up by other economists.

The most significant contribution came in September, from Professor Ota Sik, Director of the Economic Institute of the Czechoslovak Academy of Sciences, a Party Central Committee member, and very much a member of the Communist establishment. That he could write a self-critical article in *Nova Mysl*, the Party theoretical monthly, entitled "The Remnants of Dogmatism in Political Economy Must Be Overcome," was the first real indication that the regime itself had decided to take a close look at the system with a view to overhauling it.[4] By September, evidently, the full gravity of the economic situation had begun to be apparent to even the most impervious conservatives. Professor Sik, later to become the father of Czechoslovakia's new economic model, became convinced, the more he examined the situation, that only the most radical solution would suffice. He was encouraged to come to this conclusion by almost all the country's professional economists, some of whom, like Selucky and Eugen Loebl, were prepared to go much further than he.*

The discussions continued well into 1964, and it soon became apparent—in fact, it was openly admitted in the Czechoslovak press—that there were two schools of thought on the subject of economic reform. The first was the "root-and-branch" school of economists and technocrats, the second, supported by the political Party officials and initially by Novotny himself, held that there was nothing basically wrong with the existing structure, that once its many abuses were eradicated, it could provide the solution to the country's economic ills. This school had obviously not progressed in its thinking much beyond the superficially reformist outlook of 1957–59. The basis of the opposition to radical economic reform was the fear that political control of the Party would be seriously diminished; many of the vested interests built up over

* Eugen Loebl has distinguished himself as the most courageous exponent of liberalization in Czechoslovakia. Perhaps the most notable of his contributions was an article in the March 19, 1965, edition of the Slovak cultural weekly *Kulturny Zivot*, in which he argued that, even under socialism, the individual was more important than the state, a contention which brought him under heavy fire. A Slovak Jew, Loebl was sentenced to life imprisonment during the Slansky trial in 1952, but was quietly released in the mid-1950's.

fifteen years would be gravely threatened. It should not be assumed, however, that all the supporters of this school were prompted by selfishness, self-interest, or by a reactionary attitude. Some quite progressive Party officials must have realized that although a radical change was desirable for the economy, the effect of such a change on the socialist structure as a whole might be adverse. These were the men who stressed political over economic considerations, and who, therefore, appeared more conservative than they actually were.

In view of the strength of the opposition against "root-and-branch" reform and the dogmatic character of the Party leadership, it was amazing that the draft of the new system—finally published in October, 1964, and approved in January, 1965, was as radical as it was.[5] It was a tribute to Novotny's newly discovered flexibility that a document so far-reaching was approved by the Party Presidium and the Council of Ministers. But most of the tribute should go to Professor Sik, who—once convinced that no half-measures would do—conceived the new model, became its most enthusiastic salesman, and successfully accomplished the difficult task of selling it to the Party leaders.

As in all the new East European schemes for economic reform, the roles of the central planning body and the central control agencies are, in the Czechoslovak model, sharply reduced. Basically, only a long-term plan for the country as a whole will be determined centrally. There will continue to be a number of centrally determined regulations of national scope dealing with such matters as prices, basic wages, credit, and other general factors. Otherwise, the trusts and individual enterprises themselves will be, to a great extent, free of central directives.

In those basic areas in which centralized control is to be retained, it is promised—as it was in the Polish, Bulgarian, and East German proposals—that centrally made decisions will be guided strictly by economic considerations. In the Czechoslovak case, the draft model contained the instruction that, when the central planning bodies came to decide whether a particular proposal for investment would be profitable or not, they were to study similar situations abroad before making their final decision. In no case was the construction of an investment project that was not on a competitive level with respect to cost, technical standard, and quality to be permitted. Similarly, economic considerations were to play a major part in deciding whether production of a product was to continue or not. This means, in effect, that subsidies will be largely eliminated. Thus Czechoslovakia joined the general trend of cutting down free gifts to industry from the government treasury.

Although the directive powers of the central bodies are greatly reduced under the new scheme, obviously individual plants are not now free to do as they like. A new, intermediate center for decision-making and coordinating matters of quantity and assortment had to be created: the answer lay in the establishment of trusts, each trust uniting under its control all the plants and factories of a certain industry or branch of industry. These trusts would be similar to the trusts in Hungary, the Associations of State-Owned Enterprises in East Germany and the Leading Associations in Poland. The trust, or its counterpart, is to be the point of convergence of two processes taking place simultaneously: devolution from above and concentration from below. Organized through the grouping together of individual plants, they would take over many of the responsibilities that were previously held by the central planning authorities and ministries. Not only are they to prepare the plans for quantity, quality, and range of goods to be produced, within the general guidelines laid down by the central planning agencies; they are also to be mainly responsible for decisions on investments, again within the centrally outlined framework. The initiative these trusts could exercise, therefore, will be considerable indeed.

One of the most interesting aspects of the new model concerned the various proposals for pricing. Three price systems are to be established within the economy: (1) a controlled fixed-price system; (2) a controlled variable price system; (3) a free price system.

The *controlled fixed-price system* is to be used for the pricing of basic production materials and basic consumer goods. The prices of these materials and goods are, however, to cover costs of production and to be influenced by market conditions. This fixed price system is similar to one which began operation in East Germany in April, 1964.

The *controlled variable price system* is to be employed for standard products of general consumption such as bread, flour, meat, etc. Under this system, a central price bureau would set a maximum and minimum price for a given commodity. Within the range prescribed, the trusts and the plants will be able to vary the price in conformity with changing market conditions. This would considerably streamline the operation of the economic system by eliminating the frequent need to apply to a central bureau for permission to change the price whenever the market situation changed.

The *free price system* is to be based on agreements between suppliers and purchasers, taking into consideration the market situation. This system is designed for use in wholesale trade and would affect a large number of commodities sold through the domestic trade network by the various sales organizations. Obviously, this third system, taken together with the creation of the trusts, would be open to the abuses of monopoly pricing. The trust could restrict output in order to maintain prices at levels guaranteeing the highest possible profits. To counter such possibilities, the regime will establish price institutes whose job would be to prevent such restrictive practices. Another method proposed is to use imports to force a lowering of prices in a group of commodities in which restrictive practices were suspected. This would be a highly desirable method from many points of view, but Czechoslovakia's balance of payments would have to improve substantially before it could be considered a practical proposition.

One of the essential corollaries of increased enterprise or trust independence is increased financial responsibilities. One of the main aims of the whole reform is to increase the self-sufficiency of the enterprises and the trusts. This, again, is something the new Czechoslovak proposals have in common with all other new East European systems. Central investments are to be cut down to a severe minimum. Instead of having each enterprise receive the bulk of its investment funds from the treasury, as in the past, the trusts and enterprises are required to finance most of their investments themselves or get credit from the banks; investments financed out of the state budget would be limited to very large development projects. The conditions under which bank credits are to be given, however, would still be laid down by the central authorities. This is a good example of an indirect method of control to which the government will switch under the new system. It is mainly the trusts which will control the investments within their particular industrial branch; the banks, acting as state agencies, will provide the investment credit to the trusts and the enterprises, keeping in mind the minimum conditions set on a national basis and certain minimum economic requirements.

As in the case of investments, central subsidization of wage payments will be discontinued under the new model. The wage fund of an individual enterprise in Czechoslovakia, as in Bulgaria, would be made up of what was left of gross receipts after non-labor operational costs, all interest payments, credit repayments, depreciation payments, and the various payments to the state have been deducted. All rewards to workers had to be covered out of gross receipts for "realized production." In the past, the state had made payments into wage funds simply on the presentation of receipts showing that a given amount of goods had been produced and delivered. Henceforth, payments will be made to workers on the basis of receipts of actual sales.

As in the reform proposals introduced in other countries, wages and salaries will be divided into two parts: basic payments, to be determined nationally; and incentive payments, in accordance with the incentive program adopted at each plant. In the case of the workers, guaranteed payments will cover some 90 per cent of their wages; the percentage for management and executives will be considerably lower.

This new model is a far-reaching one indeed, and it puts the Czechoslovaks in the forefront of economic thinking in Eastern Europe, Yugoslavia excepted. What is unique in their scheme is the methods used in determining prices. Here, they show a flexibility and boldness that even the Yugoslavs have not yet attained. There was, however, the danger that vested interests hostile to the new proposals would seek to undermine them. The Party *apparatchiks* at the lower level stood to lose much by the new reforms, since their authority and, in some cases, their jobs would be threatened. These *apparatchiks* were supported by certain powerful men in the top ranks, who, though they could not destroy the reform plan, tried to emasculate it by stressing the elements of central control it still retained. What became apparent in 1965, when the reform began to be implemented on a large scale, was the danger that these hostile elements would form an alliance with large sections of workers, who were also suspicious because of the effect the plan might initially have on wages and even on job security. But the regime showed no sign of backing off from any part of the plan. Indeed, having embraced it, its reputation was also at stake; it seemed determined to go through with the reforms.

East Germany

The idea of Walter Ulbricht pioneering in any kind of reform is a startling one, but the fact is that in 1965, East Germany was ahead of every East European state (again, Yugoslavia excepted) in the experimentation with and implementation of economic-reform measures. The words "experimentation" and "implementation" are used advisedly, since, in *concept*, the Czechoslovak economic model was the boldest. In fact, in one very important sphere—the coordination of the planning operation with the market mechanism—the Czechoslovak proposals went beyond anything that had yet been applied in Yugoslavia. But the Czechoslovak model has still not been as fully implemented as the East Germans'. Indeed, several important reforms actually began in East Germany before Professor Sik's proposals appeared in Prague.

Ulbricht began to clamber aboard the Liberman bandwagon only three months after the professor's famous article appeared in *Pravda*. At the Sixth Congress of East Germany's Socialist Unity Party, in January, 1963, some rather vague proposals for economic reform were outlined—and none too soon.

For several years, the East German industrial growth rate had been the lowest among the satellite nations, and her economic development as a whole had been a perfect demonstration of Professor Goldmann's theory of economic cycles. The situation had been aggravated before 1961 by the constant drainage of skilled manpower to West Germany and by the inordinately large war reparations that East Germany had to pay the Soviet Union in earlier years. Both these excuses had been put forth many times by apologists for the East German regime; both had validity. With regard to the second, however, it should be pointed out that the Soviet looting of Romania did not prevent the subsequent industrial boom in that country. Ulbricht was later to blame Stalin's influence for East German economic woes. It had been responsible, he argued, for the over-bureaucratization and rigidity of the system. There was some truth in this, for the East German ailment was basically due to the fact that its advanced economy had been treated like a primitive one.

By 1963, something urgent was required. Outwardly, of course, the economy did not seem to be in bad shape, and many Western businessmen who attended the annual Leipzig Fair, always an elaborate show, came back generally impressed with what they had seen. In 1964, East German industry produced what the whole of Hitler's Germany had produced in 1938. But a closer look revealed the chronic ills that had to be tackled.

The reform heralded by the Sixth Party Congress in early 1963 assumed more specific shape in the "Guidelines on the New System of Economic Planning and Managing the Economy," approved in July, 1963.[6] These "Guidelines" called for the granting of substantial powers to more than eighty VVB's (*Vereinigungen Volkseigener Betriebe,* or Associations of State-Owned Enterprises), some of which already existed and some of which were to be set up. They were the East German equivalent of the trusts or industrial groupings being formed in other East European states. As the focal point of decentralization, they were to have transferred to them many of the planning and management functions previously held by the central ministries and agencies. At the apex of each VVB, there were to be general directorates with wide powers of autonomy, acting as clearing-houses for the directives and over-all plans for their industries that would still come down from the center, and for proposed plans that would come up to them from the individual enterprises under their control (which are known as VEB's—*Volkseigene Betriebe,* or individual State Enterprises). Once the general directorates had synthesized the different, often conflicting plans and suggestions, they were to send their final recommendations back to the National Economic Council for approval.

The VVB's took over and were completely responsible for the implementation of their particular part of the approved plan. They were to be responsible for the internal financing of investments through the profits and amortization of the enterprises under them. If necessary, they could apply to the banks for credit on a commercial basis. In any case, centrally provided investments, except in special circumstances, were to be drastically reduced. The VVB's were also responsible for the introduction of technical innovations, control of production, and distribution of profits. It was also up to them to determine the optimum size of each enterprise (VEB) under their control and to allocate manpower. The great majority of industrial enterprises in East Germany were to be grouped under the VVB's according to industry, but some were still to be directly responsible to the National Economic Council or to the local economic councils.

The "Guidelines" also announced an industrial price reform for the most important basic materials—solid fuels, power, metallurgical products, and chemical raw materials—to be carried out in 1964. This actually began in April of that year and had the effect of largely eliminating subsidies from the state treasury, which had acted as artificial price supports. To take the place of these state subsidies, the VVB's now use a system of subsidies of their own through the redistributions of profits and repayable bank credits. It was hoped that by the beginning of 1966 new prices would have been fixed for *all* industrial raw and semi-finished materials. This aim will probably be achieved, since one of the most notable features of the implementation of the whole reform in 1965 was that everything was going according to schedule.

Closely connected with the price reform was a re-evaluation of capital assets to provide for a more accurate estimate of production costs and a stricter use of capital materials. This re-evaluation was completed for most machinery and equipment stocks by the end of 1964. It was a fundamental step before a number of other necessary reforms could be carried out—the application of differentiated depreciation rates, and a system of differentiated interest charges on fixed and circulating capital, for instance.

Reforms such as these were not generally introduced before 1965 except experimentally. In April, 1965, however, they began to be applied more generally. Until the beginning of 1966, there was to be a period of "complex experimentation," after which an integrated system of economic instruments would be applied broadly. But one innovation that had been completely introduced as early as the end of 1964 was a thorough cost-accounting system covering every single cost item incurred by the VVB's, thereby laying the groundwork for a far more businesslike and "economical" approach.

As in the other East European reform models, the wage and premium system was revamped. East Germany had perhaps remained more faithful to the old Stakhanovite system of remuneration than any other country: quantitative over-fulfillment of often not very high norms had been its chief characteristic, and this had led to wage funds being increased and to premiums for over-fulfillment being paid out of them. Under the new system, the premium funds were quite distinct and directly related to profits rather than production. The general directors of the VVB's were to have the power to fix the premium funds in accordance with profits realized.

In the G.D.R., as elsewhere, profits were to be the major indicator of success or failure of an economic enterprise, and market relations (or, as Ulbricht put it, the laws of economic value) were gradually to take the place of the central directives. Contracts based on market conditions were to be the main instruments by which relations between economic organizations were to be conducted, and there were to be closer ties between the production centers and the internal and external trade networks.

By 1965, then, several basic reforms had been completed in East Germany, and various economic levers had been introduced experimentally on a fairly broad scale. The VVB's were in operation and carrying out most of the functions delegated to them; the re-evaluation of capital in the main industries and in the field of construction had been concluded; new prices for the principal raw materials had been introduced. Still being carried out experimentally were the new system of premium payments tied to profits, which actually formed the variable part of total income; the granting of credit to the VVB's on commercial conditions; differentiated capital interest and depreciation rates; and other economic instruments.

East Germany, therefore, held the lead but, by the end of 1965, as the plan in Czechoslovakia began to be more generally applied, she began to lose it. Apart from the system of *indirect* controls, an outstanding characteristic of all the East European schemes for economic reform, the Pankow regime still relied heavily on a number of *direct* controls. All the VVB's were subject to an accounting system supervised from Berlin and liable to periodic checks. Most important, central control was retained over the determination of prices. A number of provisions in the new system made for flexibility in prices in the light of changing market conditions, but, in the end, prices were centrally fixed, and the Czechoslovak proposals for variable and free prices were still absent. In its timidity, the East German scheme seemed to be more similar to the Bulgarian, which meant that one of the most advanced economies in Eastern Europe felt the same hesitations as one of the most backward on this decisive question.

But even on the question of price determination, there were indications in 1965 that some relative freedom was being considered. The truth was that Ulbricht seemed determined to make this reform work, not only for the economic benefits it would eventually bring, but also for the political advantages to be gained by accommodating the technical intelligentsia. Despite the massive defections before August, 1961, there was still much technical and managerial skill in East Germany. An essential precondition for success was present, therefore, as in Czechoslovakia. The prospects were good, if the climate remained favorable.

Hungary

Economic reform in Hungary came slowly and by degrees. There was no urgency to produce a blueprint, but, in 1965, the topic was current. Commissions had been formed to study the matter, and, from a number of regime pronouncements, it became clear that something comprehensive was being prepared. Favorable references to the Czechoslovak model and visits by Hungarian officials to

Czechoslovakia itself indicated that Professor Sik had made many converts in Budapest.

Perhaps Hungary had been slow in this regard because of complacency or perhaps because of strong opposition in conservative quarters to the idea of far-reaching reform. But probably the main reason was that ever since 1958, a number of piece-meal reforms had been introduced which now added up to an impressive total.

In 1958, the first payments were made in a new profit-sharing system. The amount of the payments given to each worker was geared to the profit his factory had made the previous year. One of the more fortunate legacies of the 1956 Revolution, the system was a small but meaningful material incentive. The next important ameliorative measure was the reform of industrial pricing carried out in 1959. Briefly, what was involved here was an increase in wholesale prices to bring them into closer conformity with industrial costs. (A similar move was carried out in Romania at the beginning of 1963.) This was an unpopular but essential prerequisite for a more rational accounting groundwork. At the same time, the Hungarian Government established a fund to promote technical development. Several billion *forint* from this fund were granted annually to individual enterprises to help toward the purchase of better machines and equipment.

In 1962, there followed the beginnings of an industrial reorganization that was to take three years to complete. In the course of this, the number of state-operated industrial enterprises was reduced, through a series of mergers, from about 1,400 to just over 900. The 900 were grouped under industrial trusts (which may have served later as a partial model for similar groupings proposed elsewhere). Once these groupings were set up in Hungary, some of the directorial control held by the ministries—in matters affecting investments, quantity, quality, and distribution plans—was delegated to them. In addition to its decentralizing aspects, this move was designed to provide more qualified and expert industrial leadership, to reduce production costs, and to rationalize the production process within the plants themselves.

Certainly the most dramatic of all the pragmatic measures introduced by the Hungarian regime was the 5 per cent interest rate fixed on gross fixed and working capital in January, 1964. Hungary was the first Communist state to make such a reform, and this "capitalist" measure is worth considering in some detail.

The measure defined "fixed" capital as including buildings (land was excluded), machines and equipment, and vehicles. "Circulating," or " working," capital was defined as including materials (raw and subsidiary materials, fuel, etc.), small tools and smaller pieces of equipment, and finished and semi-finished goods.

The principal aims of this measure were:

1. *To stimulate a more intensive exploitation of the means of production.* One of the greatest weaknesses of East European industry was that the productive capacity of the machines was not being fully utilized. In some extreme cases, valuable modern machines had been in storage for years. Even in some of the better plants, only one shift operated per day, and machines often became obsolete before the investments in them had been recouped. The interest rate was designed to encourage a more rigorous use of machines, the release of superfluous machines to other plants where they were needed, and the scrapping of machines that had ceased to be profitable. In addition, the interest rate was designed to encourage a change to the multiple-shift system.

2. *To encourage more rational investments.* Henceforth, it would not be possible to make investments "free of charge," since a 5 per cent levy would be charged on them. Directors would be inhibited from indiscriminately ordering new machines and would tend to concentrate only on capital investments that were economically worth while. As the Central Committee's political journal *Partelet* put it in January, 1964: "The enterprises will make more responsible decisions about investments if they themselves will enjoy—or suffer—the material consequences of them."

3. *To encourage a greater economy in raw materials.* Since interest had to be paid on all materials in the possession of the enterprise, the managements would think twice about hoarding these materials. It had been a universal practice among enterprise directors in Hungary (and not only there), to protect themselves against the vagaries of planning and distribution by storing up much larger quantities of raw materials than they actually needed. Here, of course, considerations of foreign commerce entered the

picture, since 60 per cent of Hungarian industry's raw-material requirements were covered by imports.

4. *To encourage a better inventory policy and more modern manufactures.* The 5 per cent interest rate was also levied on finished and semi-finished products—commission goods, i.e., commodities not manufactured by the enterprise in question but only bought for resale purposes, as well as finished products produced by the plant itself. One of the gravest deficiencies of Communist economies was the persistent manufacture of obsolete or unwanted goods that could not be sold. Since these unsalable goods would now, in effect, be taxed, the plants would be forced to produce goods the customers wanted.

The 5 per cent interest rate was a severe measure. It put many of the less efficient firms in serious financial difficulty: some industrial prices went up to enable the plants to meet the new charges; some profit shares allocated to workers went down. It was a necessary corrective measure, however, the full effects of which would probably not be felt for several years.

If the industrial price reform, the reorganization of industry, and, especially, the introduction of the 5 per cent interest rate were the most tangible features of economic reform in Hungary, they were by no means the only measures introduced to increase economic efficiency. In other respects as well, a businesslike attitude was shown by the Hungarian economic leadership. Fully realizing that Hungary heavily depended on imports, for example, they set about mounting an export offensive which, by 1963, was achieving quite good results, especially in processed foods. One should not exaggerate this success, of course, for vast improvements were still necessary. But the encouragement given to produce for the foreign market is slowly but surely beginning to pay off, and if the Common Market turns out to be a little less discriminatory than it first looked, it is probable that further successes will be achieved.

Finally, one must not overlook what might be called the Kadar regime's "personnel policy" in economic affairs. The success of even the most perfect scheme of economic reform depends largely on the managers, the technicians, and the ministry officials who run the economy. This was realized in Hungary as elsewhere; the various East European regimes were, in 1963 and 1964, anxiously casting about for trained economic personnel to replace the economically innocent Party stalwarts who had been ruining, rather than running, things for years. Kadar began his "expertise offensive" early in 1960, even giving non-Party men preference over less qualified Party members in appointments to economic positions. Slowly but steadily, he revamped his economic *apparat* until, by 1965, it was probably in better shape than any other in Eastern Europe. This in itself was a reform of the first magnitude.

A great deal has been done, but throughout 1965 it also became clear that it has not been enough. Kadar himself was among the first to criticize; it was he who announced that, after thorough preparation, a far-reaching reform would be enacted.[7] (Part of that preparation was a serious study of the new Czechoslovak system and the establishment of eleven commissions to examine different aspects of the economy.) It would appear that the reform, when it comes, will be extensive, but it remains to be seen whether Hungary will take the lead in economic de-Stalinization as she had in political de-Stalinization.

Poland

In 1963, it was clear that the Polish economy was suffering the effects of a number of long-standing ills and deficiences. Like the other countries in the region, Poland had, in the 1950's, concentrated too much investment on the heavy manufacturing industries and neglected the fuel and raw-material industries. Later, she had paid more attention to the extractive industries, but these efforts could not begin to pay off until the end of the 1960's, and the processing industries continued to expand in the meantime. In any case, Poland was suffering from an acute lack of capital with which to expand its rich raw-material base adequately. Moreover, the country's traditional exports, such as coal and processed foods, began to suffer from adverse conditions of trade. As a result, economic development began to slow down to the point of stagnation. If one adds to these difficulties other familiar ones, such as a public consumption that was too high when measured against the rise in productivity, and a growing disparity between goods produced and goods wanted by the public, the serious condition of the Polish economy becomes apparent.

Poland also had its own special problem that probably caused more concern than any other: the specter of mass unemployment. Poland was beginning to feel the effects of the "baby boom" of the first postwar years, something which no other East European country had experienced to anything like the same extent. More and more young men came onto the labor market, and it became more and more difficult to find jobs for them. The humiliating "phenomenon" of a socialist state with an open unemployment problem had come to pass: it was estimated that there were well over 300,000 jobless members of the labor force in Poland in the early months of 1964, a time when the economy was having to contract instead of expand.[8]

But if the problem was serious in 1964, it was certain to become far more serious as the years went on. The Polish Government itself estimated that between 1966 and 1970, 3.2 million youngsters would reach the age of eighteen, an increase of 45 per cent over the previous five-year planning period.[9] Retirements would provide a fairly large number of openings, of course, but it was still expected that 1.5 million new nonagricultural jobs would have to be found. (This rather unwisely assumed that the total work force in agriculture would not change.) To achieve this, the regime promised to turn to the private sector more than it had in the past, to increase the number of artisans, and to give greater encouragement to home or cottage industries. But it is difficult to see how Poland will avoid having a permanent pool of unemployed on her hands in the coming years.

It was against this background of increasing economic difficulties that in 1964 the regime once again turned to the question of comprehensive economic reform, the subject it had shelved in 1957. It is worth looking, for a moment, at those earlier proposals that would have made Poland the trail-blazer in all of Eastern Europe if they had been accepted.

The Polish economic model of 1957 was prepared by the Economic Council attached to the Council of Ministers. The father of the proposal was Professor Oskar Lange (who had taught for several years at the University of Chicago). What Professor Ota

Sik was to the 1964 Czechoslovak model, Professor Lange was to its 1957 forerunner in Poland. The Polish model called for two fundamental changes in the economic system: a thorough reorganization of the management of the economy, stressing decentralization and the financial autonomy of individual enterprises; and the introduction into the economy of quasi-market conditions in the relations between state enterprises and the wholesale and retail distribution systems. The basic aim was to bring in the profit motive and other economic incentives, and to push administrative directives as far as possible into the background.

The basic operational unit of the economy was to be the autonomous enterprise in which the director shared responsibility with the workers' councils (which had not yet been scrapped and were flourishing). The enterprise was to operate on the principle of profitability and would be allowed to sell its products to other enterprises and to the purchasing agencies at prices governed by production cost and market conditions. State subsidies were to be discontinued. To get as close as possible to real market conditions, there was to be a price and wage reform. Industrial prices were to be brought to the level of actual production costs, which meant that they would have to go up. To compensate the population, there would have to be an increase in wages and other sources of income.

The Polish model owed much to the Yugoslav example, but it went much farther than anything implemented in Yugoslavia up to that time. Indeed, it was precisely because it was so revolutionary that it was soon shelved. As the Polish Party began to recover its strength and confidence, and as Gomulka's true nature began to show itself, conservatism predominated over reformism. In 1958 and 1959, the more orthodox economic officials returned to power and initiated a policy that was at least partly to blame for the predicament in which Poland found itself in the 1960's.

Though the Polish economic model was stillborn, it was not forgotten. Its principles were kept alive in a series of experiments in a number of enterprises (mainly producing for export) which the Polish regime continued to allow. But more important was the fact that it was constantly kept before the minds of the intelligent Polish public by a stream of articles and books stressing the continued and ever more urgent need for economic reform. The standard-bearer of this crusade was the Warsaw economic weekly *Zycie Gospodarcze,* for many years the most stimulating economic journal in all Eastern Europe.

Toward the end of 1963, the Polish leaders began at last to take a close look at their economic machinery. All of them, and this included Gomulka, knew that something was wrong. Yet they persisted in their belief that the structure was by definition satisfactory and the fault lay elsewhere. But by the time of the Fourth Party Congress, in June, 1964, the more liberal economists had evidently persuaded the leadership that the structure itself needed overhauling. Some of the results of their prodding were contained in the Congress Theses[10] and in a resolution and directive published a month later.[11]

On the subject of economic reform, the Theses were rather vague and simply referred to general principles that should be followed. They did, however, contain one specific proposal designed to cushion the economy against what had become a rather alarming habit in Polish economic life: the inability to meet investment targets, which had led to abrupt cuts having to be made that seriously upset the rhythm of economic development. The Party proposed that an investment reserve pool be established to cover unforeseen demands and human errors in calculation.

The Theses also called for an analysis of various planning coefficients and the use of modern mathematical and statistical techniques to facilitate more scientific analyses. All planning in the future, they said, should be aimed solely at producing optimal economic results: "The guiding theme of change in the planning system should be a concentration on the analysis of economic returns." Efficient planning necessitated "the broad application of indicators which are the closest to net production." Such indicators were to measure profitability and reduction costs. Improvements in the price system were demanded, and an elastic system of material incentives. In the case of enterprises, the Theses called for an introduction of interest rates to ensure a better use of capital; they also suggested a reinforcement of the role of profits as "a measure of the rationality and efficiency of socialist enterprises."

Turning to the management system, the Theses called in very

general terms for greater economic independence—including more control over investments, more flexibility, greater responsibility, and more rationality. In the future, ministries would concentrate on coordinating the work of numbers of enterprises rather than directing the work of each single one. Within the plants themselves, there was to be a greater degree of joint consultation and worker participation.

The Theses were followed in July by a long resolution and directive laying down tasks for the future organization of Polish industry. These documents showed clearly the importance being given to ensuring that economic motives played a greater role in management.

The resolution and directive outlined a whole network of economic services to embrace every layer of industry. They enumerated all the official government bodies, agencies, and bureaus that were to be held responsible for "enhancing economic progress" and were to cooperate with the enterprises and the new groupings of enterprises—the Industrial Associations. Representatives from all these bodies, together with the directors of the Industrial Associations, were to form a sort of central collegium.

The most interesting change at the government level was the establishment within each economic ministry of an under secretary of state for economic affairs, who was to be directly responsible for all problems connected with the fulfillment of annual and long-term economic plans, matters pertaining to inter-ministerial and inter-branch activities, and any other issues involving central supervision and control. All other problems, relating to investments and detailed planning within the framework of the general central plan, were to be the responsibility of the lower economic bodies, mainly the Industrial Associations, which, on these matters, were to have the right of final decision. The ministries, in cooperation with the banks, however, were to conduct frequent spot-checks on their operations of the associations, and were also to offer guidance "on the basis of instructions and trends established by the Party and government." All this ensured the continuation of a considerable amount of central control.

The Industrial Associations were the key to the newly proposed structure. As in the other countries where reforms were being carried out, each association encompassed the enterprises of a particular industry or branch of industry, except for some very large enterprises that would have the status of an Industrial Association. Within each Association, a chief economist or deputy director for economic affairs was to be responsible for economic planning and analysis, employment and wage policies, finance, program development, and investment policy. He was also to cooperate with economic organizations in other countries on topics of mutual interest. Under this chief economist there would be a number of other experts to assist him in various matters.

Each large enterprise in an Industrial Association was also to have a chief economist with parallel responsibilities at a lower level. One of the most important duties of the enterprise economist would be the preparation of monthly and quarterly reports checking the status of the most important technical and economic indexes. After presentation to the manager, these reports were to be discussed with the conference of workers' self-government. Annual reports were also to be made and similarly discussed.

In addition, the resolution and directive laid down rather complicated procedures for economic accounting and the use of economic analysis. The minute detail into which they went showed that the regime was determined to leave as little as possible to chance.

After this outline of the administrative structure followed a list of the various qualifications for the personnel who were to man this structure. The ministries themselves were to define the posts to be filled by high level economics graduates. Obviously, the demand for trained economists would at first be much greater than the supply, so the regime would have to make do with fewer trained personnel. But all those to be used in the new program were to have had some training in curriculums centered on economics—technical studies, public administration, statistics, and accounting. People with ten or more years of service in any department dealing with economic subjects would qualify for at least some of the economic posts. Concurrent with the various schemes for on-the-job training, economics and technical subjects were to be given a boost in the schools and universities; existing economics courses were to be revised and modernized. The directive also outlined several incentive schemes: bonuses and premiums to be paid to workers and salaried staff who came up with good ideas or innovations; and financial encouragement to enterprises that, after ministerial approval, entered into projects involving economic risk.

Toward the end of the directive was a timetable of dates by which the various aspects of the directive were to be implemented or completely prepared. The most important of these stipulated that within twelve months (i.e., by July, 1965), the ministers concerned were to submit to the Council of Ministers a draft outlining the system of management in the Industrial Associations under their control. The main stress was to be on planning and management methods, collaboration with the controlling ministry, labor and management incentives, scientific development, and the correct disposition of investments. The directive urged the Associations to make sure that their activities were in keeping with "market and consumer demand" and the "technical-economic capabilities" of the given industry. Recognizing that conditions could change, the directive instructed the Associations and ministries to adjust production to the changing demands of the domestic and the foreign markets. The stress was on getting every economic unit in Poland away from the old axiom of production for production's sake.

At the end of July, 1965, a Central Committee plenum of the Polish Party heard a report by the Chairman of the State Planning Commission, Jedrychowski, in which he outlined further proposals for economic reform.[12] They must have come as a great disappointment to all advocates of genuine improvement, for, while stressing that profitability was to be the sole economic criterion in the future, and promising more scientific, elastic, and consistent planning, Jedrychowski made it quite clear that centralized fixing of prices would continue and that central control generally would still be the main feature of the Polish economic system. The new proposals were certainly a step forward, but they tackled the symptoms rather than the basic causes of Poland's economic ills.

The new proposals did little to relieve the concern voiced eight months earlier by the Catholic member of parliament Konstantin Lubienski. In a speech to the Polish parliament in December, 1964, Lubienski remarked:

> Today, one gets the impression that our neighbors are getting ahead of us, not only through the boldness of the questions they have brought up, but also through the speed with which they are introducing the necessary reforms in practice. . . . If things go on as they are, our economy will become a collection of experimenting enterprises. And yet the sum of experiments cannot replace a consistent and well thought-out system of new planning and administration, functioning over the whole range of our economy.[13]

The thought that they might be behind their East European neighbors in any respect has always been very galling to Poles. Now they were behind in a lot of things, nowhere more dangerously so than in the sphere of economic reform.

Romania

In 1965, the Romanian "industrial miracle" that had begun five years earlier was still in full swing. Although the growth rate had slightly decelerated since 1960, it still kept a very high, sustained pace. In 1960, the percentage increase over 1959 had been 16.4 per cent; it proceeded to drop gradually to 12.5 per cent for 1963, but in 1964 it was up to more than 13 per cent, the highest rate of increase in the Soviet bloc.

The simplest explanation for Romania's progress is that, as a backward country, it started from a very low base and that swift progress in the early stages of industrial development was a relatively easy matter. This is true, but Romania's industrial progress before World War II—and not only in her oil industry—should not be overlooked. Her industrial base was considerably larger than Bulgaria's, for example, and yet she maintained a consistently higher industrial growth rate than her Balkan neighbor.

Another basic reason for Romania's success was her natural wealth, greater than that of any other East European country. The fact that she was able to maintain this success was, in considerable measure, due to yet another "natural" cause: the continuing abundance of labor. Should her large reserve of labor begin to dry up, Romania would have to face the difficult problem of increasing productivity and keeping the increase in personal income down to a similar pace. Real wages have begun to increase steadily in Romania but are still disproportionately low. Whether the public demand for continued increases can be contained or not would be largely a political rather than an economic question.

The principal "manmade" reasons for the continued high growth rate were a 46 per cent rise in industrial investment between 1960 and 1962, and improvement in the investment structure itself. Stress had been laid on concentrating resources in industrial projects already begun, rather than in big new projects. It was possible that, in 1965 and 1966, the drain on investments for the giant, new metallurgical combinate at Galati, which was supposed to be producing 4.4 million tons of steel by 1970, and for other new projects, like the aluminum factory at Slatina, would begin to leave their mark. But the regime was convinced that it could continue its high rate of expansion, and its past economic record gave sufficient assurance that it knew what it was doing.

The very success of Romanian industry, and the apparent ability to avoid or stave off many of the ills that were plaguing the more advanced economies to the north and west, obviously made the question of economic reform less pressing. Bucharest's motto seemed to have been "let well enough alone," and it was, therefore, not surprising that by the end of 1964 there had been less economic reform or "revisionism" in Romania than in any of the other countries under review. The management and planning of the economy still presented a picture of old-fashioned orthodoxy.

This did not mean that no steps had been taken toward improvement. The main improvements had been aimed at making planning more realistic, but there had been institutional changes as well. By far the most important of these was the introduction of a new industrial price system at the beginning of 1963, a reform to which too little attention was paid in the West. The whole price system had been thoroughly re-examined between 1960 and 1962; the purpose in introducing the new system in 1963, best described by Roman Moldovan, then First Deputy Chairman of the State Planning Committee and one of the brains behind the industrial boom, was as follows:

> This perfected form of planned management [the new price system] ensures a better assessment of the real cost prices of products, as well as of profitability, and, thus, a more correct evaluation of the

required volume of investment. The new price system also eliminates, as a rule, state allocations by industrial branches, as well as exaggerated profits. In this way, the new bulk-buying prices stimulate, under improved conditions, reduction of the cost price and a more rational utilization of material resources. The new price system also permits a maximum economy of social labor, and, together with the revaluation of fixed funds of State enterprises and the elaboration of new forms for amortization on the basis of directives issued by the Council of Ministers in July, 1962, it constitutes a move of great importance for the improvement of economic planning.[14]

More "reformist" than the introduction of the new pricing system was the fact that ever since 1956 the number of centrally planned indexes had been gradually reduced. In 1956, there were 979, by 1963, 129. This was still a relatively large number compared with Poland and Hungary, for example. But it represented uniform progress, whereas in Poland the number had gone up or down according to which trend of economic thinking happened to be prevalent. As a result of this progress, the prerogatives of Romanian industrial enterprises and organizations correspondingly increased, but the area within which they were allowed freedom of movement remained restricted.

To sum up briefly: what had been carried out in Romania was a rationalization of the existing system rather than the introduction of a new one. In the article quoted above, Professor Moldovan approvingly quoted the following description of Romanian economic methods from the Italian Communist Party journal *Rinascità:*

> Within the framework of a centralized management, production programs are fulfilled gradually. The characteristic of the Romanian experiment consists rather in the distinctive way in which the general line is being applied and adapted to the specific conditions prevailing in the country, in how adequate technical solutions corresponding to the available resources are sought, and how the pace of transformation is set in terms of the objective possibilities.

As long as the goose continued to lay the golden eggs, there was no need to change this outlook, and in 1965, there was no sign that Romania's industrial boom was coming to an end. But there were signs that the rate of industrial growth was beginning to slacken. The economic planners wisely set their sights a little lower for the next five-year planning period of 1966–70: an average annual industry growth rate of 10.5 per cent, compared with the 13 per cent rate of the previous Six-Year Plan of 1960–65. (The average growth rate was actually 14.8 in that period.) But this still implies a most impressive dynamism, and, for the moment, the regime seems to have decided to leave well enough alone. At the Party Congress in July, 1965, there was little mention of reform.* Romania is "odd man out" in Eastern Europe in a number of ways and will only follow its neighbors in the sphere of economic reform when the efficacy of the present system of management and planning begins to decline. That time has evidently not yet come.

The Re-emergence of the Private Sector

The re-emergence of artisans and other private entrepreneurs in Eastern Europe should be seen as another part of the trend toward more realistic practices. It is true that the steps taken to make minor private enterprise more respectable have been rather small. "Creeping capitalism" in a socialist state is still considered doctrinally unhealthy. But in Poland, Czechoslovakia, Hungary, and Bulgaria, a break in the hostility had become discernible.

The private craftsmen had been through several vicissitudes in Poland. In 1948, there had been nearly 140,000 private workshops in Poland employing more than 300,000 workers and a large number of apprentices. By the time Stalin died, the number of workshops had been reduced to 82,000, the number of employees to 124,000. The private craftsmen had been subjected to all sorts of chicaneries: the regime paid low prices for their products and charged high prices for their materials; they were levied extra taxes that many of them could not pay, with the result that their property was often seized. When Gomulka came to power, he promised to rectify this situation, and important tax concessions were ini-

* Romania's chief economics minister, Alexandru Barladeanu, and a few other speakers did refer to the need for factories to have more independence from the central authorities, but no specific proposals were made on how this should be achieved.

tially made. By the middle of 1957, the number of private workshops was almost back to the 1948 figure, although the number of employees was still very much lower. But, as in the case of so many of Gomulka's reforms, the early promise was not kept. Local councils continued to treat the workshops unfairly in the supply of raw materials. Between 1958 and the end of 1962, their number had shrunk by another 30,000; the downward trend continued in 1963.

In Hungary, the pattern was very much the same. Before the war, there had been about 200,000 private craftsmen in the country. By 1953, there were 36,000. During the brief premiership of Imre Nagy (1953–55), their number rose markedly, but the Kadar regime further restricted them, and their number again fell rapidly. The reforms of 1963, however, rallied them once more, and by 1965 they numbered more than 60,000.

Private artisans were subject to the most drastic repression of all in Czechoslovakia. By 1961, the socialization of small traders was said to have been completed, and it is a measure of Novotny's dogmatic thoroughness that only 3,700 private craftsmen remained in the country by 1962; in 1938, there had been 380,000.

For Bulgaria, no figures showing the suppression of private craftsmen and artisans are available, but the process was the same there as in Poland, Hungary, and Czechoslovakia. In the G.D.R.—curiously enough, in view of the doctrinaire character of the Ulbricht regime—private enterprises were not suppressed to anything like the same extent. In 1963, the last year for which reliable statistics are available, there were nearly 156,000 private craft or artisan enterprises with over 383,000 employees. Pressure had been applied to force these enterprises to join artisan collectives, but it had not been strong; from 1963 onward, it seems to have almost disappeared. In Romania, the suppression since the Communist take-over was quite relentless, and there are so signs that the regime is prepared to change its policy.

There were several reasons why the Polish, Bulgarian, Czechoslovak, and Hungarian regimes decided to switch from a policy of suppression to one of mild encouragement. In Poland and Bulgaria, for example, it was one way of making the unemployment problem less acute. In Czechoslovakia, improvements in hotel and catering services were made with one eye to the tourist trade. In Hungary, exported handicrafts brought needed foreign currency. But the basic, generally applicable reason was that an improved standard of living had increased the demand for better services; East European regimes were aware that satisfying minor daily needs with shoemaking, laundries, and the like often made the difference between a moderately contented population and a thoroughly irascible one. The need was certainly great, since these minor services had been seriously neglected in the previous twenty years and the newspapers of most of the East European countries had begun to carry articles complaining about the appalling lack of plumbers, shoemakers, and other service tradesmen.

The task of filling these needs was given over to private operators because the state did not consider it an economically wise proposition to do it itself: it would require too much investment for too little return, especially in rural areas. It was much cheaper to allow private individuals to do it. The regime also wished to reduce the number of "black" enterprises. Many skilled workmen in Eastern Europe, forced to work in state enterprises or in artisans' collectives during the day, worked illegally in private, in their spare time, using state materials and often state tools for their jobs. By legalizing private work, the regimes hoped to bring this side of economic life more into the open.

In April, 1964, the Czechoslovak Government announced that, as of April 1, various minor services had been "re-privatized":[15] laundries, shoeshining, tailoring and alterations, car washing and attendance, cloakroom attendance, sales of refreshments and souvenirs, portering and running errands—in other words, hotel and catering services (the hotels, of course, still being owned by the state). Those interested in acquiring a concession were to pay insurance, a lump-sum tax, and such overhead costs as heating, electricity, etc., to the enterprise selling the concession. They were also required to get official licenses.

In July, a measure providing for a limited and controlled "reprivatization" of some rural services was also announced.[16] Local committees were authorized to issue licenses to tailors, shoemakers, carpenters, hairdressers, launderers, interior decorators, etc. As in the case of the earlier concession, it was made clear that only women, pensioners, and disabled persons would be eligible. (This clearly showed the fear of losing skilled men from the state labor force.) It was also decreed that the concessionaries could not employ additional labor. To make the area of opportunity even more restricted, private entrepreneurs were forbidden to set up in localities "served" by communal services. As can be seen, the concessions granted were not very generous, and, by the middle of 1965 only about 1,000 permits to operate private enterprise services had been granted under the new provisions. The beginnings in Czechoslovakia, therefore, were modest indeed.

The process began a full year earlier in Hungary than in Czechoslovakia, and it was more liberal. In May, 1963, the government agreed to issue licenses to any artisan who settled in an area where there was a shortage in his particular trade. They were to be granted tax exemption for a year, and an artisan who settled in the country would be allocated 30 per cent more raw materials than his urban counterpart. Indeed, the shortage of artisans in the countryside was so great that a decision was made to create an emergency service, manned by private artisans, that would work one day a week in three or four villages. In August, 1963, the government approved another decree encouraging private artisans in the villages. In October, 1964, a more generous provision was made enabling local councils in villages with a population not exceeding 5,000 to grant licenses in twenty-three trades to artisans with at least two years' practice.[17] In the cities also, the regime was more generous in granting licenses, and, by the end of 1964, there were 80,000 private craftsmen and artisans working in Budapest.[18]

In April, 1964, the Polish Government issued three new regulations concerning private craftsmen.[19] They provided for: (1) income-tax exemption for invalid or retired private artisans in towns with a population of 10,000 or less, provided they hired no employees; (2) tax relief for craftsmen who trained apprentices; (3) a two-year exemption from income and turnover taxes in towns with a population of 20,000 or less, provided that no members of the family or hired labor were employed. In July, a system of ten-year licensing for private commercial firms was introduced;[20] at the same time, the national councils were encouraged to develop private restaurants and cafés in holiday resorts and to license private traders in furniture, precision and optical instruments, and various kinds of servicing establishments. In December, private ownership of gasoline stations was authorized. By 1965, there were 135,000 private craft workshops in Poland, an increase of 2,400 over the end of 1963; it was estimated that by 1970 there would be 173,000.[21]

In Bulgaria, the regime changed its policy on the private crafts and artisans in 1965. In June, the Ministry of Finance gave permission for local authorities to give permits enabling individual applicants to perform services, work in handicrafts, and produce spare parts or semi-finished goods.[22] Those eligible were unemployed persons, employed persons working in their free time, and pensioners. In certain types of production, private entrepreneurs could employ one worker and train one apprentice; in certain cases, even two people could be employed. This was a limited measure, but it was encouraging. It was motivated both by the desire to improve the state of services in Bulgaria and the need to try to soak up the country's surplus labor.

One may assume that in the countries where the trend to revitalize small-scale private initiative has begun, it will slowly continue. For, once the private craftsmen and artisans become entrenched, they will show how indispensable they are to societies where living standards are gradually rising. Their resuscitation is another small example of the humanizing of society in Communist Eastern Europe.

Conclusion

The economic reforms reviewed in the previous pages have implications that go far beyond the purely economic sphere. Politically, they were the beginning of a development that, if carried to its logical conclusion, would bring great changes in the type and manner of political leadership in Eastern Europe. Party supremacy, as it has been traditionally understood, may gradually wither away, to be replaced by a type of control based on an empiricism and flexibility completely different from what has been known before. Politicians would, of course, still retain control; one cannot look forward to men like Professor Ota Sik becoming premier. But the new politicians may be molded by, responsive to, and thoroughly understanding of the new era of which the economic reforms are both a cause and a symptom. Similarly, as Party supremacy of the old type disappears, so will the potency of the traditionally understood ideology.

The economic reforms also had a bearing on East European relations with the Soviet Union. The fact that East Germany and Czechoslovakia could publish and begin to implement fundamental reforms of any kind without first waiting for the Soviet blueprint was a notable example of how the Soviet–East European relationship had changed in the course of Khrushchev's time. It is true, of course, that Professor Liberman's ideas and their tolerant reception in the Soviet Union acted as a great spur. But once the spur had been given, the East Europeans did not wait: they plunged straight ahead with models of their own. Thus, in one of the most fundamental reformations ever contemplated, the "satellites" and not the Soviet Union were pioneers. There was no suggestion that Czechoslovakia or East Germany acted in defiance of the Soviet Union. They were simply the first, and that was a new departure of the greatest significance.

What the economically more advanced countries of Eastern Europe were actually doing was to adopt the type of economic structure they should have had in the first place (accepting the fact, of course, that they are Communist states). By imitating the Soviet Union in every respect, they had embraced a system of planning and management much too backward for the stage of development their economies had already reached. They were now, therefore, rather belatedly catching up. Nations like Czechoslovakia and East Germany, industrially more developed than even the Soviet Union, could if they persisted on their course with boldness and consistency, retain their lead over her in the sphere of economic reform as well. They could also soon overtake Yugoslavia, where decentralization in management and planning had gone very far but where, in a sense, the economy was still too backward for some of the experiments to which it was being subjected. In this connection, it is worth quoting the Czechoslovak economist who, when asked about economic reforms in Yugoslavia, first expressed his great appreciation, then added, "you have to have an economy before you can start talking about economic reform."

Finally, two notes of caution should be sounded. The economic reforms in Eastern Europe were destined to be long, drawn-out processes. The regimes had set various dates by which the new schemes should be working, but the chances were that there would still be a great deal of experimentation, adaptation, and change long after these deadlines had passed, and that it would be several years before a recognizable and fairly stable system would emerge. Moreover, methods of planning and management might be so different in various sectors of the same country that it would be difficult to talk about a single system. It should be remembered that the new reforms were not intended to apply to industry alone. Eventually, they were to apply to *all* sectors of the economy and even, as far as principles were concerned, to local government. Within the scope of this universal application, there were bound to be many variations and a great diversity—thoroughly incompatible with the centralistic homogeneity that had prevailed before.

Just as these reforms could not be pushed through quickly, so they could not be implemented without great difficulty. There was no magician with a magic wand at work here. Severe dislocations would be caused; the situation might get worse before it got better; there was great danger that in the early stages workers' incomes would drop rather than rise. All this seems inevitable, in spite of the gradual way the reforms were introduced. The reforms also have strong opponents who would see themselves vindicated by the first disaster and would seek to capitalize on resulting discontent. The course will be a very difficult one indeed. But it has been set in the right direction; once taken, it will be almost impossible to reverse.

A Note on Comecon

In Eastern Europe, the Khrushchev era was always noted as one that saw much less interference by the Soviet Union in the internal affairs of the East European states than had been the experience during Stalin's time. This is generally true, but it should not be forgotten that, in one sense, Khrushchev tried to interfere far more in the economic affairs of these countries than Stalin ever did.

The rampant nationalism prevailing in the region before 1945 was forcibly submerged by the Stalinist system. But, under Stalin, the East European states were allowed to pursue a policy of economic autarky that was essentially a continuation of the policy each country had pursued in pre-Communist times. Thus, from 1948 to 1953, one had the paradoxical situation of Communist leaders, most of whom had been trained in Moscow in the anti-nationalist tradition, pursuing an economic policy that was to make attainment of the internationalism they proclaimed more and more difficult. They enthusiastically followed the Marxist-Leninist dictum that a heavy industrial base was a necessary prerequisite to the attainment of socialism, but it presumably never occurred to them that the construction of socialism might be carried out on a plane broader than the purely national one. Thus, the "cosmopolitan" leaders of this period unconsciously strengthened the parochial, nationalistic feelings of their populations and of the young Communist cadres maturing under them. Between 1953 and 1956, when the character of the Communist leadership changed and the "home" Communist leaders replaced the "Muscovites," this tendency was further stressed, since the new leaders' outlooks and instincts much more closely resembled those of the people they governed.

The regional pattern of trade that developed under this system was a relatively simple one. The Soviet Union supplied Eastern Europe with the necessary raw materials to mount and maintain industrialization drives, and Eastern Europe in turn supplied the Soviet Union with manufactured goods. What the Soviet Union did not want, they traded among themselves. Everything was done on a barter basis.

Very soon after Stalin's death, the new Soviet leadership saw the need to break with the absurd old system and introduce a coordination that would end duplication and waste. They had a ready-made instrument for this purpose.

The Council for Mutual Economic Assistance (CEMA or, as more commonly known in the West, COMECON) had been founded in 1949 as the Communist bloc's answer to the Marshall Plan but had never really functioned during Stalin's lifetime. It took a new lease on life after 1953 and slowly began to work toward a degree of industrial specialization among its member countries—something it was supposed to have done right from the beginning. At a meeting in Budapest in 1955, commissions were established to study its potential. These early beginnings were severely retarded by the upheavals of 1956, after which the immediate Soviet task was to bale out the groaning economies of Eastern Europe. Once the storm had been weathered, however, the Soviet Union returned to the question in greater earnest than ever before, and Khrushchev himself became the main salesman for closer coordination and greater specialization.

The first steps toward these goals were taken at a meeting of the leaders of the East European Communist parties in 1958. There, the coordination of the economic plans of the COMECON countries was agreed to, as was the drafting of long-term plans for 1960–80. The next step, a long overdue if rather formal one, was the publication in 1960 of the COMECON statutes, describing the organization, character, and aims of the institution. But in terms of making progress toward greater specialization and putting some teeth into the organization, the document proved to be a handicap rather than an advantage. By stressing the principle of voluntary cooperation and by leaving inviolate the unanimity ruling, it gave each country the legal machinery by which it could refuse to go along with any proposals it did not happen to like. (It is quite possible that the Soviet Union tried to secure the acceptance of more binding provisions in the statutes but was defeated.) At any rate, this voluntarism was to be the legal basis for Romanian obstinacy in the not too distant future.

It was obvious that for coordination to be meaningful, the earlier stress on bilateral negotiations within COMECON would have to give way to more multilateral arrangements. At a COMECON summit meeting held in June, 1962, it was agreed to form an Executive Committee, to be comprised of the member countries' deputy premiers in charge of economic development—an institutional step toward greater coordination and continuity. The Soviet Union probably hoped that, together with the Planning Board established at the same time, it would be a milestone on the road toward creation of a supranational planning body. But this same meeting proceeded to publish a document known as the "COMECON Principles." These principles stressed, in more precise terms than ever before, the notions of voluntarism, unanimous rulings, and the complete independence and sovereignty of the member countries. Soviet hopes could, therefore, be dashed by any state which chose to invoke the "June Principles." Romania very soon had occasion to do so.

In the months following the June, 1962, meeting in Moscow, Khrushchev took an active part in urging the merits of economic integration and supranational planning. In September, he made what the Soviets must have considered a great concession, one that would certainly have been unthinkable in Stalin's time. The Soviet Union, said Khrushchev, would give up the policy of developing her own industry on autarkic lines. If it were shown that other countries could make certain manufactured goods more cheaply and efficiently than the Soviet Union could, the latter would stop producing those goods. Warming to his subject, Khrushchev called for the establishment of a supranational planning body to select investment projects and allocate resources.[23]

His ideas ran into trouble immediately, however, mainly from the Romanian side. His proposal must have been debated at a meeting of the newly founded COMECON Executive Committee in Bucharest the following December, but it was not referred to in the communiqué issued at the close of that meeting. At another meeting two months later, in Moscow, the dispute came to a head, with the Romanian delegate, Alexandru Barladeanu, strongly resisting Soviet pressure. Had the Soviet Union not been so preoccupied with the great intra-bloc dispute with China at the time, it is probable that Khrushchev would have pressed his case and might even have had his way. For if it had not been for the Sino-Soviet dispute and the possibilities for diplomatic maneuver it gave the East European states, Romania, the only country to take real advantage of the dispute, would hardly have been able to challenge the U.S.S.R. Thus, Khrushchev's dispute with Mao, in addition to the other damage it inflicted on him, served to undermine one of his last great enthusiasms. At yet another COMECON "summit" meeting, in July, 1963, he finally agreed to shelve his supranational proposals.

Khrushchev's scheme had both economic and political implications. Economically, it made a great deal of sense. It was nonsense for every country in Eastern Europe to have the same kind of economic structure regardless of its resources and abilities. But if purely economic criteria were to be adopted in deciding who should produce what, then the advanced industrial countries like Czechoslovakia and East Germany would have had a tremendous advantage over the less developed countries. They would be called upon to give up certain industrial branches, but their economies would remain largely intact. Romania and Bulgaria, on the other hand, would have to remain largely agricultural and food-processing countries, with only a few heavy industries, e.g., the oil and petro-chemical industries in Romania's case. Thus, Czechoslovakia and East Germany supported the Soviet scheme while Romania opposed it. Only when the economies of all the member states were at about the same level, argued the Romanians, would integration become acceptable.

The matter was not, of course, quite so simple as this. The attitudes of the different countries toward the integration scheme were prompted by a whole complex of considerations—economic, political, personal, opportunistic, etc. Thus, the G.D.R. could not have opposed the Soviet proposal for political reasons, even had it meant she would be hurt economically. The same, to a lesser extent, was true of Novotny's Czechoslovakia. Poland, which had always preserved a degree of political independence from the Soviet Union, could not have been happy about some of the implications of supra-state planning. Yet she seems to have welcomed the proposals, mainly because she was desperately in need of outside capital to develop her own resources. Hungary, too, was overwhelmingly dependent on the Soviet Union for raw material and fuel supplies.

The case of Bulgaria was both interesting and puzzling. Because Bulgaria was the most backward of the satellites, her industrialization program would have been most seriously affected by the Soviet scheme. Yet, the Sofia regime embarked on a program of expansion that was more ambitious for Bulgaria than the Romanian program was for Romania. There was little indication, however, that Bulgaria was ever the same center of controversy that Romania was. She was evidently allowed to proceed with her expansion drive without hindrance and received a great amount of Soviet help for this purpose. One may argue that this was in return for her unflinching support of Khrushchev in the Sino-Soviet dispute, but this in fact turns the argument inside out. The question of supporting or not supporting the Soviet Union in the Sino-Soviet dispute followed, rather than preceded, the question of approving or disapproving Bulgaria's industrial expansion program. The best explanation for the strikingly dissimilar treatment of Romania and Bulgaria seems to be that Bulgarian industrial expansion, great though it was for the country herself, was too small to interfere with the Soviet integration scheme. To have a second, larger and more powerful country departing from the prescribed path would damage it much more severely. There is also the point that the pivot of Bulgaria's industrialization drive, the metallurgical combine at Kremikovtsi, was planned as early as 1958—*i.e.*, before the Khrushchev integration scheme was conceived. The center of the Romanian drive, the Galati metallurgical combine, was not begun until 1963, after Khrushchev's ideas were known.

The political implications of the Soviet proposals were very serious indeed. Had they been accepted, they would have facilitated a Soviet control over Eastern Europe far stronger and more permanent than any known before. In time, they would have also led to the disappearance of state boundaries. In this connection, it is worth recalling the famous Valev episode of the spring of 1964. Professor E. B. Valev, an economic geographer at Moscow University, wrote an article for one of the university's magazines proposing the amalgamation of a small part of the Ukraine, all of northern Bulgaria, and southern Romania into one economically integrated region in which state boundaries would disappear. Valev's article was violently attacked in the Romanian economic journal *Viata Economica*' of June 12, and *Izvestia* itself repudiated the suggestion on July 5. Whether Valev's proposal was an officially sponsored trial balloon or simply the professor's own idea is not particularly relevant. What *does* matter is that if Khrushchev's proposals for a supranational directed economic integration had been accepted, the sort of thing that Valev was proposing would have materialized at some time in the future. It was a valuable warning to all the East European countries.

The famous April, 1964, Declaration of the Romanian Party Central Committee publicly rejected the whole idea of economic integration and a supra-state planning authority.[24] It also opposed the concept of jointly, internationally owned enterprises. The declaration insisted on the right of each country to have complete control over its own economic planning. It was a thoroughly nationalist doctrine, and demonstrated how vigorous the Romanian opposition to the Soviet proposals must have been when they were discussed.

By the middle of 1963, the Soviet Union had reluctantly decided to shelve these proposals. It then switched to a renewed emphasis on bilateral development with Eastern Europe. In quick succession, it established bilateral intergovernmental economic, scientific, and technical commissions with Bulgaria, Poland, Czechoslovakia, the G.D.R., and Hungary. The obvious aim was to bind the economies of these countries more closely to her own. (Only in September, 1965, did Romania agree to such a commission.)

These were some of the political and nationalistic reasons for the failure of COMECON to achieve real integration. One must now turn briefly to the specifically economic reasons for this failure.

One prerequisite to a successful regional integration is a relatively free flow of labor. In the European Common Market, at which the Communists were always casting a baleful eye, this had been successfully achieved. By the end of 1964, it was becoming very necessary in Eastern Europe as well. But apart from the migration of a few thousand Polish workers to the Ostrava-Karvina coal basin in Czechoslovakia and a few Bulgarian dentists to the G.D.R., there had been no flow of labor whatsoever and the question had seldom been broached. Similarly, there had been relatively little mobility of capital, a fact about which the Poles complained regularly and bitterly.

But the two most serious obstacles to a unified economy were the persistence of bilateral barter in COMECON trade, and the discrepancies in the pricing and costing systems. Until a correlation could be established between industrial costs and industrial prices, there could be no specialization; for there was no reliable yardstick by which a country could be assigned the tasks it could perform most cheaply and efficiently. But, while rightly stressing the failures of COMECON, one should not overlook the considerable progress that had been made to solve the problem of pricing and costing. The internal reform measures discussed previously provided for elimination of the old, artificial prices as far as was possible. Considerable time would be needed before these measures could have an effect, but at least a beginning had been made. Toward the end of 1964, even Ulbricht was publicly voicing his belief that real COMECON cooperation would be possible only when all the member states had comprehensively reformed their economic systems.[25]

In the meantime, a step toward multilateral trading had been taken with the opening of the COMECON Bank in January, 1964. The Bank opened transferable ruble accounts for COMECON members amounting to 5 per cent of the total value of the foreign trade of each country. A year later, it was announced that a new price basis would go into operation. Obviously, a better groundwork was patiently being laid.

Among COMECON's definite achievements were the various cooperative ventures, especially in fuel and power. The completion of the "Friendship" pipeline connecting the oil fields in the Kuibyshev area with Poland, Hungary, Czechoslovakia, and the G.D.R., was a remarkable feat of engineering and could greatly lower the (previously exorbitant) price these countries paid the Soviet Union for oil. Similarly, the electric-power grid connecting the western Ukraine, Poland, Hungary, Czechoslovakia, the G.D.R., and, eventually, Romania and Bulgaria, was an immense step toward strengthening the power supply system of the whole area. Important organizational steps toward more rational cooperation were also made by the establishment of the railroad freight-car pool in 1963, joined by all countries, and of the metallurgical company, Intermetal, in 1964—at first confined to Poland, Czechoslovakia, and Hungary, but later joined by all members except Romania.

The fact remained that COMECON was still a grouping of national economies rather than a truly international organization at the end of 1964. The national economic plans of the member countries still came first; the coordination of them, a poor second. Whether this order of priorities would soon change or would ever change depended not so much on the Soviet Union as on the East European states. If they believed that the economic benefits from real integration outweighed the political dangers involved, then some kind of supranational organization was still a possibility. There were definite signs that Poland was prepared to take the chance, and there was no real choice for the G.D.R. On the opposite side stood Romania, with its completely different concept of a very loose grouping of states—a nation that received a considerable boost in September, 1964, when Yugoslavia entered into a loose relationship with COMECON. Though this was not a particularly promising development from the Yugoslavs' point of view, since it was a reflection of their economic weakness, it would certainly make COMECON an even more unwieldy body for Moscow to handle than in the past.

The Soviet Union was, therefore, faced with the problem of whether to let the pace of progress toward closer integration be set by the laggard, Romania, or to press ahead with those countries eager to do so. It was more likely that she would choose the second alternative. If she did, the independence—indeed, defection—of Romania would only become the more evident; it would amount to a tacit admission by Moscow that it was prepared to let Romania go. Conversely, if Romania could do as well for herself as Yugoslavia had done by following an independent course, other East European states might wish, in time, to follow her example. The new leadership in Moscow has showed itself hesitant to commit itself to any positive policy regarding COMECON. It has stressed bilateral ties and seems to be banking on the heavy economic dependence of all the East European states on the Soviet Union. It is sensible policy, except that there is no guarantee—as Khrushchev found—that economic dependence means political dependence.

THREE

Agriculture

BEFORE WORLD WAR II, Eastern Europe (excluding Czechoslovakia and what is now East Germany) was overwhelmingly agricultural. Easily the greater part of its labor force was engaged in agriculture, and the region as a whole was a large exporter of foodstuffs, mainly grains, to Western Europe.

This concentration on agriculture was, in itself, one of the reasons for—even a measure of—the backwardness of Eastern Europe. When one also considers the conditions that prevailed in East European agriculture—the rural overpopulation, the primitive methods, and the often miserable standard of living—it becomes a relatively easy matter to reject the idyllic picture sometimes painted of the East European countryside before the Communists seized power.

It is fairly certain that this situation would have changed after the war regardless of the type of government that prevailed. (One has only to look at developments in "backward" Greece to realize this.) The structure of the economy and the society would have altered radically with greater stress on industrialization and with agriculture relegated to a less dominant, if still an important, role. It is only fair to say, however, that any forward-looking government in post-war Eastern Europe would have had trouble with the peasantry. What the mass of peasants really wanted was land reform to alleviate the land hunger, and economic assistance from the state to cushion them against the crises that had occurred so frequently in the inter-war years. Despite the very impressive private virtues they possessed, they were collectively a reactionary element, imbued with a mystic feeling of their moral superiority, and highly contemptuous of the urban population. Even the most rational introduction of industrialization in Eastern Europe would, therefore, have met with strong opposition from the peasantry itself, from the various agrarian parties, and from the Roman Catholic and Orthodox churches, which saw their moral hold over the population threatened by the winds of change.

As long as they were out of power, the Communists had tried to woo the peasantry with promises of land reform. Once in power, however, they revealed themselves as the countryside's greatest enemy and despoiler. The Communists' priority goal was forced industrialization, with emphasis on heavy industry. This meant that agriculture had to be deliberately neglected and the rural population considered mainly as a means of providing labor and capital for the growth of industry. The Communists were also committed to a rigid system of economic planning and management obviously unsuited to any activity in which there were so many imponderables of both the elemental and human varieties. The peasants, therefore, were to be strait-jacketed and exploited to a degree never known in the past, and were to get very few of the benefits the new system might bring. Worst of all, they were to lose their very important illusion that they were the masters of their own destiny, an illusion that had often been their only source of comfort in the past.

One other Communist dogma should not be overlooked: the obsession with economic bigness or "gigantism." Of course, few would deny that, in most cases, large-scale production is more advantageous than small-scale production, in agriculture as well as in industry. But the Communists wanted bigness in agriculture in the form of large collective farms, without being prepared to make the necessary capital investments to give this bigness a reasonable chance of success. The result of their policy was that agriculture became the Achilles' heel of all the East European economies except Poland's, where collectivization collapsed after 1956.

Collectivization began in earnest in Eastern Europe in 1948. It was temporarily discontinued after Stalin's death but in most countries resumed after the fall of Malenkov. The 1956 upheavals caused an interruption that proved permanent in Poland, long-lived in Hungary and East Germany, but very temporary indeed in Bulgaria and Czechoslovakia. By the spring of 1962, however, collectivization had been completed in all the East European countries except Poland (and, of course, Yugoslavia). In Poland, 87 per cent of the arable land was in the hands of small private farmers and there were no signs that this structure would be drastically changed in the foreseeable future. Voluntary association and cooperation existed in the form of Agricultural Circles, the media by which most state aid—in the way of credit, machinery, fertilizers, etc.—was transmitted to the peasantry.

The pace of collectivization had varied from country to country. Bulgaria always led the way. By 1957, it was virtually completed in that country, and by the end of 1958, the collectives had been merged into about 1,000 giant *kolkhozes* averaging more than 4,000 hectares (or 10,000 acres) each. Czechoslovakia was a close second. Collectivization in Hungary was resumed in 1959 and continued in yearly stages until its completion in 1961. In 1960, the East German countryside was subjected to an onslaught that saw the nominally collectivized area jump from about 40 per cent to 85 per cent in a single year. In Romania, the pace had always been slower, and great stress had been laid on an intermediate form of socialization known as the Agricultural Association. But this gradualism, despite the official promise that it would continue until 1965, when collectivization was due to be completed, came to an abrupt end at the beginning of 1962. After a hectic three-month period, the Romanian regime officially declared Romanian agriculture completely collectivized. The reasons for this sudden change of plan were never officially disclosed.

"Completely collectivized" is, strictly speaking, not an accurate term; in every country, there is a percentage of land, usually in the mountains, that is not considered worth collectivizing and is left alone. But this percentage is negligible. In East Germany, moreover, most collectives in 1964 were still of a very "loose" kind, where only certain types of agricultural work were done in common. "Collectivized area" is also a term used rather generally to describe the area covered by both collective and state farms, the latter being farms owned directly by the state, and worked by state employees paid wages in the same way as industrial workers. These state farms are considered the "highest form" of rural socialist organization and receive preferential treatment in investments. The area covered by the state farms varied from country to country. In Bulgaria, they cover a very small percentage of the total arable land; in Romania and Hungary, between 16 and 18 per cent. In Poland, 87 per cent of the arable land is covered by private farms, 12 per cent by state farms and only 1 per cent by collective farms proper.

It is not possible in this short survey to discuss agricultural development in Eastern Europe in detailed terms of input and output. One should say, however, that following the disastrous period of 1948–53, a period of ruthless collectivization, peasant resistance, and financial neglect, the situation generally improved, mainly as a result of increased investments. But the increases in total output were small, they did not keep pace with the growing population, and they were very disappointing when compared with the annual targets. The demand continued to exceed the supply, and the problem was aggravated by the fact that the increase in the supply of durable consumer goods did not keep pace with the increase in real wages. Since they had nothing else on which to spend their money, the people ate more food, especially meat, and the demands on agriculture, particularly livestock, increased. Agricultural production rose most in Bulgaria and Romania, but even in those two countries the average (cumulative) increase was only about 5 per cent between 1958 and 1962. In Czechoslovakia, total output fell slightly, in Hungary, it barely increased. From 1962 to 1964, there was little progress, although 1964 itself was quite a good year for both Bulgaria and Romania, and in Hungary the regime succeeded in making the country self-sufficient in grain. In Czechoslovakia, however, 1964 saw a slight drop in production, whereas 1963 had witnessed a 6–7 per cent increase.[1] (Total agricultural production implies of course, total value—not volume—of production.)

It was during this period, especially in 1963, that all the East European countries except Romania were forced to make contracts with Western countries, most notably the United States and Canada, to purchase large shipments of wheat. They were following the example set by the Soviet Union, of course, and it was largely Soviet inability to meet its growing commitments to Eastern Europe that forced these countries to go to the West. The significant exception was Romania, which continued to have a surplus and was able to "lend" the Soviets 400,000 tons of grain in 1963.

The situation in uncollectivized Poland, though generally better than in the collectivized countries, was perhaps not so excellent as the proponents of small-scale farming might have expected. From 1958 to 1962, the average (cumulative) increase of total agricultural output was only 1.4 per cent. In the great year of 1961, however, production rose 10.4 per cent over the previous year—it was the biggest harvest in Poland's history. 1962 saw the second highest output in the nation's history, but total output was down by 8.5 per cent from the previous year. In 1963, it increased by almost 4 per cent, and, in 1964, the results were a little higher than in 1963.

By Western standards, Poland's dwarf holdings are very inefficient indeed, and their per-acre yields in the main grain crops continue to be considerably lower than those in collectivized Czechoslovakia or East Germany. Moreover, ever since 1956, Poland has imported large quantities of grain from the United States, although this is mainly a commercial proposition, in that the grain is used to feed livestock that is then exported as processed meats. Where the Polish system scored heavily over those of the rest of Eastern Europe was in its resilience, in the ability and willingness of its self-employed farmers to gather in the crops down to the last kilogram and to be less discouraged by the vagaries of the climate (which continued to be the main factor in agricultural success or failure).

The kind of success the Polish private farmers scored was reflected throughout Eastern Europe (and the Soviet Union) in the remarkable successes attained in the private plots. All the collective farmers in Eastern Europe have been allotted pieces of land they can cultivate privately. The size of this plot varies from country to country, but nowhere does it exceed half a hectare (about 1.25

acres), except in the more mountainous regions. On this land, the farmers are generally allowed to keep not more than one cow, a few pigs, and an unlimited stock of poultry. In the beginning, the private plots were intended mainly as temporary arrangements to provide the collective farmers and their families with land to grow their own food on, and were frowned on by the Marxist purists as "remnants of capitalism." They were continually being criticized, mainly because the farmers naturally tended to spend more time working on land the profits from which they could keep for themselves, than on the publicly owned parts of the collective. Until 1960, many collective-farm managements sought to cut down the size of the plots and restrict the amount of livestock that could legally be kept on them; in some cases, they simply abolished them.

Though subject to all these encroachments and often deprived of the necessary supplies of fodder and technical help, the farmers soon proved that their plots were indispensable contributors to the total agricultural output. In the main cereal crops—wheat, barley, oats, and rye—they did not compete with the collective sector, but in truck-farming and in certain orchards they played a major role, and in livestock sometimes a dominant one. Thus, in Hungary, in 1961, the private plots, covering only about 13 per cent of the total arable land, contributed 64 per cent of the total meat output of the country, 60 per cent of the milk, and 90 per cent of the eggs. (In the Soviet Union, the corresponding figures were 46 per cent, 45 per cent, and 89 per cent.) Elsewhere in collectivized Eastern Europe, the contributions were less impressive (as a result of less official encouragement) but they were still considerable.[2] The figures for the whole area provide resounding proof of the indispensability of the private sector, and the regimes, highly embarrassed though they were, were forced to swallow their ideological pride and increase their support for these rural remnants of capitalism.

The regimes concentrated on two methods to improve on the disappointingly slow progress that the collective sector of agriculture was making. The first lay in introducing technical improvements in greater volume and at a quicker rate: great stress was laid on mechanization. The number of tractors in Eastern Europe rose 300 per cent during the 1950's, although the tractor-acre ratio was still low except in East Germany and Czechoslovakia; moreover, a good proportion of the tractors nominally in service were always in the repair sheds or waiting to be put there. Equally important were the large-scale irrigation and drainage projects that were begun in the late 1950's but increased considerably in the early 1960's. New soil analyses, a prerequisite to good cultivation, were being carried out in several countries. More fertilizers were being used (though not nearly enough), as were more pesticides, other chemicals, and hybrid seeds. Better qualified personnel found their way into responsible posts on the collectives themselves (although it was still a problem to keep them there). None of these elements was new, but the urgent attention they were being given by the end of 1964 was, indeed, unique.

Whether the attention granted was adequate, considering the magnitude of the problem, was still doubtful. After 1963, investments in agriculture averaged about 15 per cent of total state investments in the economy, taking Eastern Europe as a whole. This was too low, and it was becoming obvious that the sluggishness of agriculture was having a serious effect on economic growth as a whole. The new Polish five-year plan approved at the Fourth Party Congress in June, 1964, called for marked increases in agricultural investments, as did the Romanian plan approved in July, 1965. Hungary also began an investment offensive in agriculture. Indeed, one of the planning patterns for the period 1966–70 in Eastern Europe, as in the Soviet Union, is a concentrated effort involving much larger investments than ever before, to try to overcome this chronic agricultural stagnation.

Even more vital than investments was the need to cater to the human element by providing better material incentives. The first important step toward this goal was taken in the late 1950's, when the old compulsory deliveries system was replaced by a new system of contracts. (Compulsory deliveries still remained in force in Poland, however.) The contractual system did not differ greatly in substance from the old system: the farmer was still expected to supply quantities fixed by the state; but the quotas were not so high now, and they took specific conditions more into account. Still more important was the introduction in the late 1950's in all countries of higher prices for agricultural produce, a development that continued into the 1960's. It was accompanied by other financial incentives, such as tax reductions, premiums for overfulfillment of plans, payments in advance for farm work, social-security benefits for the farmers, and the slow but steady change (in most countries) from payments in kind to payments in cash.

The basic remunerative system always used on the East European collectives had been the Soviet *trudoden* (labor-day) system. Payments under this system were determined first by deducting operating costs from the gross income of the farm, then by deducting the necessary allocations to be made to the farm's central or "indivisible" fund, and then dividing what was left of the gross income by the total number of labor-days worked on the farm; this determined the average payment per labor-day unit. The number of labor days credited to each worker depended on the work performed. For example, an operator of a mechanical harvester earned more than three times as many labor-days as a less skilled field worker. Under this system, the farmer was only a residual claimant to the farm's income, meanwhile carrying the full risk of the operation. The state, for its part, got its share of the output, depending on the harvest, without assuming any risks at all. The *trudodens* provided no incentive for the farmer, since working harder or more efficiently had little effect on earnings.

The first step away from this rigid system was the generally adopted decision to supplement the farmers' income with a share in the produce gathered over and above the goals of the plan. In principle, this was an improvement, but it seemed to have little effect on production, since whether the plan would be overfulfilled or not was only partly the responsibility of the farmers themselves. They might work very hard and yet—because of bad weather, breakdown of farm machinery, incompetence of the management, etc.—the plan might not be fulfilled or might be only slightly overfulfilled. In 1963, this prompted the Hungarian Government, the pioneer in incentives within the collectivized system, to introduce on a large scale the practice of giving the farmers a share of the *total* production, regardless of whether the plan was fulfilled or not. This was the basic element in the so-called Nadudvar system.[3]

Nadudvar is a large village on the Hungarian plain, north of Debrecen. It is the site of a large collective farm called the Red Star, covering 11,000 hectares (27,500 acres) and including 1,300 members. It was surprisingly successful from the very beginning, holding its own even in bad-weather years and always contriving to give its members a good standard of living. This was precisely because its members had been remunerated from total production rather than from production over and above the plan. The Nadudvar system had, as its basis, the two classic institutions of the labor-day and the private plot, but it grafted on two important innovations: an annual allocation to each household of a piece of the communal cropland for cultivation; and a guarantee to each household that, in addition to the labor-day payments, it would receive a specific percentage of most of the harvest regardless of total production. (Crops excluded from the scheme were those requiring less labor, e.g., wheat.)

The Nadudvar system had many characteristics of sharecropping, a system well known in the southern parts of the United States and of recent memory in Hungary itself. It was ironic that a socialist regime should have to resort to this notorious system within the framework of collectivized agriculture. The Nadudvar system, however, still continued the labor-day payments, thereby guaranteeing the farmers some kind of a basic income. But by 1963 many farms (25 per cent of the 4,000 in Hungary) had switched over to pure sharecropping and had abandoned the labor-day rate. The Hungarian regime had to tolerate this on farms that were short on manpower, but the Nadudvar system remained the model; a general change to it began in 1964.

This combination of the labor-day system and a form of sharecropping was certainly a positive measure to raise production. It was easy to operate, was understood by the peasants, and stimulated work even in bad-weather years since the farmer was always guaranteed a share of the crop. Moreover, since the payments were in kind rather than cash, they were not subject to any kind of taxation. Perhaps more important than anything, the sharecropping system appealed to the still powerful property-owning instinct of the average peasant. With the private plot, it spurred the farmers on considerably.

The Hungarian Government also took energetic steps to see that the collective farmers would have a say in the organization of the system—what types of incentives were to be introduced, what share of the crop should be distributed, etc. All this was put under the rubric of "more democracy on the collectives," a heresy stoutly resisted by many of the collective managements but one that was beginning to make definite headway.

One cannot say that the Hungarian innovations were being generally applied throughout Eastern Europe in 1965. After all, to do so, a boldness and a flexibility of outlook were required which, though characteristic of the Hungarian, was not the hallmark of the other regimes in the area. But they were given a big boost when they were discussed in an article by a senior Hungarian agricultural official which appeared in the November, 1964, issue of the chief Soviet Party journal, *Kommunist*. The timing of this article's publication was significant: the fact that it was certainly commissioned *before* Khrushchev's fall meant that he himself was prepared to give the Nadudvar system favorable consideration; the fact that it was published *after* his fall showed that his successors probably had the same attitude. The only country in which a variant of the system was known to have been applied was Bulgaria, in the tobacco-growing sector. It was possible, therefore, that, in the not too distant future, it would begin to be applied experimentally and cautiously in other East European countries as well.

The pragmatic, unostentatious approach the Hungarian regime showed in its agricultural reforms was similar to its attitude toward reforms in industry. In those other countries where new, comprehensive schemes for economic reform had been announced, it had simply been stated that the main provision of the schemes should be extended to agriculture also. But this was a long-term project. In Czechoslovakia, however, the beginnings of an important decentralization could be seen in the decision to leave most collective farms the right to draw up their own plans for crop acreage and production, with only the value of the deliveries they were to make being fixed by the planning authorities.

In East Germany, the remarkably active Ulbricht revealed astonishing vistas for the East German countryside in a speech at the end of February, 1964—vistas, however, to be unfolded only between 1970 and 1980.[4] The Ulbricht regime was actually in a dilemma over its agricultural policy. Though it had largely completed collectivization by 1961, most of the hurriedly organized collectives were still of the so-called Type I variety where the land was worked in common, but where the cattle remained privately owned. (In the rest of Eastern Europe, most of the collectives were of the advanced type with both land and livestock in public ownership.) The East German regime had tried to push through the more advanced type, but the effects on production had been such that it had had to pull back. It was trying, on the one hand, to complete real collectivization, which would harm production, and, on the other, to formulate a system of planning and management that would stimulate production. It was difficult to see how they could both be done at the same time.

Among the reform measures Ulbricht proposed were decentralization of planning and management, a comprehensive system of material incentives, and an eventual equalization of the living standards of the town and the country. To achieve this last objective, Ulbricht returned to one of Khrushchev's old hobby-horses, the *agrogorod*, or agro-city. Even before Khrushchev fell, this idea (whereby a village would take on an essentially urban character) seemed to have been dropped in the Soviet Union. However, Ulbricht spoke as if *agrogorods* would be a definite feature of the East German countryside by 1980. This would involve investments the like of which had never been made in East Europe, and it was impossible to see how anything but the smallest beginning could be made by 1980. The most interesting question for the immediate future was how soon Ulbricht would proceed with his intention of making East Germany's loose collectives more advanced. He was still delaying in 1965, in spite of continuing official statements that the intention still stood.

In Eastern Europe generally, the main question for the future was whether the regimes would intensify their movement against agricultural stagnation by stepping up both investments and the search for better and more productive material incentives. The need for a satisfactory solution of the agricultural problem was more urgent than ever. Stagnation in production was impeding economic growth, and the rural population was becoming a body of veterans (the average age on collective farms was about fifty). It was recognized that the anti-peasant mentality of the first half of the 1950's had brought near disaster. What was needed was the same kind of flexibility that was beginning to appear in other sectors of the economy.

FOUR

Cultural Developments

IN THE EAST EUROPEAN Communist states, with their totalitarian pretensions, the situation in the creative arts at any given time is largely determined by the degree of political freedom allowed. It is true, of course, that cultural ferment has often been the forerunner of political relaxation. Adam Wazyk's 1955 "Poem for Adults," the rumblings of the Petoefi Circle in Hungary in 1956, and of the Bratislava writers and journalists in 1963—these are just three examples of how the cultural milieus inaugurate a development toward greater freedom in many spheres. Except in such periods of ferment and turmoil, however, the freedom allowed in the creative arts is a reflection of the degree to which political freedoms are allowed to exist. If the political leaders cannot curb or contain freedom of cultural expression within the limits they consider safe or manageable, their authority in other fields would be so undermined that they could hardly remain in power for long.

At the time of Khrushchev's fall, therefore, the cultural situation in Eastern Europe closely reflected the political situations in each country. In Poland, the "retreat from October" had been nowhere more apparent: there was still much freedom of expression in Poland, but this was because the 1956 starting-point had been so advanced. In Hungary, the liveliness of literature, literary periodicals, and the theater exemplified the new policy associated with Kadar. In Czechoslovakia, Czech and Slovak writers, dramatists, and painters, censored and frustrated for so long, were revelling in their new-found freedoms. In Bulgaria, the ferment that began under the impact of Khrushchev's second attack on Stalin at the Twenty-second CPSU Congress had largely petered out as the de-Stalinization process ground to a halt. In Romania, the first signs of general relaxation had also brought a few stirrings in the creative arts. Rigidity was still the general rule in East Germany, but Ulbricht's belated attempts to make himself more respectable had, in turn, led to greater maneuverability for some of the writers.

Although the degree of cultural freedom varied considerably from one country to another, there was a general restlessness in the cultural life of all the countries. This restlessness, begun in 1962, had also been benefited from the new climate of "peaceful coexistence" and new opportunities for the re-association with Western cultural development that this climate made possible. Thus, artists in Eastern Europe were profoundly influenced by both East and West. Though (unjustly) contemptuous of Russian intellectual achievements, they realized that the results of attempts to gain more cultural freedom in the Soviet Union would have a considerable bearing on their own condition. Once they had gained more freedom at home, they hoped to draw on the new postwar trends in the West from which they had been isolated for so long.

One of the most notable cultural products of the Twenty-second Congress of the CPSU was the literature of de-Stalinization. The best-known example of this in the Soviet Union was Alexander Solzhenitsyn's novel about a forced-labor camp in Siberia, *One Day in the Life of Ivan Denisovich.* In fact, one can almost say that the way this book was treated in Eastern Europe indicated the degree to which each regime was prepared to allow a cultural "thaw." Solzhenytsin's novel was published in Poland, Czechoslovakia, Bulgaria, and Hungary (and, naturally, Yugoslavia). In Romania and East Germany, it was still considered too dangerous. A further subdivision can be made among those countries that allowed its publication. In Bulgaria, Hungary, and Czechoslovakia, local Solzhenitsyns appeared with novels or poems of their own about the horrors and oppressions of the Stalinist period—sometimes before the novel had actually been published in their country; in Poland, none appeared.

In Bulgaria, the most striking example of the literature of de-Stalinization was a poem entitled *Recollections*, by Nikolai Lankov, which appeared in two installments in *Narodna Kultura* at the end of 1962[1] and the beginning of 1963. Lankov had all his life been a fervent Communist who had personally suffered from what he always considered to be mere impurities of the system. He wrote of his own experience in a Bulgarian prison during the Stalinist period. The following passage, with its obvious reference to Chervenkov, was by no means atypical:

> Did I live through this night
> of cult oppression?
> Did I live?
> Oh, no!
>
> I dare not admit that
> somebody, called someone who is "9,"
> in a disgusting epoch
> shot Communists
> to clear his own path
> to a throne and personal power.

Nor was this passage, dealing with Lankov's time in prison:

> The door opens,
> the investigator enters
> and begins to rail:
> —What are you talking to?
> My head shakes
> My sleep is broken
> and on this late evening
> I hear again:
> —To interrogation,
> to interrogation.

A similar but more famous case was that of Jozsef Lengyel in Hungary. Lengyel, a veteran Communist, left Hungary after the downfall of the Bela Kun republic and eventually went to the Soviet Union, where he became a Soviet citizen. He was a victim of one of Stalin's waves of terror, and spent the years from 1937 to the end of World War II in a concentration camp. He did not return to Hungary until 1955. Lengyel's writings are, therefore, about his personal experiences of Soviet, rather than Hungarian, Stalinist terror, and his works on this subject actually appeared in Hungary before Solzhenitsyn's book was published in the Soviet Union. His most famous account, "From Beginning to End," appeared in the literary monthly *Uj Iras* in February, 1963; it was written in diary form and forcefully retold some of his own experiences.

Lengyel's work probably did much to embolden Hungarian writers to stir up their own memories, and write about the horrors of the Rakosi time. In Hungarian literature about Rakosi, a distinction should be made between those works that criticized his tyranny in a general way, and those that specifically brought up the torture and the general inhumanity inflicted on many individuals. There were many of the first kind but relatively few of the second, what there was probably owing much to the example of Lengyel. Among the most noteworthy were *The Seventeenth Sunday*, a novelette alluding to the Rajk trial by Gyula Oszko (*Kortars*, February, 1963); and "Acquaintance with Childhood," by a young writer named Bela Horgos (*Alfoeld* [Debrecen], October, 1963). Horgos's story was illustrative of the younger generation's accusations leveled against the elder, on the subject of responsibility for crimes committed in the Stalinist era.

The Czechoslovak literature of de-Stalinization was not quite so grim as that of the Soviet Union, Bulgaria, or Hungary, probably because the horrors were not so terrible and because the writers concerned did not speak from personal experience. In fact, most of Czechoslovakia's "de-Stalinizing" writers had been Stalinists themselves and only saw the error of their ways when it was relatively safe to do so. This need not detract from the quality of their work, however, the political effect of which was enormous. By far the most famous example was *Delayed Reportages*, by Ladislav

Mnacko, which appeared in 1963. Mnacko had actually written this book several years earlier, but it had been rejected by the censor. It comprised a series of dramatic sketches of various aspects of life during the era of the "cult of personality." In its comprehensiveness, it was, perhaps, the most thorough indictment of the Stalinist period that had ever been written. Two other works that also achieved great prominence were the drama *The Scar*, by Peter Karvas, and *The Spine*, a novel by Ladislav Bublik.

There is no doubt that the Polish book market would also have been flooded with de-Stalinization literature if the Polish censors, obviously acting on strict orders from the highest level, had not refused publication. There is reliable evidence to prove that many Polish authors took up the Solzhenitsyn challenge—but the crimes of the "past period" had always been frowned upon by Gomulka's cultural commissars as subject-matter for literature. Gomulka probably had this in mind when he addressed the Polish Writers' Congress in Lublin in September, 1964, and reminded his impatient audience that only to stress the evils of the Stalinist period would be to give a one-sided, distorted picture. One should also see the achievements of that period in the economic, cultural, and educational fields, he said, and take into account that this was a period when severe class struggle was necessary because of the machinations of Communism's enemies.[2] Gomulka, in short, was afraid of literary ferment. He had kept Polish writers under fairly effective control ever since the end of 1958; now, their restlessness had increased as a result of the ferment in Hungary, Czechoslovakia, and the Soviet Union. His answer was not to concede, but to continue a policy of increased watchfulness.

Lamentable as it is, it is true that Poland was behind even the G.D.R. in this respect. In the second half of 1963, at least one novel was published in East Germany which could be called a work of de-Stalinization. This was Erwin Strittmatter's *Ole Bienkopp*. In subject-matter, it was closer to the Czechoslovak de-Stalinization novels than to Solzhenitsyn's or Lengyel's. The eponymous hero, Bienkopp, is a faithful Communist who persuades the farmers in his village to form the first agricultural collective after 1945. Gradually, his and the villagers' enthusiasm is soured by the stupidity and bureaucratic behavior of local Party officials; in the end, Bienkopp dies a tragic death. Had this novel been published elsewhere in Eastern Europe (in Czechoslovakia or Hungary, for example), it would have been noteworthy for both its quality and message. But for it to have seen the light of day in East Germany was a minor sensation. Kadar, after all, had been in prison during part of Stalin's era; Novotny, as he tried to convince everyone, was "not in the highest leadership at the time."* But this could not be said for Ulbricht: he had been boss throughout. The situation that so demoralized Bienkopp was one for which Ulbricht was ultimately responsible, even if the officials directly culpable were minor ones.

Although the works exposing the horrors and stupidities of the era of the personality cult were the ones that made the headlines in 1963 and 1964, they were not the only political literature appearing. Perhaps even more important were those works that devoted themselves to the current system and practices. This literature was still anti-Stalinist, in the sense that it was reformist. It sought to point out those areas where injustice, incompetence, and bureaucracy still prevailed. In short, it was engaged, political literature in the Western sense.

In the G.D.R. and even in Romania, examples of this literature managed to get by the censors, and in Poland, such works were still published, although fewer each year. In Bulgaria they enjoyed a considerable vogue in 1962, but then seriously diminished in quantity as a result of government pressure the following year. In 1963, this literature began to appear in Czechoslovakia; it was still being published in 1965, although the tone and content were limited by the (relatively loose) confines of what the regime was prepared to tolerate as constructive criticism.

Nowhere, however, was this type of literature more voluminous or more brilliant than in Hungary—partly because of the many talented writers, and partly because of the friendliness of the censors. The Kadar regime was desperately anxious to promote the revival of literature in Hungary, once it had mopped up the remnants of the 1956 revolution. It sought not only to persuade "silent writers" like Tibor Dery and Laszlo Nemeth to resume writing, but also to harness all literary talents to the service of its policy of

* See Chapter 1, pp. 19 ff.

reconciliation and reconstruction. To do this, it had to allow far more freedom of expression that it really desired, but it succeeded in its initial aim. The "silent writers" began publishing again, without surrendering their principles or their integrity, and others also took full advantage of the new freedom. As a result, a flood of politically oriented short stories, poems, and dramatized reportages were published in the Hungarian literary periodicals. Some described conditions in the collective farms, others the factories; many of them were extremely critical, not so much of Party policy, as of the way it was being carried out. Other works castigated the low living standards and social amenities in Hungary. Among the finest and most poignant were those describing situations in which old Party stalwarts, who had given everything for the revolution and the cause of the working class, were being ousted from their posts and replaced by younger men with more technical training and knowledge. Perhaps the best of these was a story by Janos Foldeak called "Directors" (*Uj Iras,* November, 1963). This story is eminently fair to both an old factory director and a young, efficient deputy minister who orders his replacement; while recognizing the necessity of the change, it shows the fine old Communist going from factory to factory appealing for a job as an ordinary worker but being rejected everywhere: it would be bad for morale and appearances if a former director returned to the status of a laborer.

A third kind of literature in Eastern Europe turned its back on both the neo-Stalinists and the reformers and dealt with the enduring human problems regardless of political context. To the Communist ideology, this is, in the long run, the most dangerous literature of all. Perhaps anti-Stalinist literature, when it exceeded the bounds set by officialdom, was more immediately alarming to the leadership; but even the most excessive political writers were committed to socialism. Apolitical literature, however, even if written by professed Communists, as is often the case, shrugs off the whole system. It is still being written in Poland and Bulgaria, despite the many exhortations to political commitment and *partynost.* In Hungary, too, there are famous elderly representatives and a considerable younger following of this school. In Romania, a school of young writers led by the able Eugen Barbu is clearly apolitical.* In the G.D.R., Christa Wolf's novel *The Divided Sky* was mainly concerned with human and emotional problems though it was set against a socialist background and had a clear political message.

Probably the most able exponent of this trend in all of Eastern Europe is the Czech writer Josef Skvorecky, whose novel *The Cowards,* about relations between Czechs and Germans in northern Bohemia at the end of World War II, is considered by many to be a literary masterpiece in the broadest sense. *The Cowards* was first published in 1958 and was roundly attacked at the time, although later it became immensely popular. Most of these apolitical works touch on political subjects, but not in political terms. They are critical of a political system only because that system impinges on the more important human considerations which, the authors maintain, should transcend any political creed, good or bad.

An important by-product of the East European "thaw" in the 1960's was the emergence of a "conflict between generations" in those countries where the thaw was most pronounced. This subject deserves thorough study, for the difference (and often antagonism) between the outlooks of age groups in Eastern Europe is a phenomenon that could have a far more disruptive effect on society there than it would in the West. The conflict had many facets—political, social, psychological, not to mention biological—many of which are reflected in the literature that discusses the question of responsibility for the past.[3] The exposure of the sickening crimes of the "past period" evidently caught many of the younger generation in Eastern Europe completely by surprise. Once recovered from their shock, the young people naturally began to ask—as they did in a similar context in West Germany after the war—how such crimes could have happened, who was responsible for them, and how the older generation could have allowed them to occur. Young writers turned vengefully on their older contemporaries, discovered poems in praise of Stalin written by the latter and pointed the accusing finger. The elders' defense consisted mainly of the standard, not necessarily hypocritical, arguments that they knew little

* In February, 1965, Barbu was elected a member of the Bureau of the Leading Committee of the Romanian Writers' Union. This is in itself a reflection of the growing cultural latitude in Romania.

of what was going on; that, in any case, certain brutalities had to be countenanced and were even justified because of pressure from the class enemy; that they had honestly believed Stalin was infallible; etc. Naturally, the young were not convinced, and the fact that the despised older political leaders jumped to the protection of the generation under attack only increased their skepticism.

The conflict had begun in the Soviet Union, where an attractive young poet, Evgeni Yevtushenko, emerged as the champion of irreverent but sincere youth. In Eastern Europe, the conflict was perhaps most bitter in Czechoslovakia, in the years 1963 and 1964. In Hungary, however, where the Yevtushenko cult was the strongest, a young poet named Ferenc Baranyi not only called for a full reckoning with the past, but also brilliantly mirrored youth's impatience at having its progress delayed by the continued presence of so many ignorant (and probably compromised) relics of the Party's shady past. He contrasted the promise of socialism with the current reality—the squalid living conditions, the impossibility of a young couple's beginning a decent life together. His most famous tirade was his "Ballad on Pampered Youth" (*Kortars*, February, 1963), a poem that landed Baranyi into a good deal of trouble with the authorities but brought him even greater acclaim among his own generation.

There were, of course, many similarities between the conflicts of generations in Eastern Europe and in the West. In England, for example, John Osborne railed against the capitalist Establishment while Baranyi did the same against its Communist equivalent. The problem is universal, but its effect on a society that claims to be totalitarian is far greater than on a free society. Khrushchev himself realized the danger, and his statement that a conflict of generations was impossible in a socialist state reflected not so much his knowledge, but a dogmatic belief. In both the Soviet Union and Eastern Europe, this belief was steadily being eroded.

The impact of men like Solzhenitsyn and Yevtushenko showed the very strong effect of Soviet literary "revisionism" in Eastern Europe. Western literary influences, so strong until 1939, were very slight after the war—except perhaps in Poland, where Western literature has been available in relatively large quantities since 1956. In other countries, the doors were kept open only to those imports that showed Western society and the capitalist system in a bad light. By the beginning of 1963, however, most countries considered it expedient to risk a more liberal policy, and Western writers previously condemned as decadent began to appear in the bookstores of Eastern Europe after an absence of twenty-five years. They were eagerly sought by the writers and the reading public, both of whom were anxious to make up for so much lost time. Among the writers who could now be studied were Joyce, Proust, and Kafka, and even the experimenters who created the French "anti-novel." But it was around the name of Kafka that the most interesting controversy ensued, showing that at least one regime wished to retain the blinkers of the past.

Kafka, though sympathetic to radical socialism, had long been anathema to Communist cultural officialdom, which regarded his works as "decadent" and his concept of alienation as irrelevant to socialist conditions. However, many Communist writers contended that Kafka's works were, on the contrary, relevant, in that they pictured human helplessness in the face of a heartless and faceless bureaucracy not unlike that under which the Communist states had recently suffered. Pressure for his rehabilitation naturally was strongest in his native Prague and, indeed, was finally successful in 1963. In May of that year, a "literary colloquium" was held near Prague to commemorate Kafka's birthday. It was attended by many writers and cultural officials from Eastern and Central Europe; general agreement was reached on Kafka's rehabilitation. The East German delegation, however, persisted in the old view of Kafka's decadence.[4] With the exception of some support from Bulgaria, this conservatism was rejected, even by the Soviet Union.[5] But the obstinacy of the East Germans continued, leading to sharp exchanges between Prague and Pankow, with the Czechoslovaks privately accusing the East Germans of interference in their cultural affairs.* The East Germans held out on Kafka until after the fall of Khrushchev, but, in 1965, they quietly published him;

* At an SED Central Committee plenum held February 3–7, 1964, Horst Sindermann, candidate-member of the Politburo, openly accused certain Czechoslovak artists of trying to revise Marxism-Leninism. There was no direct reply to Sindermann from Prague, but the reliable Hamburg weekly, *Die Zeit*, of March 13, 1964, reported the presence in East Berlin of a Czechoslovak delegation there to remonstrate against Sindermann's attack. According to *Die Zeit*, this delegation had said that Czechoslovakia refused to be treated as an "East German protectorate."

though Bulgaria was still holding out, strong pressure was mounting there, also, for his rehabilitation.

It will be some time, of course, before the influence of Kafka or other Western writers can begin to have an effect. But Western literature is back in Eastern Europe in fairly good force. The problems facing the censors when its presence begins to be felt even more strongly will be difficult indeed.

Western drama, also beginning to reappear on the East European stage, is no doubt having a quicker and more direct effect. While East European audiences could see only the Western classics until fairly recently, the 1964–65 season featured a wide variety of Western plays—plays as dissimilar as Kafka's *The Trial* and Edward Albee's *Who's Afraid of Virginia Woolf?* In Prague, one could see Samuel Beckett's *Waiting for Godot,* Tennessee Williams' *A Streetcar Named Desire,* William Faulkner's *Requiem for a Nun,* Eugene O'Neill's *Mourning Becomes Electra,* and Jean-Paul Sartre's *The Prisoners of Altona.* Bucharest audiences were having their first glimpse of a play by one of their famous expatriates, Eugene Ionesco's *Rhinoceros* (performed in Prague the year before). Even the Bulgarians were sampling Sartre's *No Exit.* Plays by Friedrich Duerrenmatt were running in at least two capitals.

Domestic dramatists were also writing more interesting plays. In Bulgaria, Emil Manov's *Abel's Mistake* proved that this talented and courageous writer had not succumbed to any of the threats or blandishments to which he had been subjected since 1956. In 1963, the Polish satirist Slawomir Mrozek wrote a play called *Death of a Lieutenant,* which survived a number of critical reviews and showed that Poland's censors were much more tolerant toward the spoken than the written word. Satire was lively on the Budapest stage and in the Hungarian cabarets. Here, the sharp barbs directed against the regime, including Kadar himself, were tolerated with surprising good humor.

In both drama and films, it was Czechoslovakia that really caught the eye. The Prague theater was once again becoming the excellent center it had once been, famous not only for its productions of classic plays but also for its original works. Karvas' heavily political play *The Scar* has been mentioned earlier; but other works, less political and probably more enduring, were also performed—among the most notable, Josef Topol's *The End of the Carnival* and Vaclav Havel's satire *The Garden Party*. Even more engaging, and often amazingly irreverent, were some of Prague's little cabaret theaters, like Semafor and Na Zabradli—young people's theaters that old people also liked.

In 1964, the Czechoslovak Semafor company gave some performances in West Berlin; it did not get the reception it perhaps deserved—mainly because some of the humor was lost in German. However, those who were privileged to see a number of Czechoslovak films in West Germany, France, and England in the fall of 1964 got more than their money's worth. These films display a mastery of technique, a level of acting, and a political fearlessness that clearly indicate that the Czechoslovak Barandov has replaced the Polish Lodz as the film capital of Eastern Europe.

The reactions of the Communist regimes to these various developments have differed widely. In general, much depended on whether the initiative for change and relaxation came from above or below: where the impetus came from the rulers rather than the ruled, it was usually a question of tolerating, even encouraging, new trends in literature and drama because of the considerable political benefits they brought. Later, however, when they tended to get out of hand and began to bring political harm rather than advantage in the regimes' views, attempts were made to push them back within acceptable limits. This was the case in Hungary where, beginning in the second half of 1963 and continuing throughout 1964 and 1965 there were many instances of official criticism of "liberal," "nationalist," "bourgeois," and other harmful tendencies in literature, and even cases of certain writers being penalized. But until the Kadar regime was able to produce a clear definition of what was permissible and what was not—in short, until it developed a cultural policy—it was very difficult for it to conduct a successful campaign against the kind of literature it did not like. Practically all the writers supported the regime, albeit some less ardently than others. All could, therefore, claim that their works were designed to assist, rather than impede, the regime's efforts. In 1965, regime pressure for more conformity and for "safer" literature did increase. More writers were penalized, there was stricter censorship, and the editorial boards of some magazines were changed. In March that year the Party Central Committee approved a set of "Ideological Guidelines" strongly critical of those writers who strayed from the path of "permissible criticism."[6] But there was still no adequate definition of what this term meant. Hungarian literature, though not as lively as in 1963 and 1964, was still in considerable ferment.

The situation in Bulgaria was similar to that in Hungary—but also very different. Here, too, the impetus for reform came from above; for in 1962, the Zhivkov leadership took its cue from Moscow and once more became a proponent of de-Stalinization. This gave the writers their chance, though it soon became clear that they were anxious to go much further than the regime, which soon reverted to its old conservatism. The writers had to be checked. This was done by Zhivkov himself in a brutal speech of April, 1963.[7] The infamous old catalog of literary sins was once again read off, some of the worst offenders publicly pilloried, and *partynost* and socialist realism reaffirmed as the two essential guidelines in Bulgarian literature. Yet literature did not subsequently return to the Stalinist dark ages; instead, more and more writing became apolitical. Though this was directly contrary to what the regime intended, it became obvious that no attempts were being made to use coercion. Thus, there was wide discrepancy between the official line and what was actually being written. It was almost as if the regime was content with having submerged dangerous political writing and did not care to make too big an issue over nonpolitical expressions, the danger of which, though great, was not immediate.

In 1965, however, there were signs that a period of cultural relaxation might be beginning once more. At the beginning of the year, a number of changes were made in the executive bodies of the Union of Writers; several older, "Stalinist" writers went, and more courageous ones, who had previously been criticized by the regime, came in. In July, Emil Manov, perhaps the regime's greatest "problem" writer, was the leading member of the Bulgarian delegation to the PEN Club conference in Bled, Yugoslavia. New and slightly warmer winds seemed to prevail.

The outstanding example of reform coming from below was Czechoslovakia. Novotny would have liked to ignore the Twenty-second Congress of the CPSU altogether, but a combination of circumstances forced him to make one concession after another. It was the writers who played the dominant role in this process. Indeed, for a few months in 1963, the Czechoslovak writers mirrored the political, economic, and social grievances of the whole people and became the "conscience of the nation" (in this case, the two nations), a role that no group of writers had played in Eastern Europe since the Polish and Hungarian revolutions. The reaction of the Novotny regime was to try to stifle the literary opposition. The well-controlled Party press, together with the regime's ideological and cultural spokesmen, delivered broadside after broadside against the rebellious writers. These proved ineffectual throughout 1963, and during that year an area of cultural and intellectual freedom was opened up that would have been considered impossible a short time before.

In 1964, however, the regime's attacks continued and, combined with occasional acts of repression, had a noticeable effect. Eventually, an informal and uneasy compromise was reached: the regime had to abandon its previous positions, and the writers rested, for the time being, with what they achieved. They had, after all, gained a great deal; though they might still heartily despise Novotny and his associates, they had to concede that the Party was at last beginning to move along the right lines. For those still anxious to continue the fight, the astonishing political resilience of Novotny, plus the realization that the "revisionist" Khrushchev was strongly supporting him, must have made all but the lion-hearted few thankful for what they had already gained.

In East Germany, the initiative most definitely originated from below. Restlessness in the cultural world and the universities had increased considerably after the building of the Berlin Wall in August, 1961, and had been answered by very severe repression. After about two years, however, the Ulbricht regime evidently decided that some concessions were necessary if any kind of *modus operandi* were to be worked out. It had also begun to take a belated and startled look at its own international image. These concessions became apparent not in any change of principle—the official "line" in culture remained the same, as was seen so clearly in the Kafka controversy—but in a certain tolerance in dealing with offenders and a readiness to allow far more discussion than in the past. Although Professor Robert Havemann was dismissed from his positions at East Berlin's Humboldt University, no further measures were taken against him; he was even allowed to retain his title. Had he given his interview to the Hamburg paper and delivered such obviously "subversive" lectures several years earlier,* he would undoubtedly have received a considerable prison sentence. Similarly, if the novels by Erwin Strittmatter and Christa Wolf, referred to earlier, had somehow been published sooner, not only would they have been the targets of the most savage abuse; their authors would probably have been victimized, as well. In 1963, however, nothing of the sort happened. Both novels were criticized, but both also received much praise. Christa Wolf's novel *The Divided Sky* was actually given the Heinrich Heine Prize, a major literary award in East Germany, and was made into a film that aroused a great deal of favorable and unfavorable discussion. The cases of Strittmatter and Miss Wolf were typical, and they indicated a slight but perceptible loosening of the reins in the G.D.R.

In every East European country, a distressingly large proportion of the intellectual community has always shown themselves to be either Party hacks or opportunists ready to vacillate with the prevailing political winds. The courageous rebels have been relatively few. The Romanian regime has, by and large, shown itself most adept at "buying off" its intellectuals by combining enviable rewards in the form of sinecures at publishing and newspaper offices, with the occasional show of force or terror. There were inspiring cases of individual rebellion, such as that of the writer Alexander Jar in 1956,[8] and of a group in Cluj centered on the cultural magazine *Steaua*. But proceeding from a policy of intimidation to one of bribery, the regime managed to keep the intellectuals well under control. Not that it was able to force everyone into the socialist-realist strait-jacket—far from it: ever since 1956, there have been constant complaints in the press about the "apolitism," "evasism," "escapism," etc., of many Romanian works of art. The fact remained that creative artists in Romania had never, until 1964, been the problem their counterparts in most other countries of

* See Chapter 1, p. 38.

Eastern Europe had been. Relaxation in culture, as in other spheres, was something introduced from above in Romania; in allowing the relaxation, the regime was very careful to prescribe limits.

Realizing that it was impossible to remain frozen when thaw was prevalent, and that even the most pliant body of intellectuals eventually would grow impatient with the prevailing circumstances, the regime set about gradually easing its Zhdanovite grip. A slight cultural thaw became noticeable in 1964; the censors seemed prepared to allow a more flexible interpretation of socialist realism, and even articles urging that all authentic art could be placed within the framework of realism were published. For example, a book by the French Communist writer Roger Garaudy called *Realisme sans Rivages,* which had been discussed in every East European country except East Germany, was commented on favorably by some Romanian critics.

Apolitical literature, which had once been severely criticized, also began to be tolerated more, and the publication of certain novels showing Communist officials in a bad light was allowed. But the would-be Mnackos and Foldeaks of Romania still had to tread carefully. In 1963, a witty play by a young dramatist, Teodor Mazilu, called *Stupid People in the Moonlight,* won much critical and public acclaim, but the Party daily *Scinteia* stepped in with its censure and the play subsequently closed.[9] Yet the stakes were slowly moving forward into the undefined, but probably still narrow, latitudes the regime was prepared to allow.

The most spectacular concession allowed in 1964 was the publication of large numbers of Western books that previously had been on the official index. This concession should be seen in the context of Romania's general policy of *rapprochement* with the West. At a time when Bucharest was extending its economic, cultural, and even political relations with Western Europe and the United States, it would have been pointless to maintain a barrier to Western books. The concession was quite large, and implied, at least in theory, that practically every type of Western literature could be studied freely in the country. However, the regime meant to manage the whole process from start to finish, and at a meeting of the Writers' Union in March, 1964, its spokesmen set out the strict conditions under which the imports were to be studied.[10] What was good in them from a Marxist-Leninist standpoint was to be utilized; what was not was to be discarded. The regime was taking a chance, of course, and knew it. But after the death of Gheorghiu-Dej in March, 1965, the Ceausescu regime amplified this general line. In a speech to Romanian writers in May, Ceausescu said that the particular style a writer chose was not important; what mattered was the content.[11] The term "socialist realism" was officially discarded—an important concession. Though the regime went on urging the importance of realism and of socialist themes, the fact that writers could now express themselves as they wished was an opportunity that, only a few years earlier, they could not have dreamed of.

The attitude of the Polish regime and of Gomulka, personally, toward the literature of de-Stalinization has been described above. It was typical of their approach to artists in general and writers in particular. Basically, Gomulka must have wished that the Twenty-second CPSU Congress had never happened, for it is evident that he viewed its message and its implications with the greatest alarm. This may seem an odd thing to say about a man who, in 1956, had benefited so greatly from its forerunner, the Twentieth Congress. But, though naturally grateful that the Twentieth Congress had brought him to power, he had disapproved of much of it—particularly the "spontaneity" it produced: the spirit of questioning, of rebellion, and of iconoclasm generated by it. To his orthodox mind and authoritarian temperament, these were dangerous features that had to be destroyed. Once firmly in power, he set about doing precisely that, and nowhere was the retrogression from the Polish October more severe than in culture. (Cultural freedom had not been destroyed; it was probably still greater in Poland than in any other country east of the Elbe, though this was cold comfort to the Polish intellectuals who saw their liberties steadily being encroached upon.) This campaign against the intellectuals had just begun to produce a situation of relative calm when the unpredictable Khrushchev started the whole process up again in 1961. Once again, writers went on the offensive in the Soviet Union and many parts of Eastern Europe; the fever naturally spread to Polish writers, the most restless section of a congenitally restless people. Any concessions by the regime at this critical juncture would have been seized and enlarged upon, the whole process of pacification undone. Under these circumstances, Gomulka could afford to make no concession; instead, he tightened the screw. But here his usually deft touch deserted him: he tightened it a little too much and produced the last thing he had wanted—a burning political issue. Two respected and lively cultural magazines, *Przeglad Kulturalny* and *Nowa Kultura,* were closed down and replaced by an almost unreadably conformist journal called *Kultura.* Newsprint for literature became increasingly scarce; writers were discriminated against through legalistic niceties. At the Central Committee Plenum in July, 1963, Gomulka delivered his ill-conceived harangue against Poland's artists which wounded their sensitivities and insulted their intelligence. It was a speech in tune more with the spirit of 1953 than 1963.[12] This blunder was the basic reason for a protest of thirty-four intellectuals in March, 1964, drawing attention to the disastrous consequences of the regime's policy, which convinced writers that something had to be done while there was still hope.

Gomulka paid dearly for his blunder. The publicity given in the West to both the protest and the victimization of some of its signatories seriously damaged the Polish regime's reputation, as did the blatantly propagandistic "counter-protests" organized throughout the country. The more reasonable among the Polish leaders, notably Premier Cyrankiewicz, to whom the protest had been originally addressed, urged moderation and certain concessions, especially regarding the supply of newsprint. Then followed the most absurd blunder of all. The regime ordered the arrest of Melchior Wankowicz, a veteran writer, an American citizen, and one of the signatories, on charges of passing slanderous information about Poland to his daughter in the United States. The trial terminated in November, 1964, and Wankowicz was sentenced to eighteen months' imprisonment.

If the incident of the thirty-four intellectuals made the Polish regime look rather sinister, the Wankowicz affair made it look ridiculous. It made of a rather vain old man, who should have been left alone in obscurity, a willing martyr and the focal point for general dissatisfaction and contempt. Wankowicz, glorying in his unexpected publicity, refused to appeal the verdict. The regime had maneuvered itself into an absurd impasse and sought to extricate itself by leaving Wankowicz alone: he was excused from serving his sentence on the grounds that there was no room for him in jail!

After this serious moral defeat, the regime seems to have made a conscious effort in 1965 to woo the intellectuals by bettering their working conditions and giving them greater opportunities to publish their works. Even in an orthodox journal like *Kultura*, writers have been allowed to express opinions on their literary freedom. On the other hand, the trials of the three writers accused of "slanderous" attacks on Poland in emigré journals (see Chapter 1), although an exceptional case, showed that the writers' movements were being watched closely by a regime that neither liked nor trusted them, and that showed no skill in dealing with them.

Summing up briefly, one may say that by 1965, in cultural life as in other spheres, Poland was, if not falling behind, then going in the opposite direction from, other East European states. In the latter, creative artists had hope; in Poland, this was replaced in many cases by a bitter hopelessness.

FIVE

Relations with the Soviet Union

SINCE STALIN'S DEATH, his system of control in Eastern Europe has had no recognizable replacement; there have simply been reactions, both dictated and spontaneous, against it. The general dissatisfaction that found its outlet immediately after his death, and its dramatic expressions in Poland and Hungary in 1956; Khrushchev's acceptance of the fact that more autonomy for each country was necessary for a viable system; the influence of Yugoslavia—these, together with the Sino-Soviet dispute and the beginnings of a Western policy aimed at exploiting the centrifugal forces at work in Eastern Europe, were perhaps the main factors responsible for reviving the marked diversity that had always characterized Eastern Europe.

Before 1948, it was by no means certain that the Communist parties in the countries of Eastern Europe would imitate the Soviet Union. Most of their leaders, even Comintern stalwarts like Dimitrov and Rakosi—not to mention the "home" Communist Gomulka—indicated that the policies they would adopt would embody a form of socialism tailored to some extent to the nature and traditions of their own countries. This position has often been dismissed as a propaganda smoke screen, and to a certain extent it was, but there was also an element of sincerity. It is certain that the different Communist parties plunged into the affairs of their own countries too deeply to satisfy Stalin, to whom a foreign Communist was first and foremost an agent of the Soviet Union. It was the diversity and divergencies caused by this "domesticism" which led, in part, to the establishment of the Cominform; the defection of Tito served to accelerate rather than to cause it.

Khrushchev gave this domesticism (or internal autonomy) the green light; the result was a gradual return to the old diversity. However, Khrushchev's concept of autonomy had strict limits. Though obviously wishing that every country would conform to the Soviet model of Communist practice, he was prepared to tolerate deviations, as in the case of Gomulka's agrarian policy. Still, he insisted that no regime hold up its deviations as a legitimate example for others to follow, and that there be complete obedience to Moscow in foreign policy and intra-bloc policy (when the latter became relevant). Yugoslavia failed this test on both counts, while Albania and, later, Romania, failed on the second; because of this, these three countries became, in different degrees, the "odd men out" in Eastern Europe.

The Sino-Soviet dispute introduced to bloc relations a new element and a new potential: China emerged as a challenger of Moscow for the political and ideological leadership of the Communist world, an alternative center of power and authority. The emergence of this alternative opened up a number of possible courses of action for the East European states. Albania, for example, was able to break completely with Russia and become a Chinese satellite. Romania played Peking off against Russia so as to force the latter to concede her the right to adopt a full-scale industrialization policy. (*See* Chapter 6.) The possibility also arose of using the Sino-Soviet dispute to extract concessions from the Soviet Union. But no East European country has yet done this. East Germany and Bulgaria have fully supported the Soviet Union, but this support has not been given in the expectation of corresponding reward; it derived rather from the regimes' great weakness and was given simply so that the U.S.S.R. would help them to stay afloat. Hungary's support of the Soviet Union has been equally prompt—in this case not so much because of weakness as because of Kadar's close personal and political association with Khrushchev, which goes back to November, 1956, when together they crushed the Hungarian Revolution. Personal gratitude on Kadar's part, combined with the feeling that his destiny was closely linked to Khrushchev's, seem to have been stronger factors than his probable hesitation over pressing the quarrel with China; at the same time, they perhaps precluded his seeking a *quid pro quo* for his support. (Economically, Hungary was always dependent on the Soviet Union, especially for raw materials. Her commercial connection with Moscow steadily grew closer toward the end of the Khrushchev era, and has become closer since.)

Antonin Novotny's Czechoslovakia came closest, in some ways, to implementing the third option. From 1962 to 1964, Novotny faced problems of severe economic stagnation, mounting demand for internal reform, and a resurgence of Slovak national feeling. At first, he showed little inclination to solve them with flexible reform. While the Twenty-second Congress of the CPSU provided the encouragement a man like Kadar needed to press ahead with reform, it produced something akin to paralysis in Novotny. He seemed bent on paying only lip service to de-Stalinization, and there is little doubt that this rigidity, and such incidents as the Barak affair, did not endear him to Khrushchev. Yet Novotny, whose instinct for survival had always been of the highest order, realized that what Khrushchev now needed more than anything else was implicit loyalty in his struggle with China. This he gave him; in return, his survival was ensured, and he was left to deal with domestic affairs as he saw fit. The relaxation that came in Czechoslovakia was probably due to the pressure from below and Novotny's slow retreat before it, rather than to Soviet interference.

After Gomulka came to power in 1956, Poland was never a Soviet satellite in the way that her neighbors were. In certain of her domestic policies, most notably in agriculture, she pursued a different course. In foreign and intra-bloc affairs also, her support of the Soviet Union was seldom as automatic as that of the other East European states. Similarly, Gomulka fully supported Khrushchev on the main issues in the Sino-Soviet dispute—*détente* with the West, peaceful coexistence, non-inevitability of war, etc. But he did not support Khrushchev over the Soviet leader's desire to settle the conflict by formally expelling China from the world Communist movement. A year before his ouster, Khrushchev had been mainly preoccupied in trying to organize an international conference of *all* the Communist parties in the world (similar to the one held in Moscow in November, 1960) in order to provoke a showdown with China and have her expelled. Support for the Soviet Union on this issue was made a test case of loyalty to Moscow, and it was here that Gomulka balked. He was not opposed to a conference at which the participants would try to heal the Sino-Soviet breach, but he strongly disliked the idea of expulsion, "excommunication," as it came to be called. His attitude may have been prompted by personal dislike of factionalism, whether national or international; by his concept of the Communist camp as a loose commonwealth based on the principle of "live and let live"; or by his awareness that situations can change with bewildering rapidity. (Who would have thought that Tito could work himself back into a position of grace and favor? Who would have thought in 1949 that Gomulka himself would be the "savior" of his country in 1956?) Finally, there must have been the fear that, if Khrushchev succeeded in this plan of excommunicating China, he might follow it with attempts to restore a greater degree of unity and cohesion to Eastern Europe. Indeed, in the course of 1964, it became evident—in statements made by Khrushchev and other Soviet leaders—that this was precisely what the Soviet Union had in mind.* Gomulka naturally opposed the idea.

Some of the motives that prompted Gomulka also prompted Gheorghiu-Dej. He shared Gomulka's fears, but, unlike Gomulka, found himself involved in a very serious dispute over COMECON policy with Khrushchev—a dispute that forced him to flirt with China and openly defy the Soviet Union. Gomulka's stand was, in a sense, more disinterested. More analogous to it was Yugoslavia's. Despite the hatred between Peking and Belgrade, Tito hesitated to endorse any move that would formally expel China from the Communist camp, mainly on the ground that this would revive the practice of excommunication (of which he himself had been the first victim).

* See, for example, Khrushchev's strong hint in Budapest on April 4, 1964, that it would be desirable to have some kind of joint body to coordinate foreign policy (MTI, April 4, 1964).

Among the Yugoslav, Romanian, and Polish Communist parties, therefore, one could see a unity of outlook based on a similar concept of what the character of the Communist world should be. But while the Yugoslav Party had complete freedom of maneuver because of its unique position outside the Soviet bloc, and the Romanian Party, carried forward by the dynamic of its quarrel with Moscow, created a great degree of freedom for itself, the Polish leaders' elbow-room was much circumscribed.

The Romanian example illustrated the limitations of the Soviet ability to coerce the East European regimes in the last two years of Khrushchev's rule. Four factors were primarily responsible for Romania's successful independence: a ruthlessly united Party; the Sino-Soviet dispute and the freedom of maneuver it gave; the example of Yugoslavia; and the beginning of something like an "activist" Western policy toward Eastern Europe. The last two deserve brief examination.

The question of where Gheorghiu-Dej was going was one that Gheorghiu-Dej himself could not answer for a long time. It would be a great mistake to imagine that he (or any leader) coldly sets forth his objectives and marches inexorably toward them. He moved from one brilliant improvisation to another until he found himself at, or close to, the point of no return with Khrushchev. It was probably then that he decided to take Yugoslavia as a model for what his relationship with Moscow and the bloc should be. This did not mean that he was so foolhardy as to want formally to renounce Romania's institutional ties with the bloc—COMECON, the Warsaw Pact, etc.—but that he would simply use them when necessary, at the same time feeling free to follow whatever intra- or extra-bloc policy suited him. This justified his closeness to Tito and represented the first success for Yugoslavia's East European policy since 1955 and early 1956. However, it was a success that must have been rather embarrassing to Tito, for it came at a time when his own relations with Khrushchev were very good. Indeed, Tito may have tried to urge some restraint on Gheorghiu-Dej in order not to endanger his own connection with Moscow.

The change in Western policy toward Eastern Europe played a small but important part in aiding the Romanian deviation, and its implications for the other Communist countries were obvious.

When Gaston Marin, the Chairman of the State Planning Committee, visited Washington in May, 1964, when Premier Maurer visited France the following July, and when the number of economic agreements between Romania and the West continued to grow—all these developments represented political and economic insurance of great present, and even greater potential, value to the Romanian regime. The Romanians, maneuvering cleverly within the framework of precisely that peaceful coexistence which was one of the main planks of Soviet foreign policy, used this policy for their own ends; on occasion, they even pointed out that they were only doing what the Soviet Union both preached and practiced. Hence, it was difficult for Khrushchev to take a public stand against such action, on the part of Romania or any other East European country that chose to take advantage of it. Of course, other East European regimes began to increase their trade with the West considerably, but this has not had the same political significance that the Romanian action had.

Khrushchev also had mainly Romania to thank for the failure of what might have been a most subtle and powerful unifying instrument in Eastern Europe—the Council for Mutual Economic Assistance. The political implications of COMECON were always as important as the economic. Although much was (rightly) made of Romania's opposition to proposals that would have greatly circumscribed her schemes for economic expansion, the real, long-term importance of her success was that it contributed to the abandonment of the goal of political unification, achieved through economic means, which would have been far stronger and more lasting than the system associated with Stalin. Economic integration through division of labor would, in itself, have had many advantages. But its logical conclusion would have been a blurring of national divisions, mainly in the interests of the Soviet Union. This Romania effectively sabotaged, and the rest of Eastern Europe had cause to be grateful.

One should not, however, exaggerate the effect of Romania's defiance on the rest of Eastern Europe. The example she set was too quickly generalized; the fever, while rightly diagnosed as highly contagious, was prematurely considered to be raging far and wide. Closer examination revealed that, at the fall of Khrushchev, five of the regimes—Poland, Hungary, East Germany, Czechoslovakia, and Bulgaria—seemed bent on tightening, rather than loosening, their ties with Moscow, at least in the economic sphere; and the Soviet power of economic coercion over Eastern Europe was still great. All the same, conditions had been created, even before the fall of Khrushchev, that made the assertion of more independence by all the East European regimes possible, and examples were at hand to show it could be done.

The following country-by-country summary deals with the main features of the East European states' relations with Moscow, and their attitudes toward the Sino-Soviet dispute, up to the fall of Khrushchev.

Bulgaria

In Chapter 1, the weak internal position of the Zhivkov regime in Bulgaria was probed. This essential weakness made independent action extremely difficult and, indeed, forced it to lean more and more heavily on the Soviet crutch. In 1964 alone, Bulgaria made economic agreements with the Soviet Union involving loans of 530 million rubles (or approximately $589 million).

Her unconditional support for the Soviet Union in the Sino-Soviet dispute is, therefore, not surprising. It is not a reflection, as is often thought, of the overwhelming sympathy of the Bulgarian people for the great Slav brother and liberator. (Over the last twenty years, Russia had used up much of her spiritual credit in Bulgaria, because of her dominance and the Sofia regime's servility.) It was basically due to the government's weakness and lack of confidence.

This unconditional support was first shown when the Central Committee of the Bulgarian Communist Party announced its "ardent approval and unanimous support" of the first CPSU Central Committee proposal to call an international conference of Communist parties. This statement was published in the Bulgarian Party daily *Rabotnichesko Delo* on April 5, 1964, only two days after *Pravda* had printed Suslov's speech to the Soviet Central Committee Plenum of February in which the conference had first been proposed. Bulgaria's prompt and unequivocal endorsement clearly revealed that the loyalty of the Zhivkov leadership to the Soviet Union never wavered. Throughout the year, Soviet-Bulgarian relations remained much the same as they had been ten years before; the centrifugal forces at work in the Soviet bloc had not yet touched Sofia. The Soviet Union's subsequent proposal for the twenty-six–party preparatory conference in December, which would help to organize the full international conference met with equally whole-hearted and prompt approval: in August, *Rabotnichesko Delo* reported that the BCP "fully endorses the proposals made by the Central Committee of the CPSU and will participate actively both in the preparations for the conference and in its work."[1]

Bulgaria's official reaction to Khrushchev's downfall showed, perhaps more clearly than anything else, this dependence on Moscow. There was not even a parting nod to the fallen leader who, until the very moment of his eclipse, had been virtually idolized in Bulgaria. Contemptible though this attitude might be deemed, it is understandable; Moscow was the only place Zhivkov could go, regardless of who held power there. Until he could strengthen his position at home, he would have no other course.

Yet even as late as 1964, there were probably many disaffected men in the Bulgarian Party, without much influence but with more than a little nuisance value, who not only resented the servility to Moscow but were drawn to Peking. These men, especially strong in the provinces, who are still loyal to the disgraced Chervenkov or Yugov, inclined to Peking mainly because of a chain reaction of circumstance having little to do with the basic issues dividing the Soviet Union and China. Having been either disgraced or threatened by Zhivkov, they could hardly feel much sympathy for Zhivkov's benefactor in Moscow; hence, they were drawn to Khrushchev's great and powerful enemy in Peking.

In fact, one effect of the Sino-Soviet dispute throughout Eastern Europe could be the creation of "Chinese" factions out of disaffected groups in pro-Soviet parties, or "Soviet" factions in parties which are pro-Chinese (Albanian) or strive to be neutral (Romanian). The factions concerned may have little or no ideological sympathy for the protagonist whose cause they embrace, but are simply drawn to one or the other out of self-interest or the hope of survival. In Bulgaria, however, these men were not sufficiently organized to be called a faction. They were simply the sullen mass of "outs" to whom China represented a possible ray of hope.

Czechoslovakia

At first glance, there would seem to be little difference between the policies of Bulgaria and Czechoslovakia toward Moscow. Khrushchev had equally strong support from Novotny and Zhivkov, although, as said earlier, Novotny's was based on an awareness that Khrushchev needed him almost as much as he needed Khrushchev. There was, that is, something of a bargain between Prague and Moscow—unspoken, unwritten, but nonetheless understood.

Novotny's reaction to the fall of Khrushchev showed the essential difference between his attitude and Zhivkov's. Circumstantial evidence, backed by unofficial reports, suggests that there was considerable coolness between Moscow and Prague over the fact and the manner of Khrushchev's dismissal. Novotny evidently objected forcefully to the treatment of Khrushchev, and the Soviets replied by not answering the protocol telegram of congratulations that the Czechoslovak Party and government had sent the new leaders. Novotny countered by refusing to attend the "summit" meeting in Moscow on the forty-seventh anniversary of the October Revolution; instead, he sent his number-two man in the Party, Jiri Hendrych. Later, of course, Novotny visited Moscow (in December, 1964), and relations became closer, almost assuming normalcy. But the unpleasantness over Khrushchev's dismissal served notice to the new Moscow leadership that even the Czechoslovak regime was not to be trifled with.

Hungary

In the degree of his support for Khrushchev's policy against China, Kadar lay between East Germany, Bulgaria, and Czechoslovakia on the one hand, and Romania and Poland on the other. He was seldom as prompt to back the Soviet leader as the first three; he was never so reluctant as the other two. The Hungarian Communist Party did not publicly support the proposal for an international conference until April, 1964, and only after a personal visit by Khrushchev to Budapest.[2] But the "special relationship" between Budapest and Moscow was always there while Khrushchev was in power. With his fall, however, this relationship ceased to exist. After an initial outburst in favor of his old protector, Kadar accepted the change in the Kremlin as a fact of life, but he must have had deep reservations about it. On the other hand, while there can be little doubt that this very human person was profoundly affected by the fall of his friend and protector, the personal loss could well have been a political blessing. In Hungary, Kadar would, in the future, be judged on his own merits; he would no longer be regarded as the stooge of the man who destroyed Hungarian independence in 1956. In intra-bloc and international politics, he would no longer feel bound by personal loyalty to follow the wishes of the man in the Kremlin. Kadar would have followed Khrushchev even to the point of reading China out of the "socialist camp," but the reluctance he displayed showed that he would have done so against his better judgment. The fall of Khrushchev freed him to embark on a more independent course. He knew that, if he did so, he would further enhance his prestige among his own countrymen.

Poland

If Gomulka's prestige inside Poland had never been so low as at the time of Khrushchev's fall, in the socialist camp as a whole it had probably never been so high. That Brezhnev and Kosygin paid him the courtesy of visiting him on Polish territory to explain Khrushchev's dismissal and presumably to reassure him on certain points, is in itself significant: it seemed to indicate that, in the Soviet view, Poland and her regime were sufficiently independent and influential and yet—and here is the contrast with Romania—sufficiently loyal to be worth the trouble of prompt and personal reassurance.

Before Khrushchev fell, Gomulka had already clearly distanced himself from the Soviet leader's implacable hostility to China. Though roundly condemning Chinese policy, he constantly stressed the need for patience and perseverance, and supported the proposals for a conference to restore harmony, rather than one to impose sanctions. At the Fourth Party Congress in June, 1964, he advocated a world conference of Communist Parties, but one to be held only after the most careful and complicated preparation.[3] That Gomulka's feelings on the Sino-Soviet dispute remained much the same were shown after his meeting with Brezhnev and Kosygin in October, 1964. He urged the Soviet Union and China to negotiate again; then steadily, layer by layer, he argued, confidence could be built up that would make a conference worth while.[4] His views had become identical with those of the Romanian regime, with whose attitude on this subject he had always had much sympathy.

Romania

An interesting comparison could be drawn between the intrabloc policies of Gheorghiu-Dej and Gomulka. From the beginning of 1963, the Romanian attitude toward the Soviet Union resembled Poland's in 1957 on the basic issue of the Soviet Union's position in the socialist camp. Although Gomulka has made his peace with Moscow, the similarity to some extent remains. The Polish leader, in his quieter way and in different circumstances, was as concerned as Gheorghiu-Dej over the prospect of a strong reassertion of Soviet hegemony. But, while Gomulka regarded some measure of economic integration as advantageous, Gheorghiu-Dej saw this as a serious threat. The Romanian dispute with the Soviet Union began precisely on this point.

The dispute always had political overtones, of course, and they continued after the purely economic issues seemed to have been settled (in Bucharest's favor). As early as July, 1963, Romania was allowed to proceed with her industrialization campaign, but things were never again the same between Khrushchev and Gheorghiu-Dej. Gheorghiu-Dej used the Sino-Soviet dispute as an instrument in his dispute with Khrushchev and even went as far as a flirtation with Mao. After winning his point, however, he still needed Mao in his camp, for he realized that China was the best guarantee against the assertion of control in the Communist movement from a single center, the best guarantee that Romania could continue on her own course. Moreover, Mao and the whole Sino-Soviet dispute provided a tremendous boost to the prestige and self-respect of the Romanian Communist Party. Always considered one of the weakest in the bloc, it now assumed an importance second only to that of the Soviet and Chinese parties. By its spectacular efforts at mediation, it gained considerable admiration. Such newly found prestige might also stand the Romanian regime in good stead in the future, since it could be another factor protecting it against any move Moscow might wish to make.

The Romanian policy on relations with other Communist countries was laid down in the famous Central Committee Declaration of April, 1964, following a Plenum called to discuss the mission led by Premier Maurer to Peking the previous month. It has been aptly called the Romanian "Declaration of Independence," since it places on record the regime's opposition to all (Soviet) schemes for suprastate planning, and to any forms of economic cooperation that would involve even the most indirect infringement upon national sovereignty. It repeatedly stresses the complete independence of all Communist parties, pointedly proclaims that there is no such things as a "parent Party" or "son Parties," and comes down heavily against any attempts by one Party to interfere in the affairs of another. On the Sino-Soviet dispute, it strongly supports the Soviet Union—criticizing China for its proclivities for disruption, but also making indirect criticisms of the Soviet Union for its part in the public polemics. It is quite clear that Romania considers that the days when Communist parties can be read out of the Communist camp are over.

On the question of a world Communist conference, the document contains proposals similar in many respects to those Gomulka suggested at the Polish Party Congress two months later, and identical with those he made after meeting Brezhnev and Kosygin.

> We address a heartfelt call . . . for preparing a conference of the representatives of the Communist and workers' Parties with a view to defending and strengthening the unity of the camp of the socialist countries, of the world Communist and working-class movement. The Romanian Workers' Party deems it necessary that immediate consultations should be started between the CPSU, the CCP, and the other fraternal Parties with a view to setting up a commission

> consisting of representatives of a number of Parties. This commission should proceed to a conference of representatives of the Communist and workers Parties. Such a conference should be organized only on the basis of the participation of all Communist and workers' Parties and should be convened only after having been thoroughly prepared. The Romanian Workers' Party Central Committee considers that a conference with the participation of only part of the Communist Parties would run counter to the cause of unity, and would lead to an aggravation of the situation, to the isolation of some of the fraternal Parties, to the establishing of a split in the world Communist and working-class movement.[5]

The April Declaration was both the justification of previous Romanian policy and the basis for future action. Bucharest continued its attempts to mediate between China and the Soviet Union. In August, invitations were sent to (and accepted by) every ruling Party to send representatives to the twentieth-anniversary celebrations of Romania's liberation; and in September, Premier Maurer again went to Peking to attend the fifteenth-anniversary celebrations of the Chinese People's Republic. Up to the very end of the Khrushchev era, the Romanians continued on their own road in intra-bloc and international policy.

East Germany

In that artificially created political unit which is the German Democratic Republic, it is impossible for the regime in any way to reflect the nationalism of its population, i.e., the nationalism of the German nation, expressed by the simple desire for absorption into the German republic of the West.

One need not belabor this point, but in the context of the Sino-Soviet dispute, one should bear it in mind, since it was the utter dependence of the Pankow regime on the Soviet Union, regardless of the character of the leadership in Moscow, which made Ulbricht perhaps the most dependent of all the East European leaders. The East German regime supported Suslov's call for a world Communist conference without delay and accepted the invitation to a preparatory conference without demur. Ulbricht and other prominent East German leaders were the loudest critics of

China. (For the sake of irony, one should perhaps recall that it was Ulbricht, the dogmatist, who [obviously at Soviet orders] broke an East European tradition of fifteen years by inviting a representative from revisionist Yugoslavia to the congress of his Party in January, 1963.)

Yet, despite his "Muscovite" background, Ulbricht was always a Hoxha at heart—but without the opportunity and probably without the courage. Many of the circumstances that prompted Hoxha to "defect" from the Soviet bloc also faced Ulbricht: the fear of a neighboring power (Yugoslavia; West Germany); the suspicion that the Soviet Union might make a deal at his expense; the threat to his repressive rule by Khrushchev's liberalizing policy. But, unlike Hoxha, Ulbricht had twenty Soviet divisions in his domain, and his geo-political position made such defection impossible. All the same, it was not difficult to detect where his heart lay. In 1958–60 and for some time afterward, the East German press was full of laudatory articles on China, and relations between Pankow and Peking were very close. Of course, when the full gravity of the Sino-Soviet conflict became apparent to Ulbricht, his attitude changed. To learn what Ulbricht *really* thought about Khrushchev's foreign policy, however, one should read occasional articles in the Chinese or Albanian press. The *People's Daily* of September 8, 1964, for example, said that "the Soviet Union was planning to sell the G.D.R. out"; four days later, Radio Tirana accused the Khrushchev clique of "betraying the interests of the G.D.R." This was undoubtedly what Ulbricht himself thought, but such was his unenviable position that his press on occasion even denounced these embarrassing charges as interference in East German affairs.[6]

What Ulbricht thought was of little consequence to Khrushchev, however, or to the other East European leaders, for that matter. Alexei Adzhubei's visit to West Germany in July, 1964, the conference of several Communist-bloc foreign ministers (excluding East Germany's) in Prague the following September, and the announcement of Khrushchev's intended visit to Bonn—these were enough to illustrate Ulbricht's pathetic lack of influence. Even more galling from the East German point of view must have been the trade agreements reached between West Germany and Bulgaria,

Romania, Poland, and Hungary. These not only established West German trade missions in the capitals of those countries, but also stipulated the inclusion of West Berlin in the West German currency area. East Germany openly showed her pique over this last insult but was calmly ignored by her allies. The painful truth was, and Ulbricht knew it, that he would always be a satellite Moscow could afford to ignore.

Yugoslavia

For several years before the fall of Khrushchev, Yugoslavia's foreign policy had gravitated toward the Soviet-led part of the Communist bloc. To account for this, one must look in the first place at her domestic situation—complex and controversial, a mélange of progress, stagnation, retrogression, and nervous uncertainty about the future.

Liberalization in Yugoslavia's domestic affairs began about 1950 and continued until 1961, probably reaching its height in 1958–60 with the new program approved by the Seventh Party Congress in April, 1958. This liberalization, both political and economic, left an impression that almost certainly would never be eradicated. But a strong group of conservatives had always opposed it, and they saw their chance, in the economic crisis of 1961, to press for a tightening of the reins, more centralization, and a curbing of what they considered to be excessive political freedom. A serious split in the Yugoslav League of Communists consequently developed, with the "liberal" Edward Kardelj and the "conservative" Alexander Rankovic, the leaders of the two warring factions, emerging as contenders for Tito's throne. The conservatives seemed to dominate for two years; but in 1964, the liberals made a strong comeback—especially in the economic sector—and succeeded in getting several of their important proposals adopted at the Eighth Party Congress in December, 1964.

The retrogression in Yugoslav internal policy, beginning in 1961 and continuing well into 1963, can be explained partly by the domestic crisis and partly by Tito's wish to remove obstacles to a *rapprochement* with Moscow. This did not mean giving up any essential independence; it was a gesture of accommodation. But it was a measure of the decline in Yugoslavia's self-confidence after 1955 that Tito thought he need accommodate at all. The main reason for this decline was fear of the future—particularly of what would happen after Tito's death. If he had been younger, the split in his Party would certainly not have been so serious or so overt. By 1964, however, the contending forces were now strengthening themselves in patterns that in many ways reflected Yugoslavia's most chronic problem—the nationalities.

Nowhere is the problem of nationalism more acute than in the Federation of Yugoslavia. It has several aspects—of which the Serb-Croat antipathy is only one. Perhaps more fundamental is the complete difference in outlook toward the Federation between the "have" republics (Slovenia, Croatia, and parts of Serbia) and the "have-nots" (Bosnia-Herzogovina, Macedonia, and Montenegro). The decentralization tendency has always been strongest in Slovenia, the most prosperous republic, which has suffered most from federation. The "have-nots" take the opposite line, since, without the aid extracted from the more prosperous federated republics, they would be even more backward than they are now. Tito—of Croatian descent, but quintessentially a Yugoslav—has always been the one uniting and placating force. Rankovic is a Serb, powerful in Serbia but with little authority and less prestige elsewhere. It is difficult to see how he (or anyone else) can counteract the centrifugal forces of the country except with a severe tightening of central control. This the Slovenes and Croats would find intolerable; to them, it would simply be the resurrection of Serbian hegemony.[7]

The second half of 1964 was a period of great diplomatic activity on the part of the Yugoslav regime in general and Marshal Tito personally. In early June, he met Khrushchev in Leningrad; later in the same month, he saw Gheorghiu-Dej in Romania; at the beginning of July, he was in Poland; early in September, he met Gheorghiu-Dej again to inaugurate the Iron Gates project, a huge scheme for a dam and hydro-electric plant on the Danube to be undertaken jointly by Romania and Yugoslavia; almost immediately afterward, he visited Kadar; later in September, he was host to Novotny; lastly he entertained Ulbricht when the latter was returning to East Germany from Bulgaria.

What did all this diplomatic activity signify? The end of Yugoslavia's ideological and political independence? The beginning of a gradual but inexorable process of Yugoslavia's reabsorption in the Soviet bloc? Or, on the other hand, the signal for a new offensive by Tito who, taking advantage of Khrushchev's predicament, sought again to play a major role in East European affairs? These were important questions, since they concerned the future of the first state in the Communist camp to become an example of polycentrism.

Though Tito was prepared to accommodate himself to some extent to Soviet wishes, he was not prepared to abandon his independence, as his foreign policy and his reluctance to support the Soviet Union on the issue of excommunicating China prove. But in one basic respect, Tito changed: his essential quality in intra-bloc relations was not that he was a revisionist, but that he considered himself an example of revisionism that others should follow—the anti-Pope in Belgrade, or at least the ardent proselytizer. By 1964, however, he no longer had the disruptive potential that had characterized him in 1955 or 1956. Wisely, he realized this and did not attempt to revive it.

Why this change? There were three probable (mutually connected) explanations. The first was the deterioration in Yugoslavia's domestic affairs, which considerably shook the confidence of the Yugoslavs, in consequence moving the regime closer to its old camp: the decision to enter into association with COMECON, announced in mid-September, was strongly influenced by the country's economic difficulties. It can be argued, of course, that Yugoslavia's association in COMECON only diluted it and, made it more unwieldy and difficult for the Soviet Union to control. But those who expect Yugoslavia to have a disruptive effect on the organization will probably be disappointed. She entered COMECON to gain economic advantage; she will hardly spoil this opportunity by being too awkward.

It was Khrushchev's eagerness to strengthen his position in Eastern Europe which enabled the Yugoslavs to draw closer to the Soviet bloc without giving up the essential aspects of their independence. Khrushchev was never averse to Yugoslav independence as such, but he objected to Tito's proselytizing and independent role in foreign policy. One of his first moves after it became obvious in 1960 that the point of no return with China had been reached was to effect yet another reconciliation with Tito. This was completed in 1962, and it probably implied tacit concessions on both sides: Tito stopped the proselytizing he was no longer in a position to carry out; Khrushchev refrained from insisting on obedience in foreign or intra-bloc policy, which he would never have been able to exact. No one can say that both sides were satisfied, but the unwritten agreement was acceptable because both sides realized they were less strong than before.

The third reason Tito would never again be the disruptive force he had been in the past was that much of his attractiveness to other East European states evaporated. After 1956, when his prestige throughout the area suffered a serious blow, his influence began to deteriorate sharply. Even if this had not been the case, he must have realized (his vanity notwithstanding) that events in the Communist bloc had overtaken him and made his example largely irrelevant. The Sino-Soviet dispute and the beginnings of an activist policy by the West (*see* Chapter 7) created opportunities for a more independent policy by the East European countries toward the Soviet Union. Everyone could get in on an act that he had once monopolized—an act that he, as the East European states realized, had to some extent abandoned in order to draw closer to Khrushchev. It was true, of course, that Romania was trying to achieve a status essentially similar to Yugoslavia's but this does not invalidate the argument. Romania was a special case because of her direct dispute with Moscow; in any case, times had so changed that by the autumn of 1964, Belgrade was trying to soothe, rather than aggravate, Romania's relations with Khrushchev.

The fall of Khrushchev created a great deal of nervousness in Belgrade. What concerned the Yugoslavs most was Moscow's future relations with Peking. Though Tito may have opposed Khrushchev on the issue of the Chinese, he realized that the Sino-Soviet dispute as such brought him many advantages. A genuine *détente*, on the other hand, might work against him. The fact that one has not occurred must have brought Tito great relief; as we shall see later, his relations with Moscow since Khrushchev's fall continued to be cordial.

Albania

Probably from the beginning of 1961 and certainly since Khrushchev's open attack on Premier Hoxha at the Twenty-second Congress of the CPSU, Albania has been China's bridgehead in Europe. The bridgehead has been maintained, but it has not expanded. It remains an isolated segment of an anti-Soviet alliance, sustained by a steady influx of slow boats from China, which have completely replaced the quicker vessels from the Soviet Union as the country's lifeblood. The Hoxha regime's value to China in its struggle against the Soviet Union has become almost entirely one of prestige, yet for that reason it must still be supported economically and politically. Chou En-lai's visit in January, 1964, was a political gesture designed to boost Albanian morale and assure Peking's isolated ally that she was not forgotten. If the Chinese ever hoped that Albania would positively help to spread Chinese influence in Europe, if they hoped that the bridgehead could be widened, they must have been quickly disillusioned.

China's bridgehead in Europe became a propaganda pocket—not a very effective one, at that. The days when Albanian pronouncements were useful because they showed what the Chinese were thinking came to an end in 1962 when the Chinese began to express their own thoughts. The tirades from Tirana were sometimes as picturesque as ever, but little notice was taken of them; after 1962, the East European press virtually ignored Albania; politically, she had almost become an "uncountry."

However, in one important sphere—commerce—Albania actually strengthened her ties with the East European Communist states after her break with the Soviet Union. Since 1963, the annual trade treaties concluded with the East European states have provided for considerable increases over the previous year. At the same time, the nature of the trade with these countries changed to the "mutual benefit" of both parties. In other words, Albania no longer traded on the basis of deficits, entailing credit from her former friends—a healthy improvement that seems to have been effected by increasing her exports and modifying the structure of her imports. The complete industrial products that once constituted the bulk of Albanian imports were partly replaced by semi-manufactured materials, to be converted into finished products in Albania. (This also reflects the development of Albania's economy.)

From the political point of view, however, the important thing about the continuing and developing trade between Albania and the East European states was that it existed at all. While the Soviet Union boycotted Albania, her allies did not. This was not due to economic considerations alone; for example, although Czechoslovakia had a serious lack of chrome and nickel of which Albania had important reserves, such deficiencies could have been made up elsewhere. That the Soviet Union permitted this open trade policy probably indicates that she wanted to prevent Albania's going to the West to obtain those vital commodities with which China could not supply her. This may seem an odd explanation, in view of Albania's alliance with China and her regime's interminable anti-Western diatribes. But the Soviet Union must certainly have remembered the lesson of Yugoslavia after 1948; also, it was becoming clear by 1964 that China herself was not averse to commercial deals with the West if they were necessary. Soviet policy was evidently predicated on the assumption that Albania the Chinese satellite had a better chance of returning to the fold than an Albania fallen under the commercial and political influence of Western countries.

If this was the Soviet motive, it was largely successful; Albanian trade with the West did increase. It was by no means insignificant that Tirana and Rome, then Tirana and Paris, agreed to raise their diplomatic missions to the embassy level. Still, commercial and diplomatic contacts with the West increased less than one might have expected; more than 90 per cent of Albania's foreign trade in 1964 was still with Communist countries.

The chance of Albania's returning to the fold of the Soviet bloc in the near future seems remote, indeed. Unlike their Chinese ally, the Albanians lost no time in registering their jubilation over Khrushchev's downfall, but they made it quite clear that this was only the first, and not the conclusive, victory for the true Marxist-Leninist cause; what was needed now was a renunciation of Khrushchev's entire policy. Tirana's initial tirades on this subject showed that Albania had little confidence that Brezhnev and Kosygin were the men to repudiate their predecessor. There was no doubt that this was exactly what the Chinese felt, too; Albania thus reverted, for a short time, to its pre-1962 role as the spokesman for Chinese attacks on the Soviet Union. She did not maintain the role for long; the Chinese soon began to speak for themselves.

Relations with the Soviet Union Since Khrushchev

Khrushchev fell in October, 1964, leaving his unsolved problems to his successors. It is too early to speak of any new Brezhnev-Kosygin policy toward Eastern Europe as a whole. What the new Soviet leaders do seem to be stressing are the economic ties between the Soviet Union and her allies. It is a sensible course of action, since this is one of the few remaining areas where the two sides share common interests. The economic dependence of the East European countries on the Soviet Union is still very great. The publicity that their developing economic relations with the West has received should not blind one to the fact that the Soviet Union still dominates the East European economies. Even rebellious Romania still does about 42 per cent of all her trading with Russia. The long-term agreements signed by the East European regimes and the Soviet Union to cover the 1966–70 planning period mostly provide for great increases in trade turnover. It is too early to talk of a *shift* in trade from East to West. But while the implications of Eastern Europe's economic dependence on Russia should not be overlooked, this dependence, as Khrushchev realized only too well, is no guarantee of Soviet control, nor is it a real substitute for the kind of unity Khrushchev tried and failed to impose.

Otherwise, the new Soviet leaders have seemed to be content simply to try to avoid trouble. It is unlikely that their two ventures in join consultation so far—the top-level meeting of Warsaw Pact members in Warsaw in January, 1965, and the nineteen-party preparatory conference in Moscow in March—have convinced them of the usefulness of multilateral meetings in the future. The Warsaw conference ended with a series of unconstructive platitudes, and the Moscow meeting was a serious diplomatic and propaganda defeat for the Soviet Union. It is more likely that, in the future, to avoid public disunity and embarrassment over failures to promote joint action, Moscow will rely more and more on bilateral consultations with the East European regimes. Understandably enough, they seem to have abandoned Khrushchev's ideas for tighter political unity. Any such form of institutionalized unity is, for the near future, out of the question.

One international development that, under normal circumstances, might have been expected to produce an impressive demonstration of unity has significantly failed to do so. This is the United States' air offensive against North Vietnam. Just as one of the factors tending to further disunity in Eastern Europe is an atmosphere of international *détente*, so—conversely—the jeopardizing of that *détente* by the American actions against North Vietnam should, in theory, have helped to restore some unity among Warsaw Pact nations. This has not happened; even the Soviet Unions' minimal gesture of offering to send volunteers to Vietnam has not met with a unified response from Eastern Europe. There has been an impressive display of sentimental solidarity with Hanoi, but only Bulgaria and Hungary have specifically followed the Soviet example of offering volunteers. If the Soviet Union were to take the initiative for more direct military intervention, Romania would certainly not be the only ally who would balk.

So far, there has been no clear evidence that the Soviet Union has had trouble with its Warsaw Pact allies over membership in or participation in the activities of the Pact. It is worth noting, however, that Article 43 of the new Romanian constitution, published at the end of June, 1965, includes a passage saying that a state of war can be declared only in case of aggression against Romania or against allies with whom Romania has mutual defense obligations, "if the situation occurs on which the obligations of declaring war are based."[8] This proviso, which did not occur in the old constitution, may reflect the desire not to be drawn into any unwelcome conflict, whether in North Vietnam or elsewhere.

In some specific areas of Eastern Europe, Brezhnev and Kosygin seem to be continuing Khrushchev's policy and in others abandoning or modifying it. With Yugoslavia, for example, there has been continuity. The new leaders appear to have persuaded Tito that his fears of change in Soviet policy were unjustified, and Tito's visit to Moscow in June, 1965, was marked by great cordiality on both sides. With East Germany, however, policy has changed in a way that is highly gratifying to Ulbricht. Khrushchev never sought to undermine East Germany or to repudiate its leader. But his moves in 1964 toward *rapprochement* with Bonn certainly caused consternation in Pankow. These moves have been discontinued by his successors, who have seemed anxious to reassure Ulbricht and who have urged that trade relations between the East European states and the Federal Republic should not be increased at the expense of East Germany. In the case of Albania, the new leaders seem to have tentatively tried, and decisively failed, to improve relations. Radio Moscow's Albanian broadcasts have been much more moderate in tone than they usually were under Khrushchev, and the Soviet Union, probably at the suggestion of the Poles, did agree to invite Albania to the Warsaw Pact meeting in January, 1965. But she was rewarded with a torrent of abuse from Tirana that destroyed all hope for a normalization of relations.[9] With Hungary, relations have improved considerably since their low point immediately after Khrushchev's fall, when Kadar was the most outspoken of all in the defense of his old friend and protector. But the Hungarians have made it clearer than ever they did under Khrushchev that the Soviet Union is no longer the center from which inspiration must come.[10] With Czechoslovakia, as has been said, relations are correct but more distant than they were under Khrushchev.

A special note should be made of the new Soviet leadership's relations with Poland, Romania, and Bulgaria.

The particular relationship between Gomulka's Poland and Khrushchev seems to be continuing under Brezhnev and Kosygin. Less than two weeks after the fall of Khrushchev, the latter met with Gomulka and Premier Cyrankiewicz on Polish territory. Immediately after the Warsaw Pact conference in Warsaw in January, 1965, the same four men conferred together near the Mazurian Lakes, and the following April, Brezhnev headed a Soviet delegation to Warsaw. The new leaders were obviously eager to reassure the Poles that they contemplated no basic changes and prepared to listen to Gomulka's exhortations and advice—showing not only their respect for Gomulka but recognition of his influence in Eastern Europe. It revealed once again the Soviets' awareness of Poland's importance in their whole European policy and strategy. As pointed out by Professor David Dallin—in his book *Soviet Foreign Policy After Stalin*—East Germany, Czechoslovakia, and Poland form a northern tier of states in Eastern Europe that include the greater part of the industry of the whole area and well over half its population.[11] These three countries are considerably more important to the Soviet Union than the southern tier, comprising the Balkan states (with Hungary providing the link between the two), and Poland's strategic position in this northern tier is particularly important. She is the military and economic link between the Soviet Union and East Germany. Any defection on Poland's part or any dangerous display of independence—even on the Romanian, let alone the Yugoslav, model—would gravely weaken the Soviet Union's position in Central Europe and endanger the very existence of the East German state. The Soviets have always been aware of this basic fact, which explains the much greater concern Khrushchev showed over the October, 1956, events in Poland than he did initially over those in Hungary. Gomulka, of course, is not likely to display too much independence, still less to defect: the Soviet Union is still the only guarantor of Poland's western frontier, and Polish economic weakness is such that Gomulka has always been prepared to sacrifice a good deal of independence for the benefits he thinks economic integration might bring. But, in on the whole unenviable circumstances, he is still not without a certain bargaining power. He knows it, and so do the Russians—hence the special place they have accorded him. What applies to Poland also applies in lesser degree to Czechoslovakia. Moscow's future reactions to the new course Novotny appears to be adopting should be of particular interest.

The northern tier has, on the whole, held firm for the Soviet Union. The southern tier, less important but still of great value, has been disastrously eroded. First Yugoslavia and then Albania broke off completely; more recently, Romania has become a doubtful element. Any hopes the new leaders may have had that Khrushchev's elimination would facilitate bridging the gulf between Moscow and Bucharest must soon have been dispelled. Khrushchev's removal only confirmed the Romanian victory. Nicolae

Ceausescu, the new Romanian Party leader, is, if anything, more militant in his nationalism than was Gheorghiu-Dej. Since October, 1964, the Soviet leaders have adopted a policy of sweet reasonableness, almost of turning the other cheek, with Romania. They have avoided any move that might worsen relations between them; the presence of Brezhnev at the Romanian Party Congress in July, 1965, and the friendly speech he made were clearly meant as conciliatory gestures. The Romanians, for their part, have been very correct but have shown no signs whatever of retracting.

The deterioration of relations with Romania was probably one of the reasons why the Soviet Union, under both the old leadership and the new, has striven for better relations with Yugoslavia. The development of very close relations between Gheorghiu-Dej and Tito in late 1963 and early 1964 did not go unnoticed in Moscow. A Belgrade-Bucharest axis would have meant the isolation of Bulgaria, the Soviet Union's only remaining trusted ally in the Balkans. Soviet efforts to prevent such an axis seem for the time being to have succeeded. Yugoslav relations with Romania since Tito's visit to Leningrad in June, 1964, have not developed with their previous momentum, although they are still cordial. At present, Moscow is more important to Belgrade than is Bucharest.

The deterioration of the Soviet Union's position in the Balkans has made Bulgaria more valuable to her now than at any time since 1945. Her strategic importance as an outpost bordering two unstable Western allies—Greece and Turkey—has always been generally recognized. But now Bulgaria has become the only state in the whole of southeastern Europe on which the Soviet Union can rely. Up to now, mainly because of its own weakness, the Bulgarian regime has been steadfastly loyal, and the U.S.S.R. has accepted the loyalty and turned a blind eye to the weakness and the incompetence. But in April, 1965, when the anti-regime conspiracy motivated by strong dissatisfaction over the Zhivkov regime's subservience to Moscow was uncovered in Sofia,[12] Moscow thought it expedient to send as authoritative a man as Suslov to make an on-the-spot investigation. This was the Soviet Union's way of telling everyone that Bulgaria was a sphere of interest she was determined to preserve.

Indeed, "hold on to what we have" seems to be the policy of

the Brezhnev-Kosygin regime for all of Eastern Europe. It is a negative, defensive policy. Perhaps it is meant only as an interim one. But it is difficult to see how it can be successfully replaced by something more positive. The Soviet Union will remain the major factor in the East European situation for many years to come, but its power to lead has already diminished greatly and seems hardly capable of being restored. It remains to be seen whether Brezhnev and Kosygin, or any future leaders, will defy the odds and try to restore it or whether they will take the line of least resistance by making the best of what has already become a very unsatisfactory situation.

To all friends of Eastern Europe, this must appear a desirable situation; nevertheless, it contains an element of danger. Between the wars, Eastern Europe was a hotbed of nationalism and chauvinism, the enmity of one state felt for the next making the area easy prey to outside intervention. Soon after World War II, however, the whole region was embraced by "proletarian internationalism." The evils of nationalism, it was argued, sprang primarily from economic causes; hence, a change in the ruling class and in economic and social relations would remove them. It is true that, after 1948, Eastern Europe was united, but it was a different unity from what was advocated and, perhaps, envisaged.

Under Stalin, proletarian internationalism became a euphemism for one of the most severe and ruthless imperialisms the region had ever known. The interstate hatreds that existed before the war were now submerged beneath a common hatred for the Soviet Union. Thus, there arose a negative type of unity which was fruitful nonetheless: many Eastern Europeans realized that, however serious the previous rivalries and conflicts among themselves may have been, they were paltry in comparison with the predicament they now faced. This, in turn, led to a feeling (especially among the younger generation) that when the opportunity arose, East European countries should ensure that they were strong enough to forestall any repetition of the experience. Thus the word "unity" came to have a pressing significance it had never had before.

Certain preconditions for unity were being created in the meanwhile. The economic and social structure of the region was radically and brutally changed; the differences of centuries were unceremoniously brushed aside. Before the war, the area as a whole had been mainly agricultural. Still, there had been a world of a difference between egalitarian Bulgaria and nonegalitarian Hungary; between the well-balanced class structure in Bohemia and the dangerously uneven spread of wealth and rights in Poland. Now, the state controlled industry in every country, and agriculture was being collectivized in most countries. Many of these economic measures were unwise, but they had the potential of solving a vital problem that would survive Communism.

One can say, therefore, that the Stalinist system consciously and unconsciously welded the East European states together to an extent previously unknown. Under Khrushchev, Soviet policy toward the satellites changed considerably, and this slowly began to have an important bearing on the question of unity. The new policy of autonomy; the Yugoslav example; the Sino-Soviet dispute, and the consequent inability of Moscow to coerce its satellites as before; and the beginning of a more active Western policy in the region—all these developments, favorable though they were, tended to undo some of what Stalin had accomplished. In the last few years of Khrushchev's period in power, disturbing signs of some of the old irritations, rivalries, and distrust among the East European countries began to reappear. The revival of nationalism was not directed solely against Soviet tutelage; it was also stirring up old feuds among neighbors.

Economic nationalism was the most conspicuous. It was the reef on which Khrushchev's COMECON schemes foundered; it also revealed itself in the contempt, suspicion, and envy different countries manifested toward each other. There were also signs of a revival of political nationalism. As will be seen in the next chapter, it was mainly the traditional fear of the Serbs that prompted Hoxha and his regime to secede from the Soviet bloc. One could hardly expect another Albania in Eastern Europe, but it was becoming clear that the old territorial issues were far from dead. Hungarians, for example, had never reconciled themselves to the loss of Transylvania; in the 1960's, there was growing resentment in Hungary over the attempts of the Romanian regime slowly but steadily to assimilate the Magyar minority in Romania. The Bulgarian-Yugoslav dispute over Macedonia remained dormant as long as there was a *rapprochement* between Belgrade and Moscow, but were this *rapprochement* to be interrupted, the quarrel would almost certainly flare up again. Finally, as pointed out in Chapter I, one of the less fortunate products of relaxation in Czechoslovakia was a resurgence of Slovak feeling against the Czechs.

The Soviet Union is itself very vulnerable on the territorial issue. Bessarabia, Ruthenia, large sections of prewar eastern Poland, and parts of East Prussia were annexed by the U.S.S.R. after World War II. The East European peoples had not forgotten this, and China too, in the course of 1964 showed its readiness to use the issue as a means of embarrassing Moscow. The Romanians, who never brought up the subject of Bessarabia directly, made it clear to all concerned that they had not forgotten the postwar annexation.*

Thus, almost every country in Eastern Europe has some claim against the next. The Soviet Union, because of her predominant power, can resist any pressure applied against her (in the unlikely event of there being any) and, if the need arose, could seek to retain her sway by a policy of *divide et impera*. If she ever chose to do this, her range of opportunity might be depressingly wide.

* The most notable example of this was the publication in Bucharest in December, 1964, of an unedited manuscript of Karl Marx criticizing Czarist annexation of and repression in Bessarabia. A. Otetea and S. Schwann (eds.), K. *Marx—Insemnari Despre Romani* (Bucharest: RPR Academy of Science, 1964).

SIX

Nationalism in Albania and Romania

THE PROBLEM OF East European nationalism and how to counter it was one that always plagued Khrushchev. Nationalism was one of the main reasons for both the Hungarian and Polish upheavals in 1956; it was also one of the main reasons that COMECON failed to fulfill the hopes he placed in it. Though Khrushchev never countered nationalism successfully, he granted a series of concessions throughout the 1950's that prevented it getting out of hand and disrupting the East European calm. In the 1960's, however, first he lost Albania, and then Romania outmaneuvered him on one point after point until she had shaken off her satellite status and become a nation thinking and acting almost completely on the basis of what she considered her own interests to be. The following is a brief study of the nationalist "deviations" of these two countries.

Albania

The Balkans have traditionally been prey to the ambitions of the great powers, and foreign penetration has been facilitated by convenient communication routes through the difficult mountain terrain. If the Balkan area has been fairly easy to control from the outside, it has also lent itself to the most serious type of internal fragmentation. A number of causes—geographical, historical, ethnic, and religious—have generated schisms and enmities that have given the Balkans an unenviable notoriety. Always conscious of its past glories, and intoxicated by the joy of delivery from servitude, each new state saw itself as the direct heir of its medieval forerunner. It was impossible wholly to fulfill such aspirations, and disastrous clashes resulted after independence. Nor did the interference of the great European powers, whether motivated by direct self-interest or the desire to preserve a balance of power, help matters. The state boundaries that emerged in the twentieth century left a trail of bitterness and resentment, and the still unsatiated territorial demands of some of the larger Balkan states created genuine fear among the smaller.

The smallest state in the Balkans is Albania, a country that has never been taken seriously by anyone in the Balkans or the Adriatic. For, despite a strong folk tradition and a worthy national hero (Scanderbeg), Albanians seem to have found it much easier than their Balkan neighbors do to be absorbed in a foreign pattern. The Albanian state was created in 1913—mainly because Austria wished to check Serbian designs on the area. When independence came, Albanian patriots had not only to begin stirring up the dormant national consciousness of their people, but to evade the greedy demands of their more powerful neighbors that Albanian territory be divided.

Still, the danger persisted—most immediately from fascist Italy. Albania's "natural" enemy, however, was Serbia, now the conscious master of the new Yugoslavia, which included some 800,000 Albanians of the Kossovo-Metohija region—the Kosmet, which had been ceded to Serbia in the Treaty of Bucharest of 1913. Palpably dependent on foreign support for its very survival, Albania's problem was how to take money without rendering service. In 1924, the north Albanian landlord-chieftain Ahmed Zogu rode into Tirana on a white horse (provided by the Yugoslavs) with promises of financial support from Yugoslavia. But the Yugoslav pump went dry, mainly because of internal economic and financial difficulties.

Zogu (now Premier, soon to become President and then King Zog) next turned to Italy, submitting to the fatal embrace which, though it benefited Albania a good deal materially, was to result in the presence, on Good Friday, 1939, of Italian troops in Tirana.

After the war, the players were different, the game very much the same. The Italian danger had gone, but Communist Albania was now the puppet of Communist Yugoslavia. Despite the ideology both countries now shared (at least superficially), there were understandable reasons for Albanian hatred and fear of Yugoslavia. Yugoslavia was now quite clearly the strongest nation in the Balkans, and there was no longer an ambitious power across the Adriatic against which she could be played off. Tito was regarded as Stalin's favourite protégé, and the Soviet Union was overlord of the whole area. Moreover, Tito was dizzy with success: under the guise of a plan for Balkan federation, he was seeking to bring Albania, Pirin Macedonia, and even all of Bulgaria under his control. Balkan federation looked like Serbian chauvinism writ large.

For Albania, there was both greater will and a greater need to resist Yugoslav domination than ever before. In the first place, a real Albanian national consciousness had now come into being, fostered by King Zog, who, for all his concessions to Mussolini, had done much to further the notion of Albanian unity. This consciousness had been tremendously strengthened by the wartime struggles of both Communist and other resistance movements, like the Balli Kombetar and Legaliteti. At the end of the war, most Albanians were ready to resist Greek claims to northern Epirus and resented Yugoslavia's re-acquisition of the Kosmet, with its preponderantly Albanian population.

It was this question of the Kosmet that brought a new element into the Albanian regime's fear of Yugoslavia after 1945. The Albanian people are divided into Ghegs and Tosks, differentiated by the two principal dialects of the Albanian language and separated roughly by the Shkumbini River. Historically, the Ghegs, north of the Shkumbini, had dominated the Tosks. A primitive people, with a society organized on closely knit tribal lines, they had lorded it over the slightly less primitive Tosks, who consisted largely of a few landowners and many exploited peasants. Educational standards in this area were relatively high, and some students went abroad to study. Many came back confirmed radicals. The first break with the traditional Gheg predominance came in 1924, when the Harvard-educated Orthodox Bishop Fan Noli, a typical example of the first radical wave of returning students, assumed power for a few months, having overthrown the government of Ahmed Zogu.* The latter, himself a Gheg chieftain, soon regained power, and the country settled down to another 15 years of Gheg predominance. During this period, the Albanian Communist movement slowly evolved; most of its leading members were Tosks. Enver Hoxha, the young man who was to become their leader, was a Tosk from Djinokaster who spent the six years from 1930 to 1936 as a singularly unsuccessful wandering scholar in France and Belgium. The Tosk majority in the upper echelons of his regime after liberation was quite strong.[1]

Thus, in 1945, the Tosks had political as well as numerical predominance for almost the first time in the nation's history. They meant to keep it that way and cowed the Ghegs with severe oppression. Fear of Gheg predominance persisted, however, now transferred largely to the Ghegs in the Yugoslav Kosmet. If these ever joined forces with the Ghegs in Albania, the Tosks would lose their numerical and political domination, and many of them would lose their heads as well—hence Albania's gripping fear of Tito's ambitions, no matter how well hidden in the "internationalism" of the Balkan Federation scheme. The Cominform's denunciation of Yugoslavia gave Albania its chance to throw off the Yugoslav domination and danger established during and after the war.

When the tough, experienced Yugoslav Communist emissaries had gone to Albania at the beginning of World War II, they had found the Communists there (or at least the people who called themselves Communists) divided into many factions. With professional skill and ruthlessness, they had reduced the chaos to manageable dimensions and launched the Albanian Communist Party on November 8, 1941. They agreed to Hoxha's leadership, but never really trusted this cosmopolitan dandy who had picked up too much education and too many bourgeois habits during his

* Bishop Fan Noli later fled the country and became head of the Albanian Orthodox Church in America. He died in Boston in March, 1965.

years in Western Europe. Their man was Koce Xoxe, a worker like themselves. Xoxe became the Yugoslav's principal agent within the Albanian Party. As Minister of the Interior after the war, he was probably the most powerful man in the regime after Hoxha. He built up an impressive apparatus with Yugoslav support and seems to have pursued a steady policy of isolating Hoxha. By 1948, both Tito and Hoxha saw the writing on the wall. In Tito's case, the writing was Stalin's; in Hoxha's case, it was Tito's.

Tito's 1948 expulsion from the Communist camp caused serious upheavals among all the ruling Communist parties in Europe. The fantastic indictments against practically all the victims of these upheavals included adherence to Titoism or "national Communism." In the Balkans alone, Lucretiu Patrascanu was imprisoned in Romania, Traicho Kostov was hanged in Bulgaria, and Koce Xoxe met his death in Albania. The Tito incident, in fact, served to intensify the Soviet Union's efforts to tighten its grip on the satellites and to standardize their political, economic, and social development. Purges in the parties elevated to positions of real influence only those people of whom Moscow could be absolutely sure.

In Albania, Enver Hoxha became the most Stalinist of them all. Now leader of a full-fledged Soviet satellite, he revelled in the anti-Tito onslaught and could afford to ignore the disturbing rumor that Stalin had once offered Albania to Yugoslavia.[2] The situation had changed, and he knew it. He was safe, the Tosks were safe, the country was safe. But situations have a way of changing more than once. In 1953, Stalin died, and no one watched the ensuing struggle in the Kremlin more keenly than did Hoxha. The man who emerged victorious exceeded his worst fears. In intra-bloc policy, Khrushchev immediately showed himself to be a fence-mender. His first objective was to improve relations with the two Communist countries in which "national Communism" had done the most harm—China, at the far eastern end of the Communist world, and Yugoslavia, at the far western end. In 1954, Khrushchev visited Peking, and generous terms of alliance were drawn up; in May, 1955, he visited Belgrade. His aim was to bring Yugoslavia back into the fold; to do this, he was prepared to make a number of concessions. At the meeting, Tito made part of his price the removal of some of his enemies—Rakosi, probably Chervenkov, and, of course, Hoxha. It required no great perception on Hoxha's part to realize that something like this was brewing. The following eighteen months were probably the most trying he had spent since coming to power. Two of Tito's arch-enemies, Rakosi and Chervenkov, were removed; Stalin was denounced at the Twentieth Congress of the CPSU; and the whole foundation on which Hoxha had built his power seemed to crumble. Finally, the tremors from the Hungarian Revolution reached Albania. Still, Hoxha survived —not because he had a determined and united party behind him, but through a combination of traditional Albanian clan nepotism, patronage, terror, and skill, plus a fortunate geographical isolation from the rest of the "socialist camp."

The Belgrade meeting of 1955 was, therefore, the beginning of an entirely new situation for the Albanian Communist leaders. Tito was being courted by Moscow and was agreeing to the courtship only on conditions highly dangerous to them. Again, as in 1948, the question of power was involved, as was that of national interests. The circumstances of Albania's differences with the Soviet Union beginning in 1955 and the Yugoslav differences with Moscow prior to 1948 were not the same, of course, but, in the last analysis, the contended issues were similar. With both Tito and Hoxha, it was a question of power and survival. In the case of Hoxha, the question of survival was probably the more pressing. One must assume that, after 1948, the Soviet ambassador in Albania did not consider the feelings of Hoxha or Premier Mehmet Shehu when he wanted to get information or to summon an Albanian official to his embassy. Hoxha was cheerfully prepared to accept this affront to his dignity as long as his clique stayed in power and his country was protected from Yugoslavia. After 1955, he was not sure of either. Once he had survived the Hungarian disaster of October, 1956, he was probably glad it had occurred; perhaps it would keep Khrushchev from further dalliance with the Yugoslavs.* In fact, the Khrushchev-Tito courtship was broken off in 1957, and after the Yugoslav Party's program in April, 1958, there seemed little hope of reconciliation. During this period,

* The first attack on Tito after the Hungarian Revolution was Hoxha's, in *Pravda*, November 8, 1956.

Hoxha may have persuaded himself that Khrushchev had ended his attempts at *rapprochement* with Belgrade; Khrushchev, for his part, occasionally found Hoxha's constant and virulent attacks on the Yugoslavs useful. In 1959, however, the Soviet leader renewed his effort to improve relations with Yugoslavia. Khrushchev's trip to Tirana in May of that year was probably an attempt to forestall dangerous repercussions of his courtship of Tito. His disillusionment complete, Hoxha soon fell into the arms of Mao, who was similarly unconvinced when visited by Khrushchev later in 1959.

After October–November, 1959, Albanian speeches, broadcasts, and articles took on a "Chinese" tone on questions of international policy. It was a matter of emphasis rather than fact—but it was there. The first striking indication of differences between Moscow and Tirana came in June, 1960, when neither Hoxha nor Premier Shehu attended the Communist "little summit" meeting in Bucharest, held during the Third Congress of the Romanian Communist Party. Hysni Kapo, Albania's number-three man, who went instead, gave a speech at the Congress which was "Chinese" in emphasis but which implied no open breach with the Soviet Union. At a secret session in Bucharest, however, the differences became both profound and bitter. Kapo solidly backed the Chinese delegate Peng Chen, with arguments that apparently echoed the famous anti-Soviet article ("Long Live Leninism!") which had appeared in the Chinese Party journal *Red Flag* the preceding April.[3] It was here that the Albanian deviation probably began in earnest. Albanian anger, pent up for four years, finally exploded. Peking's cause became Tirana's; the dispute was on.

Shortly before this Bucharest meeting, an incident occurred that may have persuaded Hoxha to throw caution to the winds. At the end of May, 1960, Khrushchev gave an interview to the Greek Liberal Party leader Sophocles Venizelos. According to Venizelos, Khrushchev promised to discuss the question of internal autonomy for northern Epirus with the Albanian delegation at the forthcoming Bucharest conference.[4] Hoxha must have heard of this very quickly, and it may have finally decided him on desperate measures. In the interests of a "peace offensive" in the Balkans, Khrushchev was now cultivating the Greeks as well as placating the Yugoslavs—all at the expense of Albania's national integrity.

In the interval between the Bucharest meeting and the September session of the U.N. General Assembly in New York, the Albanians continued to give evidence, in articles and broadcasts, of their affinity with China's "line." Delegations of many kinds plied between the two countries with notable frequency, and the most laudatory protestations of friendship were uttered. In early September, the first sign of the strain that the new policy imposed on the Albanian Communist Party appeared. It was announced that Liri Belishova had been dismissed from her Politburo and Secretariat positions, and Koco Tashko from the chairmanship of the Central Audit Commission. In November, Maqo Como, Belishova's husband, was replaced as Minister of Agriculture. These three were considered pro-Soviet; Mikoyan confirmed this at the Twenty-second Congress of the CPSU.

When the September session of the U.N. General Assembly convened, Hoxha again stayed away. He sent Shehu, who was cold-shouldered by his Communist peers, but who said nothing publicly to cause concern. He was biding his time. In a report to the Albanian parliament the following month, he attacked Gomulka's proposal for the "freezing" of military bases on foreign soil, and Zhivkov's proposal for drastic reduction of arms in the Balkans as a prelude to world-wide disarmament.[5] He did not mention the two leaders by name, but he left no doubt to whom he referred.

Shehu's attack came on the eve of the world conference of eighty-one Communist parties in Moscow. Hoxha went to this meeting, as did Shehu. In a speech of which a fragment was afterward revealed, he vilified Khrushchev in a manner that evidently embarrassed even China; Shehu made a few remarks that were brought up against him at the 22nd Congress. The two left early and have never returned to Moscow.

After this, Albanian relations with the Soviet bloc deteriorated steadily, if not too obviously; relations with China rapidly and ostentatiously became closer. The first official admission that there had been trouble at the 1960 conference in Moscow came from Ulbricht. Addressing the Socialist Unity Party Central Committee on his return, he remarked that the Albanians had advanced "dogmatist and sectarian" arguments at the conference.[6] Then, in a classic venture into esoteric communication, the CPSU omitted the word "comrades" in its New Year message to the Albanian Party. Immediately after, the Bulgarians referred simply to "Enver Hoxha."

In January, perhaps in a last attempt to bring Hoxha either to heel or to reason, Moscow sent an experienced *apparatchik,* Josif Shikin, to Tirana as Ambassador. (His appointment had been announced the previous November.) The Albanian Party Congress, twice postponed, was now scheduled for February, and this may have been considered the last hope for a change in attitude. Shikin's speech to the Congress was admonitory, but it was the Polish delegate, Roman Nowak, who explicitly appealed to the Albanians to mend their ways. However, the Congress changed nothing; the Albanian leadership and line remained the same. Hoxha continued his tactic of swearing eternal fealty to the Soviet Union but on his own terms; several speakers, notably Shehu, carried on an almost open ideological wrangle with Moscow; the Soviet delegation was treated like a poor relation compared to the Chinese; Khrushchev was treated like a nonentity. The differences between the Albanian speeches and the Soviet and Soviet-bloc speeches were all too clear. Finally, Hoxha revealed a "plot" hatched the previous autumn, he said, by some Albanian traitors inside and outside the country, by the Yugoslavs, the Greeks, and the American Sixth Fleet, aimed at overthrowing the "Peoples' Republic."[7] Most outside observers agreed that this was actually a Soviet plot to unseat Hoxha: Hoxha's disclosure met with virtually no response from the Soviet bloc; some of the culprits, who were later given a "show trial," had maintained very close Soviet connections.

Shikin's failure to affect the Congress probably set the seal on any hope of bringing about a change in Albania. Yet, there was still no open condemnation of the Albanian policy from Moscow. Other evidence pointed to a widening of the gulf. Both Hoxha and Shehu failed to attend the important Warsaw Pact conference in Moscow at the end of March. Speaking to a trade-union congress in Tirana in late April, Rita Marko, a prominent Albanian Politburo member, expounded a fire-eating theory of international relations that was diametrically opposed to "peaceful coexistence."

A year later, in early June, 1961, the Adriatic-based Soviet submarines left their base at Valona and never returned. Perhaps more important was the steady withdrawal, throughout the year, of Soviet and East European money and men from Albania. Having failed to browbeat or overthrow Hoxha, Khrushchev obviously now hoped to force him economically to his knees. (He had actually begun to do this in the autumn of 1959, for this was one of the bitter complaints Hoxha had made in Moscow.) The Soviet, Czechoslovak, and East German governments cancelled the credits they had promised to Albania; later, they began to withdraw the technicians and specialists they had sent. In other circumstances, this combination would have brought a collapse of the Albanian economy. But Hoxha turned to China. At the end of April, the regime announced that the Peking government had agreed to supply Albania with credits to the value of about $125 million. Chinese specialists began to arrive—perhaps a bit slowly for the Albanians' liking, but at least in some number. East Europeans became conspicuous by their absence. Throughout the year, the exchange of compliments and delegations between Tirana and Peking multiplied.

The situation was heading for a showdown. On August 3–5, 1961, a Warsaw Pact conference was held in Moscow to discuss the German problem. A communiqué issued at its close stated that the conference had been attended by the First Party Secretaries of the Warsaw Pact countries. Yet, a subsequent Albanian announcement made it fairly clear that Hoxha had not attended and that whoever had led the Albanian delegation had not gotten much further than the front door. The following month (September), there was no Albanian representative in Pankow at the celebrations of the twelfth anniversary of the G.D.R. In October, there were no East European representatives at the fifth congress of the Albanian Women's Union. A few days earlier, Radio Moscow, in its broadcasts beamed to Albania, had given its listeners a lecture on the evils of the personality cult. The stage was being set.

On October 17, 1961, the opening day of the Twenty-second Congress of the CPSU, Khrushchev openly attacked the Albanian Party, accusing it of "dogmatism" and of pursuing a domestic policy of repression and inhumanity. By its attitude, he said, Albania was weakening the socialist camp and playing into the hands of the imperialists. The Albanians immediately counterattacked:

Khrushchev and his clique, they said, has succumbed to Yugoslav revisionism and had openly collaborated with the imperialists.

The conflict was now open. The Soviet Union had lost a satellite; China had gained a bridgehead in Europe.

Romania

At the time of Khrushchev's fall, in October, 1964, Romania owed its prominence in world affairs to its successful policy of independence from the Soviet Union—a policy that would have seemed utterly improbable five years earlier, not only to outside observers, but possibly to Romania herself.

Why Romania? What prompted a government noted for a rather Byzantine prudence to enter a game that was bound to be dangerous no matter how skillfully played? Indeed, the game was not even of Romania's choosing. Once it had started, however, there was nothing to do but play to the end, with neither side ever really knowing where that end was going to be.

The Romanian Government found itself in a quarrel with the Soviet Union over an issue on which it had staked much prestige. Once the issue had been joined, Romania felt it could not withdraw. To explain this issue and the importance attached to it, one must go back to the early years of Communism in Romania and the circumstances under which the Communist Party came to power there.

Communism never had a strong tradition in Romania. It had first appeared there, toward the end of the last century, in the person of Mikhail Katz, a Jewish emigré from Russia. He later became Constantine Dobrogeanu-Gherea, the only serious theorist the Romanian Communists have ever had. Communism in Romania was an internationalist creed in a fiercely nationalistic land; it drew its inspiration from Russia, a country that most Romanians feared and despised; many of its proponents were Jews in a country in which anti-Semitism was strong. Between the two wars, it was doubtful whether the Romanian Communist Party ever had more than 1,000 members. It was considered not only un-Romanian but anti-Romanian, for it constantly supported the Russian cause when it conflicted with the interests and sentiments of the Romanian people, e.g., on the Bessarabian issue.

In 1945, Communism was officially imposed on Romania by Russian troops. The Communist regime sanctioned the ceding of Bessarabia and northern Bukovina to Russia; it condoned the most blatant economic exploitation—first through open looting, then through the notorious Sovroms, which were the joint Soviet-Romanian companies which managed the more important industries. With Russian troops in support, it quickly tightened its grip on a demoralized and sullen nation. To swell its meager ranks, the Party welcomed the scum of society: former fascists, members of the Nazi-like, reactionary Iron Guard, careerists, opportunists, criminals. This further disgusted the mass of the population. Even the most tyrannical dictatorship, if it is to function at all, needs the support of some sectors of the population. In this respect, the Romanian Communist dictatorship could hardly have made a worse start.

Its first step toward full identification with the Romanian people came about 1950, when it conducted a series of purges that weeded out many of the unsavory elements that had joined the Party immediately after the war. The Party was drastically trimmed, and a new cadre policy was aimed at the younger generation. The purges culminated in 1952 with the dismissal of the two Soviet-trained Party leaders, Ana Pauker and Vasile Luca. "Red Ana," the daughter of a Jewish rabbi and a "cosmopolitan" Communist *par excellence*, with her loyalty to Moscow as the seat of the world revolution, had been the real ruler of Romania since 1945, although the nominal power was Gheorghiu-Dej's.

With the "Pauker clique" out of the way, the "home" Communists began to dig in. Of course, they had no intention of pursuing any nationalist policy at that time; they were interested solely in power. Later, however, they hinted strongly that a nationalist policy was, indeed, their intention, and Gheorghiu-Dej argued that, by getting rid of Pauker in 1952 (i.e., one year before Stalin's death), he was the first in the Soviet bloc to de-Stalinize. His specious claims, with their anti-Semitic and even anti-Russian overtones, showed skill in the manipulation of public opinion and prejudices.

The decade of the 1950's showed that Gheorghiu-Dej could be as ruthless as any other dictator in consolidating his power. During the years of the "new course," after Stalin's death, he combined concession with terror to stay in power. No sooner had he weathered this storm than Khrushchev upset the calm at the Twentieth CPSU Congress. Gheorghiu-Dej's responses were the same—purges in the Party, accompanied by intimidation of the population at large. By 1958, the situation was once again in hand. Soviet troops left the country in the summer of that year; at the head of a now thoroughly united leadership, he could plan for the future.

It was probably at about this time that Gheorghiu-Dej convinced himself (or was convinced by others) that a more positive policy was both opportune and necessary. Ever since he had assumed the leadership of the Party in 1945, he and his group had been forced to spend most of their time either fighting for power, protecting it, or consolidating it. Now came the time for them to deepen it and broaden its base. They also had to run the country, a task in which they had failed lamentably in most respects, nowhere more so than in the economy, for which their planning had been just as ambitious and ill conceived as in other East European nations. It can be argued with some justice that there were mitigating circumstances—that Romania had the burden of having to pay tremendous war reparations to the Soviet Union, and of having to organize and support the Sovroms, which were only dissolved between 1954 and 1956 (an act for which Gheorghiu-Dej later quietly claimed credit). There was also the political instability that characterized all of Eastern Europe for the five years after Stalin's death. By 1958, however, these drawbacks no longer were relevant, nor was another, more serious handicap, which had played a large part in undermining the Communist economic effort—the absence of some kind of technical intelligentsia.

Immediately after the war, the policy had been to reject the old, bourgeois technical elite as being tainted and unreliable. Much of the economy, therefore, was managed either by naïve and untrained Party hacks or by fledglings with no experience and little training. Still, the Romanian regime had provided for the education of large numbers of technical cadres very early in its rule. It was forming a new class, in effect, ambitious for both place and privilege, and not devoid of patriotism. This class presented both a challenge and an opportunity to the regime. Its ever-growing numbers had to be satisfied with jobs in an expanding economy; if their demands were met, the technical elite could become a large and powerful support to the regime. Thus, the one thing Communism had previously lacked in Romania—a strong base of support—was by 1958 in an advanced stage of formation. The regime was also very fortunate to have, in its vanguard, men who were both confirmed Communists and able economists—men like Alexandru Barladeanu, now Romania's COMECON delegate, Gheorghe Gaston Marin, the Chairman of the State Planning Committee, and Gogu Radulescu, the Minister of Trade. Capable leaders like these could win the confidence of the upcoming technocrats. Finally, Gheorghiu-Dej himself was believed to have developed more than a passing interest in technical and industrial matters, an interest genuine enough to make him realize that too much Party interference would be detrimental to incentive and initiative.

This, then, was the potential base of support the regime needed. Romania's leaders could harness the ability, the ambition, and the patriotism of this class if it gave it the green light with a comprehensive industrialization policy. One must also assume that the leadership was not simply prompted by power cynicism. Its actions were probably also motivated by genuine national pride, conveniently buttressed by the Marxist-Leninist craving for a heavy industrial base for the economy.

Nor did Gheorghiu-Dej at first have any serious reason to believe that Romania's program of economic expansion would be found objectionable by the Soviet Union or its COMECON partners. But after the COMECON summit meeting of May, 1958, it became evident that the economically more advanced East European countries, most notably Czechoslovakia, were arguing that countries like herself, East Germany, and the Soviet Union should monopolize heavy industry while the less advanced nations, like Romania and Bulgaria, should concentrate mainly on agriculture, food processing, etc. The Soviet attitude was at this time not clear. Until 1960, at least, Moscow was still publicly advocating that each COMECON member should build its own integral economy. The Romanians pressed on regardless, and at their Third Party

Congress in 1960, approved a program designed to make Romania a considerable industrial power by 1975.*

It was after this congress, however, that the Soviet Union definitely came around to the viewpoint held by Czechoslovakia and East Germany, and publicly showed her attitude toward COMECON cooperation—now favoring specialization by whole industries and advocating that a country like Romania concentrate on agriculture and industries, such as the petrochemical, for which it already had a good foundation. The Romanians may have gotten wind of these intentions as early as the Twenty-second CPSU Congress, in October, 1961; throughout 1962 and early 1963, Soviet intentions became ever clearer—just when the Romanians' "economic miracle" started to be noticed as a major development by analysts in both East and West.[8]

Gheorghiu-Dej's dilemma is not difficult to understand. Here was a leader who had made prudence the hallmark of his political activity, so successful a trimmer in his relations with the Kremlin that he had remained in power for more than fifteen years. Yet one of his basic policies, on which he had embarked in the confident belief that there would be no opposition to it, had been challenged by the very nation to which Romania looked for trade and aid in carrying out her program. On the other hand, Gheorghiu-Dej knew that if he bowed to Soviet wishes, he would lose prestige in his own Party, and his Party would lose prestige among the people—especially among the class on which it depended most heavily for support. Then came the momentous event that rescued him—the open eruption of the Sino-Soviet dispute.

With daring shrewdness, Gheorghiu-Dej soon recognized the implications of the Sino-Soviet dispute for the East European satellites. He saw that they were now given much more scope for maneuver *vis-à-vis* the Kremlin than ever before. On the overt basic issues in the Sino-Soviet dispute, he was always wholly pro-Soviet; there was virtually no danger of his ever becoming a Maoist. Mao, to him, became simply a means of winning concessions from the Soviet Union. He knew that Khrushchev was preoccupied with China and that he could not afford another Albania in Eastern

* Khrushchev himself attended this congress and heartily endorsed the Romanian program.

Europe. He realized the possibilities of the situation, and he was forced to exploit these possibilities. Thus, in 1963, Romania's "flirtation" with China began. Throughout the year, there was no real attack on Peking in the Romanian press; the press of the other satellites abounded with them. While the rest of the East European bloc cut its trade with China, Romania increased hers by 10 per cent; simultaneously, she restored her diplomatic relations and increased her trade with Albania.

In the summer, two more serious events occurred. It was obvious that Moscow took violent exception to Peking's letter to the CPSU of June 14, containing the twenty-five points on which China proposed the talks between the two parties should be based. Every regime in Eastern Europe published *Tass'* statement that the letter contained slanders and distortions and would not be published in the Soviet press—every regime, that is, except in Romania, where a long account of the letter, itemizing all twenty-five points, was published.[9] This was open defiance of Khrushchev, and it is quite likely that this question of the Chinese letter was closely linked to the other striking example of Romanian divergence from the Soviet bloc—the absence of Gheorghiu-Dej from the "little summit," organized in East Berlin at the end of June, at which all other bloc leaders were present.

All this occurred during a year that also witnessed provocative interviews with Western journalists on the Romanian view of COMECON, and flamboyant commercial sorties to the West. These sorties had begun earlier but were now paying off with startling success. They could not be considered merely as part of the general East European trend to open up trade with the West; for many of them were designed to get either equipment that Romania's COMECON partners could not provide, or equipment superior to that which they were producing.

This defiance of the Soviet Union brought Gheorghiu-Dej a popular support much broader than that which he could summon from Romania's new technical elite. He had done little to stimulate, and nothing to deserve, the support of the toiling masses from which he himself had sprung. Though the standard of living had risen in Romania, it was pitifully low; the "economic miracle" was based on this hard fact. The great masses of the population had, indeed, very little for which to thank the Gheorghiu-Dej regime. But, in one respect, he did satisfy the people's emotions, if not their needs: he responded to one of their strongest sentiments, or prejudices—anti-Russian feeling. He must have realized that his defiance of the Soviet Union on the COMECON issue would win the strong emotional support of the population, but would also divert attention from the issue at the center of the dispute—Romania's insistence on comprehensive industrialization—and would limit greatly the possibilities of early improvement in the general standard of living.

This may have been the main reason why Gheorghiu-Dej made sure that the masses knew what he was doing. He did not, of course, publish his case in the daily press; he simply saw to it that every Party member was informed, and Party members were by no means sworn to secrecy on the matter. This development seems to have taken place shortly after the February, 1963, meeting of the COMECON Executive Committee in Moscow, at which Romanian economic policy was evidently subjected to severe criticism.

Gheorghiu-Dej did not stop there. He further titillated the anti-Russian sentiments of his people by a number of acts designed to play down the Soviet presence and influence in Romania. The first instance of this was the Romanian attack, in late 1962, on the Soviet historian Ushakov, for a book in which, it was claimed, he failed to give the Romanian Communists sufficient credit for the role *they* claimed to have played in the liberation of the country in 1944. Ushakov had simply told the old Stalinist history, which gave all the credit to the Red Army. The Romanian Communists now insisted that they played the major role, and they even gave credit to King Michael and certain bourgeois groups for having recognized what was inevitable and for cooperating with the Communists. The truth of this version need not be discussed here, but two points can be noted: first, the Party's attempt to present itself as the inheritor and torchbearer of all that was finest in the Romanian progressive tradition, to embody itself in the nation; and second, the Romanian people's propensity to approve disparagement of the Soviet Union's achievement, even though they were not likely to be taken in by the Romanian Party's claim to predominance in the 1944 events.

Their emotions were fed by other little gestures of anti-Russian nationalism—renaming streets, squares, cinemas, etc., or, more important, the closing of the Maxim Gorky Institute in Bucharest, which had been the bastion of Soviet cultural influence; the demolition of the Russian bookstore in Bucharest; and the discontinuation of the Romanian edition of the Soviet *New Times.* All these acts were noticed and talked about.

The most daring anti-Soviet gesture made by the regime was the condoning, even the encouragement, of popular agitation over the Bessarabian issue. Bessarabia, a Romanian province, had been annexed by the Soviet Union in 1940, along with northern Bukovina. In private and in public, the Romanian people began to demand the return of Bessarabia; fuel was added to the fire late in 1964 when the Romanian Academy of Sciences published an unedited version of a pamphlet by Karl Marx called "Notes on Romanians," in which he attacked Russia for its oppression of Bessarabia when it was under Russian control in the nineteenth century.[10] All these gestures, or the condoning of them, won credit for the Romanian regime in circles where normally it would have been disliked or even opposed.

It is probably correct to assume that the regime's defiance of the Soviet Union was prompted mainly by its desire to win points on its comprehensive industrialization program. But it seems that the animosity this defiance engendered persisted after the issue that caused it was settled. Most observers agree that the strong objections to Romania's program expressed by the Soviet Union and her more advanced COMECON partners, like East Germany and Czechoslovakia, were finally dropped at the Moscow COMECON meeting of first party secretaries in July, 1963. One can assume that Romania's obstinacy won the day, and that her flirtation with China and ambivalence on the whole Sino-Soviet dispute had contributed to this victory. After the victory, however, this ambivalence did not diminish but became more marked. There was no settling back into true satellite status. De-Russification continued, top-level commercial delegations were still sent to the West; most important of all, Romanian policy toward China took a turn more displeasing to the Soviets than before.

The COMECON dispute, and the tactics used in it, proved that things would never be the same again between Khrushchev and Gheorghiu-Dej. The causes and consequences of the dispute evidently had created a momentum that could not be reduced. There was no reconciliation. Instead, there was dislike on the one side, fear on the other. Once his victory had been won, therefore, Gheorghiu-Dej had more, rather than less, need for Mao, with whom he was basically not in sympathy, but who had become the guarantor of his security. This being the case, the Romanian leadership had two things to fear. One of them—a real reconciliation between Khrushchev and Mao—seemed almost impossible; the other—the formal expulsion of China from the world Communist movement—seemed, in the autumn of 1963, to be a distinct possibility. With China publicly expelled from the movement, Khrushchev would have a much freer hand in bringing East Europe to heel. With China remaining in the movement, there would still be that element of uncertainty and fluctuation which would give small powers room to maneuver.

Thus, Romania put herself in the van of the growing number of Communist countries or parties urging restraint, an end to polemics, and a renewal of some form of Moscow-Peking contact. The first public expression of this view was an article by Premier Ion Gheorghe Maurer in the November, 1963, issue of *Problems of Peace and Socialism,* in which he indirectly chastised both disputants, called for a renewal of bilateral contacts, and supported the summoning of a world conference of Communist parties after the necessary preparations could be made. Maurer's article, with other, earlier appeals, may have done much to deter Khrushchev, who was believed to be eager to force the issue with the Chinese at that time. The most dramatic expression came in March, 1964, when Maurer and other Romanian leaders departed for Peking—a trip that can best be interpreted as an eleventh-hour attempt to prevent the final, irrevocable split which would have greatly lessened Gheorghiu-Dej's power of maneuver with Khrushchev.

In April, 1964, came the famous Central Committee resolution, which has been accurately called Romania's Declaration of Independence. Then came Deputy Premier Gaston Marin's visit to Washington and Premier Maurer's visit to Paris—the two most dramatic examples of Romania's rapidly improving relations with the West. The defiance continued right up to the moment of Khrushchev's fall. Though the Romanians were clever enough not to say so, Bucharest must have regarded it as setting the seal of success on its policy. If the April resolution had declared Romania's independence, Khrushchev's departure guaranteed it.

SEVEN

Relations with the Western Powers

At the end of the Khrushchev era, relations between the Soviet Union and Eastern Europe on the one side, and the United States and Western Europe on the other, were better than they had been since the end of World War II. Economic and cultural relations were developing at a brisk pace, even political relations were improving steadily. This improvement had taken place under the rubric of "peaceful coexistence."

Both the main protagonists in the East-West confrontation saw peaceful coexistence as presenting two opportunities: it could facilitate the establishment of certain international guarantees that would greatly diminish the danger of war; and it also implied the mutual recognition that each side had certain claims, interests, and privileges the other would respect and that if these were not respected, the injured party would ring down the curtain on peaceful coexistence. The cold war would thus be renewed, the international confidence that had been built up would be destroyed, and the danger of nuclear war would re-emerge. Within this broad framework, however, both sides were free to pursue their own political, economic, or ideological interests, often at the expense of the other. Hence, the numerous political, economic, and cultural agreements should be seen as having a twofold character: they reinforced the guarantees against nuclear war by creating a better international climate and by strengthening the vested interests in the preservation of peace; but they were also attempts directly to probe the weaknesses of the other side, or to gain political or economic advantage. If any of these efforts showed signs of ruining the international climate, however, the side making it pulled back—a basic rule in a game dictated by the balance of terror. The Soviet withdrawal of missiles from Cuba was the most striking illustration. There have been no such clear-cut examples on the Western side, since the West has been largely on the defensive. If the more activist Western policy continues, there will almost inevitably be future cases in which withdrawal or restraint will become necessary—barring a drastic and unforeseen shift in the balance of strength.

Subject to these basic limitations, each side has tried to gain the advantage over the other. The East has used peaceful coexistence to try to weaken the West by dividing the NATO alliance and by ruining Western prestige in underdeveloped countries. It also became a means of obtaining Western technology and industrial equipment on relatively good terms; the Communist countries could then challenge the West more strongly in economic competition. Similarly the West has tried, with some success, to weaken the Eastern alliance, and Eastern Europe's readiness to buy or borrow opened up possibilities of weakening the Soviet Union's hold in the area and also of slowly undermining the Communist system. Western economic assistance was predicated on the assumption that the long-term political advantages it would bring outweighed the shorter-term economic advantages that would accrue to the East.

East-West coexistence meant different things to different countries. To Romania, it meant an added means of distancing herself from the Soviet Union; for her purposes, President Johnson and Mao Tse-tung made excellent bedfellows. To Great Britain, it was a means of alleviating serious economic difficulties. (To many businessmen everywhere, it was a means of boosting profits.) West Germany saw in it the possibility of isolating East Germany and making the day of German reunification slightly less distant; it was also a way to reintroduce the German presence in Central Europe. For the France of General de Gaulle, it provided not only a means of increasing French prestige in Eastern Europe but was an instrument for furthering her policy of a united Europe as a third force in the world.

When considering the part East European states played in the workings of peaceful coexistence, one must distinguish among three types of actions: those they took, or tried to take, independent of the Soviet Union; those actions that were part and parcel of Soviet-inspired international strategy; and actions that, if not directed by the Soviet Union, were either encouraged or not opposed by her. Obviously, the Sino-Soviet dispute, the fact of peaceful coexistence itself, and the more activist Western policy made independent action more possible than ever before. Only in the case of Romania, however, was it absolutely clear that this possibility was being used to break away from Soviet control. In the case of the other countries, it was still a question of the future whether western probing tactics would meet with similar success.

It is not necessary to catalog the many steps—political, economic, cultural—that Romania took to strengthen her Western contacts. The most spectacular were Gaston Marin's visit to Washington and Maurer's to Paris, but there were many other delegations that traveled to the West. Not all of these visits produced concrete results, but, by the end of 1964, it was already possible to see that the Romanian offensive was having some success. Complaints from Moscow and other East European capitals were countered cleverly by the argument that Romania was, after all, simply putting into practice those principles of peaceful coexistence that everyone, and especially Khrushchev, preached. It was a difficult argument to answer, especially when Bucharest could cite impressive statistics showing, for example, that all other East European regimes were also increasing their trade with the West.[1] Everyone knew, of course, that though Romania might be keeping to the letter of the law, she was not adhering to its spirit. But under the circumstances, there was little or nothing that could be done about it.

If the case of Romania is clear, what of the others? Excluding the very special case of the G.D.R., all the East European countries tried hard to mend there fences in the West. Economic delegations from Czechoslovakia, Poland, Hungary, and Bulgaria were a common sight in Western Europe and the United States during 1964. As with Romania, the number of specific agreements reached was fewer than the number of journeys made. But each country could point to beneficial results. On the political level, Hungary began talks with the United States designed to normalize the relations so severely strained as a result of the 1956 revolution. Relations between Budapest and Vienna became more and more cordial. At the beginning of 1965, Hungary's Foreign Minister, Janos Peter, made a successful visit to Paris—and later an equally successful visit to London. After years of being the socialist camp's truculent bastion in the West, Czechoslovakia showed a friendlier face. She made successful attempts to strengthen economic ties with Western Europe; and, on the political level, the Czechoslovak Foreign Minister, Vaclav David, was received in London and Paris, and talked with Secretary of State Dean Rusk when in New York to attend a session of the U.N. General Assembly. Bulgaria succeeded in increasing her ties with the West, though the December, 1963, show trial in Sofia of Assen Georgiev, accused of being an "American spy," and the subsequent riot in front of the United States legation, rather undermined her efforts in Washington. Poland also improved her relations with Western Europe; although, as in the case of Bulgaria, relations with the United States were somewhat soured by certain anti-American gestures and an intensification of anti-American propaganda after 1963.

All these gestures reflecting better relations were welcome to the Western powers. But it should not be considered that they were necessarily unwelcome to the Soviet Union or carried out in defiance of her. Except in the case of Romania, it can be validly argued that although better relations between Eastern Europe and the West might in the future facilitate a drawing away from the Soviet Union, they were for the present being used by Moscow in a diplomatic campaign against the West.

The East European response to General de Gaulle has been a case in point. The similarities between the position of France in the Western alliance and that of Romania in the Communist alliance have often been pointed out. Both were rebellious, concerned with independence, and a thorn in the side to the respective leaders of the alliances. Thus, both presented opportunities to the other side. The United States wished to exploit Romania in order to weaken the Soviet alliance; the Soviet Union and its allies wished to exploit France in order to weaken the West. Even without her interest in Eastern Europe, France would have been the subject of much attention; as it was, her eagerness to re-enter the region only increased it. Of course, the French Government was well aware of the fact that France was being courted by the East for a definite purpose. But France had something to gain and little to lose, and she could rightly argue that a successful French presence in Eastern Europe would weaken the Soviet Union and benefit the West as a whole. The Soviet bloc evidently was confident that the French presence could be contained, and that there were greater advantages in France being increasingly at cross-purposes with her allies than there were risks involved in helping to bring this about. This would seem to be a better explanation of, for example, Hungary's flirtation with France at the beginning of 1965, than one which interpreted this as a sign of Budapest's eagerness to escape from the bear hug.

An even clearer case of an East European state using peaceful coexistence to press an initiative which, if accepted, would weaken the West was Poland and the Gomulka Plan. This plan was a refined, up-to-date version of the Rapacki Plan, and it called for a freezing of nuclear weapons and bases on the territories of NATO and Warsaw Pact states. It was officially presented at the beginning of 1964, although Gomulka had first aired the idea as early as 1960, at the U.N. General Assembly. Its main aim was to prevent the nuclear rearming of West Germany, a step that many people in the West were also anxious to see avoided, and to torpedo the American plan for a multilateral nuclear force that would, of course, include German personnel. Throughout 1964, the Poles conducted a campaign in Western Europe using their civilized and personable Foreign Minister Rapacki himself as their chief salesman. The Poles, with their fear of Germany, were obviously most directly concerned with getting the Gomulka Plan accepted and were gratified at the increased prestige or prominence accruing from their initiative. But very few would claim that this was a genuine act of independence on the part of Poland. If not Soviet-inspired, it was a Soviet-supported initiative designed to weaken the Western alliance.

If Moscow were ever to show signs of wanting a real *rapprochement* with Bonn, it is quite possible that Poland would adopt a policy of genuine independence, i.e., defiance, of the Soviet Union in foreign affairs. Toward the end of the Khrushchev era, when the Soviet leader was dallying with West Germany, there were definite signs of Polish nervousness. Under the new leadership, Khrushchev's policy seems to have been abandoned, at least for the time being, perhaps partly as a result of Polish pressure. If it is ever resumed, there could be a danger of real estrangement between Warsaw and Moscow.

Although the Polish initiatives won most publicity in the West, perhaps the best example of the success of Communist diplomacy in recent years was the series of Bulgarian-Greek agreements signed in July, 1964.

The two non-Communist Balkan states, Greece and Turkey, long were targets of a Communist "peace offensive." This offensive had been prompted by the Soviet Union but spearheaded by Romania and then Bulgaria. Turkey had been completely unresponsive to these overtures until the very end of 1964; then, mainly as a result of disillusionment with its Western allies over the Cyprus question, it began to respond more favorably to Soviet gestures. In November, 1964, the Turkish Foreign Minister Mr. Erkin, went to Moscow and in May, 1965, Gromyko was in Ankara.

Greece, with its very large Communist or pro-Communist minority, was always the more likely target. Prior to 1964, the Communist gambit had been mainly to appeal to the Greek population over the heads of government officials. Mainly because of Greek dislike for Bulgaria, this had proved largely unsuccessful. The Greek Government's insistence that before any purposeful negotiations with Sofia could begin, the Bulgarians would have to show themselves willing to pay their war reparations, grew stronger. These reparations had been fixed by the 1947 peace treaty between the two countries at $45 million and subsequently ignored by the Communist Bulgarian Government. In 1964, however, aided by Greek animosity toward the West over Cyprus, the fortuitous assumption of power of a more conciliatory government in Athens, and a greater showing of reason on their own part, the Bulgarians met with swifter success than they had ever dared expect. In July, a number of agreements between the two countries were signed in Athens.[2] Bulgaria agreed to pay Greece a sum of $7 million in goods against its war reparation obligations. This was a far lower sum than the Greeks had envisaged, and their acceptance of it constituted a real Bulgarian victory. A number of other agreements were signed at the same time, involving trade, collaboration in improving communications between the two countries, cultural cooperation, and tourism. The Bulgarian Foreign Minister visited Athens, and a friendlier era seemed to have been ushered in for these traditional enemies.

The agreements were a victory for Bulgaria, not for Greece; for the East, not for the West—testimony that peaceful coexistence is a game that has defeats as well as victories for the West, and that an improvement in East-West relations has its dangers. Still, the centrifugal forces in Eastern Europe are so powerful that they give the West a ready-made advantage over the Soviet Union. If the game is played with skill, if realism prevails over naïve optimism, nowhere are the chances of winning stronger than in Eastern Europe.

Economic Relations

It is in the sphere of economic relations that the West's best opportunities lie. In 1963, more than 65 per cent of East European exports went to COMECON member countries, about the same percentage of imports came from these countries, and the volume of intra-COMECON trade continued to mount each year. (The G.D.R. is excluded in all these approximations.) After 1962, the volume of Soviet and East European trade with China and her Asian allies dropped drastically, but, though at a slightly slower rate, trade with the industrialized Western powers increased steadily. In 1963, it amounted to about 17 per cent of the total.[3] When the situation was measured in terms of total world trade, however, it could be seen that total East European trade, including trade with the West, still counted for little. During 1960–63, the proportion of exports originating in Eastern Europe rose from just over 10 per cent to just over 11 per cent. In 1963, only 4 per cent of all the goods sold by Western Europe went to Eastern Europe. On the other hand, in the same year, some 18 per cent of total East European exports went to Western Europe. Thus, Western Europe continued to be more important as a market for Eastern Europe than as a supplier to it.

(The role played by the Soviet Union varied from country to country. In 1963, about 57 per cent of her exports went to her COMECON partners, and about the same percentage of her imports came from them. She had a favorable trade balance of about $15 million with Eastern Europe. Her share of each East European nation's total trade ranged from well over 50 per cent in the case of Bulgaria, to about 33 per cent in the case of Poland.)

The biggest exporter to Western Europe was Poland, with about 29 per cent of her exports in 1963 going West. In imports from the West, Poland was level with Romania, each having about 22 per cent. In both exports and imports, Bulgaria was at the bottom of the list, with Czechoslovakia, despite its traditional commercial gravitation toward the West, next to the bottom in both imports and exports. Trade between Eastern Europe and the United States had, with the exception of Poland, always been negligible.

Eastern Europe's trade balance as a whole with Western Europe remained favorable in 1963, though it had steadily declined since 1959. Not every country, however, maintained this position; in this, they contrasted with the Soviet Union, which always had a favorable trade balance with Western Europe. Poland's excess of exports over imports was generally large; it was usually the size of her surpluses that kept the total average for the region high. In the late 1950's, Romania had a strong favorable balance, which, in the 1960's, she lost—mainly because her increased imports of industrial equipment were not matched by success in placing exports.* Bulgaria's very large deficits in 1959 and 1960 were probably covered by Soviet hard-currency loans; thereafter, she managed to keep herself on the positive side of the ledger, but by the smallest of margins. In most years, Czechoslovakia had surpluses, while Hun-

* In 1964, Romania's trade deficit amounted to about 1 billion lei (six lei to the dollar).

gary showed a surplus for the first time in 1963. The biggest sources of the region's surpluses were Great Britain and Italy.

It is virtually impossible to obtain accurate information on the balance-of-payments situation because of the lack of data on "invisible" exchanges, i.e., noncommercial trading items. But if one takes into account the increasing number of Western tourists visiting Eastern Europe, and items like emigrant remittances (which, in the cases of Hungary and Poland, must be considerable), it is quite possible that the balance of payments for the region as a whole is positive, also.

The continuing favorable trade balance made the claims of some regimes about the discriminatory character of the two Western trade blocs, especially the Common Market, sound somewhat captious; Poland, for example, still had a sizable margin to import goods from the West without having to appeal for credit. But in view of the heavy purchases of Western capital goods that all these countries wished to make, the margin of any country was small. In these terms, therefore, their complaints about discrimination against their exports arose from a genuinely difficult situation.

Up to the middle of 1965, the countries of the Common Market were still undecided about what trade policy their organization should pursue in dealing with Eastern Europe. (The deadline for working out a common trade policy was set for January 1, 1966.) A number of discouraging restrictive practices have already crept into EEC policy, however; they appear in several forms, of which three are the best known: the traditional technique of introducing common external tariffs higher than the organization's internal tariffs, which makes for higher prices on imported goods from nonmember countries; the "sluice-gate" system, which sets up minimum prices for several types of imported goods, below which third-party products cannot come in; finally, the so-called *montant évaluatif*, a value-estimate measure used to control the entry of agricultural products from third countries—a particularly important system because of the part agricultural products continue to play in the East European export structure. It specifies that each member country submit estimates to the EEC's controlling body of its requirements and expectations, based on its bilateral agreements with the East European countries. These estimates of imports from

Eastern Europe are watched very closely whenever they reach 80 per cent of the 1960–61 total of agricultural imports to the country concerned. When they reach 120 per cent of this total, the EEC may intervene. This has not yet caused any great hardship; but if not altered in the future, it may constitute the most serious form of discrimination.

The European Free Trade Association uses fewer discriminatory measures against third parties, and trade between its member countries and Eastern Europe grew more quickly than the Common Market's. But the presence of two trade blocs in Western Europe presents a constant danger of restrictions on the flow of trade. The best answer to the tendency toward closed trading blocs seems to lie in the broader GATT approach.

The General Agreement on Tariffs and Trade was established in October, 1947. (One of its founders was the then democratic Czechoslovakia, whose membership was nominally retained by the subsequent Communist government.) By 1965, GATT had more than sixty full members and many associate and acting members. Poland became an associate member in 1959; unlike Czechoslovakia, she enjoys "most-favored-nation" treatment with the U.S. Romania regularly sent members to GATT's plenary sessions; Bulgaria also did so, but with less regularity. During 1964, these two countries and Hungary expressed interest in becoming more closely associated with the organization.[4]

For a country to gain the full benefits of membership in GATT, it had to abide by four basic rules: there must be no discrimination in its trade; its domestic industry must be protected only through the use of tariffs and not by any kind of quota system; changes in tariffs should be preceded by consultations with all parties concerned; all negotiations resulting in agreements must be made public in legal documents.

If both East and West fully abided by GATT's basic principles, all would obviously benefit—the East European states no less than the others. The EEC clearly violates one or more of these principles as a group; but so do East European states. It is worth examining some of the basic obstacles presented by the Communist regimes themselves to a freer flow of trade.

Perhaps the biggest obstacle of all is the fact that foreign trade continues to be run largely by state monopolies. This system imposes a bureaucratic intermediary that prevents the necessary direct contact between those producing for the foreign market and the buyer, and between those buying on the foreign market and the retailing organization that must sell the goods on the home market. A second hindrance is the obsession with bilateralism in trading (bartering would be a better word) and the insistence that the flow of goods between the two trading partners be in balance. This bilateralism means that trade ends up where it started, and balances earned with one country cannot be used in trade with another. Thus, the refinements and advantages of multilateral trade are lost because of unwarranted concern over the balances with each particular country, rather than the balance with *all* the countries with which trade is carried on. A third impediment is the deliberate policy of minimizing imports of consumer goods and maximizing their export. Nowhere is the Communist propensity to mercantilism more clear than in regard to this kind of merchandise. The immediate effect is to lower the standard of living at home; foreign trade becomes an indirect means of forcing the population to save more, without immediate benefit, in order to provide a further source of capital. In commerce itself, this policy is self-defeating, in that it reduces the range of commodities that can be traded.

The fourth basic impediment harks back to the early years of the Communist regimes in Eastern Europe—that of producing for the Soviet market. In dealing with economic development, we have seen how, in the beginning, the Soviet Union supplied practically all the raw materials for East European industry, while the latter, in turn, concentrated on manufactures for the Soviet market. This market was constant and would take almost anything, regardless of quality. Under these conditions, foreign trade was very simple; all it involved was fulfilling a rigid plan. Since the buyer was not too concerned about technological development or quality, neither was the supplier. The bad habits bred by this system made East European products singularly ill suited to compete on the world market. Another impediment was closely connected with this: the tendency to regard trade with all countries outside COMECON as "residual" trade. Since the great preponderance of Eastern Europe's trade was done within COMECON, the demands of its member countries set the tune. Anything the COMECON countries did not want could go elsewhere—unsuitable goods at "dumping" prices. This attitude was hardly calculated to win either approval or success in the West.

It is fair to say that the East European states have recognized these self-made difficulties and are tackling them (with varying degrees of vigor). Their various schemes for economic reform have provisions to free foreign commerce from the more crippling kinds of bureaucratic interference. The stultifying effect of bilateralism is also understood, and the first gropings toward a multilateral trading system have been made. There are attempts to study Western market conditions and to adapt East European industry to them. It will take several, or perhaps many years for East European goods to begin to compete; but a definite shift in the right direction has already been made and will certainly continue.

The East European regimes have also become aware of the importance of the payments problem. When imports from the West were relatively small, this problem was never acute; but as soon as large imports of heavy industrial equipment from both Western Europe and the United States were about to be made, the problem loomed very large indeed. Without, or in addition to, resorting to Western credit, there were several ways the East European states tried to help themselves in this matter: various "scrape-the-barrel" campaigns whereby citizens were exhorted (theoretically, with no questions asked) to trade their remaining collections of gold, hard currency, jewels, or art treasures for local currency; or the exploitation of whatever gold deposits a country might still have. Czechoslovakia was doing this in 1964, but Eastern Europe's gold deposits have never been considerable. Czechoslovakia and Romania had had considerable quantities of uranium, but this had always gone to the Soviet Union (at unknown prices); there was, in any case, a strong suspicion that they were becoming depleted.

By far the most effective earner of hard currency was foreign tourism. Since 1960, all the East European states have taken steps to encourage foreign tourism generally, with Western tourists as the prime target. Westerners have been given the benefit of a simplified visa-granting system, easier customs procedures, and favorable currency-exchange rates. Large new hotels have been built, especially on the Black Sea coasts of Romania and Bulgaria;

all kinds of tourist services and facilities have been either improved or begun. The 1964 season saw a very large number of Westerners in Eastern Europe, and plans were being made to welcome many more in future years.

Number of Foreign Tourists (approximate)[5]
(in thousands)

Country	1960	1964*
Bulgaria	8	400
Czechoslovakia	40	744
Hungary	50	164†
Poland	64	100

* Includes visitors in transit.
† January to September.

Satisfactory as this progress is, all these East European countries have a long way to go before they can begin to compete with Yugoslavia in the tourist business. In 1964, 2.2 million Western tourists visited Yugoslavia, compared with just over 1 million in 1961.[6] Still, it was a good beginning, and the financial benefits were considerable.

Tourism, incidentally, is not one-sided. Since 1956, considerable numbers of Poles have been able to travel to the West; in 1964, this figure was about 47,000.[7] In this area, however, Czechoslovakia had taken the lead; 153,000 Czechs and Slovaks visited the West in 1964.[8] The number of Hungarians is only slightly below that figure. To complete the picture one should mention the very large amount of travel in Eastern Europe and the Soviet Union. In 1963, for example, more than 422,000 Hungarians traveled in Eastern Europe;[9] in 1964, the number for Czechoslovakia reached 1.46 million.[10] Thus, there was still a far higher rate of travel in the East itself than between East and West. Here the 1964 Yugoslav figures present another striking difference: as opposed to 2.5 million visitors from the West, there were only 100,000 from the East.[11]

Looking at the rapidly increasing travel to the West in purely economic terms, it constitutes a loss to Eastern Europe, but a slight one in comparison to what was gained from the influx of Westerners to the East.

The net gain from tourism is, then, considerable, and it will certainly grow. In a sense, it is a further strain on the economies of the countries concerned, since the investments being made in the tourist industry could have been used for such necessities as housing or schools. Moreover, the regimes are using only a small part of the earnings gained from tourism to enable their own subjects to visit the West or obtain consumer goods. The balance is being used to help finance the purchase of industrial equipment.

Yet the regimes know only too well that the hard-currency earnings from tourism and other means will not suffice. This is why the issue of Western credit has become so important.

Short-term credits (up to three years) and medium-term credits (up to five) have always been available to Eastern Europe and have frequently been granted by Western countries. But under the Berne Convention, signed in 1961, seven of the largest Western creditor nations agreed not to extend credits for periods of more than five years. By 1964, however, as the demands from East European countries became greater, this agreement was practically dead. A rather undignified scramble for Eastern orders began, and the pressure on different Western governments to break the agreement mounted. A British-Czechoslovak transaction for a fertilizer plant in Bohemia, involving a credit of up to twelve years, was made; the Japanese were reported to have given the Soviet Union an eight-year credit on another fertilizer plant. A group of major French banks signed preliminary agreements with the Soviet Union granting ten-year credits in the amount of $350 million. The commercial treaty signed by Romania and France in December, 1964, is reported to involve France's granting seven-year credits. None of the governments of the Western countries involved in these deals has officially announced its withdrawal from the Berne Convention, but it is obvious that they now regard it as obsolete and a hindrance to trade. Barring a serious deterioration in international relations, it is only a matter of time before officially guaranteed, long-term Western credits to Eastern Europe will be an everyday fact of life.

This is the background against which businessmen of the West and East held their meetings and clinched their deals. That the Western governments, and not only Western businessmen, were eagerly interested in developing trade, was shown by an important number of official agreements, visits, or statements. The agreement between West Germany, on the one side, and Bulgaria, Hungary, Poland, and Romania, on the other, to exchange official trade missions (negotiations were also taking place with Czechoslovakia) was a very important step in re-establishing the German economic—and political—presence in Eastern Europe. In July, 1964, the British Parliamentary Secretary to the Board of Trade, Edward du Cann, visited several East European countries. Early in 1965, the French Minister of Finance, Valery Giscard d'Estaing also made a tour. Italian interest had been shown by several high-level visits. Though the United States has made no top-level visit of this kind, former Secretary of Commerce Luther Hodges was known as an ardent exponent of a more liberal trade policy toward Eastern Europe; this subsequently has become a part of the Johnson Administration's approach.

The upshot of this activity was a series of trade agreements between East and West European countries, usually providing for large increases in the volume of trade, and a sizable number of East European agreements with individual Western firms. Here, American industry, taking advantage of the Administration's growing generosity in granting licenses, has begun to play a role. For example, as early as the fall of 1963, the Commerce Department granted a license to an American firm, authorizing it, in effect, to build a steel mill for Romania's gigantic Galati combine. Some smaller agreements between American firms and East European countries followed; at the end of 1964, it was announced that the Romanian Government would buy a complete rubber plant from the Firestone company, and a catalytic cracking plant, for the processing of oil residues, from the Universal Oil Products Corporation in Illinois.* (In 1965, however, Firestone withdrew, on the grounds that public pressure against trading with a Communist state had been too strong.) The United States was still very much behind Western Europe in the race for Eastern markets. But if American credit restrictions could be eased, American products

* This deal actually involved Administration approval of a seven-year credit to Romania. The plant cost $22 million; toward payment of this, an Illinois bank was to lend the Romanian Government more than $16 million, repayable over seven years.

were certain to be very strong competitors in the near future. As for American imports of East European goods, it seemed likely that they also would increase through the gradual granting of most-favored-nation status to all or most of the states concerned. Only Poland (together with Yugoslavia) already enjoys such treatment. She was granted it in 1960, and has retained it, in spite of strong efforts by Congress to withdraw it because of the increasing unfriendliness of the Polish regime. The Administration seems prepared to grant it to Romania, and possibly also to Hungary, although in 1965, the deterioration of East-West relations over the Vietnam crisis increased opposition in the United States to such a move.

In addition to the development of normal trading relations, 1964 also witnessed examples of joint cooperation between economic enterprises in Eastern Europe and private firms in the West. These were a sign of recognition that the West could help in the search for higher standards of managerial and organizational skills, high technical standards, access to the best production equipment and techniques, and the most effective marketing methods. One example of this was the arrangement between a British company and the Czechoslovak Foreign Trade Corporation, Kovo, by which the two partners were jointly to market an automatic production line throughout most of the world, including Eastern Europe. Another was the agreement, in 1965 between the Hungarian Government and the West German firm of Krupp on "cooperation in machine tools." An American company, the Simmons Machine Tool Corporation, agreed to market a broad line of large precision tools produced by the Czechoslovak Skoda works in accordance with specifications provided by Simmons. The number of such cases is growing rapidly. Even Bulgaria, the laggard in cooperation with the West, has an agreement with a Dutch firm for marketing and servicing Bulgarian machine products in Holland. This trend toward agreements on joint production continued in 1965, and several further projects between West European firms and Eastern Europe were decided on.

Romania, for a time, seemed to be willing to entertain the even more radical idea of allowing Western capital within her boundaries. In November, 1964, in an interview given by Gaston

Marin to William Randolph Hearst, Jr., the Romanian planning chief invited American companies to produce their commodities in Romania. He casually mentioned Ford and General Motors. Firms thus established would be owned by Romania, but the American companies would be assured a liberal profit. Later, however, the Romanian attitude changed, and at the Romanian Party Congress in July, 1965, the idea of inviting foreign capital was specifically rejected.*

It was, perhaps, too premature a notion. But it had been canvassed, and this in itself was a measure of the progress made in East-West relations. In the not too distant future, it might well be canvassed again.

* In August, 1965, Gaston Marin was removed from his post as Chief of the Planning Committee. The issue of foreign capital may have been one of the reasons for his dismissal.

EIGHT

A Summing Up

IF STALIN WAS A MAN who created situations, Khrushchev was a man who responded to them. His main preoccupation, throughout his years of power, was the attempt to respond successfully to the situations he had inherited from Stalin.

The outstanding characteristic of the Stalinist system had been uniformity enforced by terror and coercion. This had been true for both the Soviet Union and Eastern Europe. In the Soviet Union, it lasted for three decades; in Eastern Europe for less than one. When Stalin died, it was obvious that the system could only lead to destruction. But breaking the *mythos* Stalin had created required someone with courage and authority. That man was Khrushchev, and he did it with great success. However, he was completely unsuccessful in building up a new order: there was never such a thing as a "Khrushchevian system." Even if the situation had been conducive to such a system, it is doubtful that a man like Khrushchev could ever have constructed anything of the sort. In any case, he never had a chance to try; from 1953 to 1964, the situation was never appropriate. Khrushchev was continually having to react to problems not of his own making, both in the Soviet Union itself and within the Communist bloc. His rule was marked by a series of improvisations, rather than by a policy. Some of his improvisations were brilliant, others only added to his problems. In the end, they became so inconsistent that his colleagues decided he had outlived his usefulness. As an expurgator of Stalinism, he had been indispensable and had secured his place in history; as a builder of something to replace Stalinism, he simply would not do. To what degree his inconsistencies were due to his own volatile temperament, rather than to the fact that the situation itself was largely uncontrollable, will be shown now and in the future, with other men at the helm in the Soviet Union.

He certainly left these men a problem in Eastern Europe. From Stalin, he inherited an empire, to Brezhnev, he bequeathed a commonwealth—one which, though still much more tightly knit than the British, had already begun to develop clear centrifugal tendencies. Because of his personality and prestige and because he had deliberately cultivated personal ties with most of the East European leaders, Khrushchev had managed to contain some of these tendencies. Even so, Albania had bolted, and Romania was skillfully edging toward a "Yugoslav" type of association with the Communist commonwealth. If Khrushchev had any system at all in Eastern Europe, it was a personal one; his attempts to create institutional ties through a strengthened, supranational COMECON had failed. When he left the scene, therefore, his personal system went with him. It was the unenviable task of his successors to close the stable door before more horses could take an interest in what was going on outside.

Once terror and direct coercion are abandoned as instruments of government, they must be replaced by attempts at consensus. This is true both in international and domestic politics. Having necessarily abandoned Stalin's practices, Khrushchev was forced to give the East European regimes a much greater say in their own affairs and in their relations with the Soviet Union. Similarly, the East European regimes themselves, once they abandoned terror and coercion as the main tools of their own policy, had to identify more closely with the peoples they were governing and had to reflect their traditional nationalism, even if only in a limited way. (This generalization can be faulted in certain cases and for certain reasons: the G.D.R., because of its peculiar character, could never reflect the nationalism of its people; Bulgaria, because of internal weaknesses, was almost as much of a satellite in 1964 as she had been in 1953. Yet the general movement was in the direction of more independence, and in Eastern Europe this meant away from the Soviet Union; after Khrushchev, it seemed certain that this trend would gather momentum.) The need for consensus at different levels was not, of course, the only reason for this movement. The Sino-Soviet dispute, with the opportunities it presented, and the activist Western policy within the framework of coexistence—both played important roles.

Most decisive in this connection was the decline in the Soviet Union's prestige—the Sino-Soviet dispute and Khrushchev's debacle in Cuba in 1962 being important factors. Another was the growth in self-confidence of the new elites of Eastern Europe, who had been nurtured in the belief that the Soviet example was the correct one to follow in everything—a belief about which many had been skeptical from the very beginning. As they grew more entrenched and more aware of their own importance, they became increasingly impatient of Soviet tutelage.

Two developments only served to strengthen this impatience. One was the revelation of earlier, Stalinist excesses in the Soviet Union (later, of course, Khrushchev's fall was another damaging blow); the second was the opening of a window to the West in the late 1950's, and of the door in the early 1960's. Economic, scientific, and technical cadres were now given a chance to compare East and West, and they knew which impressed them more. The decline in the prestige of the Soviet Union through the exposure of her own internal weaknesses was perhaps just as important in Eastern Europe as the decline in her prestige through the reverses she suffered in intra-bloc and foreign policy.

She was no longer the model nor the accepted pioneer. The fact that East Germany and Czechoslovakia, always considered two most devoted satellites, could launch far-reaching programs for economic reform in 1964 without waiting for the Soviet Union to do so was a most significant development in Soviet–East European relations.

All this is not meant to imply that the Soviet Union had "lost" Eastern Europe by the end of the Khrushchev era. There were still strong ties binding the two. Despite the failure to establish a supranational planning authority, bilateral economic cooperation was still very close and, in many cases, becoming closer. Even the renegade Romanians still did 42 per cent of their trading with the Soviet Union. Dependence on the Soviet Union for raw materials and for help in exploiting domestic resources probably would increase, rather than diminish, in most countries. The impact of the developing trade with the West was still slight. Moscow would dominate the economies of Eastern Europe for many years to come. This was a basic, centripetal factor that would have to be balanced against the centrifugal forces undoubtedly at work.

A big change had taken place in the *status* of Eastern Europe vis-à-vis the Soviet Union. One country, Albania, had defected to the Chinese side. Of the rest, only two—the G.D.R. and Bulgaria—remained satellites in the old sense of the word. The rest had become allies, troublesome allies at times, with Romania an ally only where and when it suited her to be one. Yugoslavia, independent since 1948, had shown interest in closer association, but not on terms that would deprive her of basic freedom.

Just as the Soviet Union had to strive for consensus with the East European regimes, so these regimes had to do the same with their own peoples. The pace at which this was done varied greatly from nation to nation. In 1965, the "de-Stalinization race" stood as follows: Poland was in first place, with the narrowest of margins over Hungary and every possibility of being soon overtaken. In third place, after showing an amazing spurt, was Czechoslovakia. Fourth was Romania, having moved up in 1964 and 1965. Bulgaria and the G.D.R. would come last.

The main reason for the retrogression in Poland was that her 1956 revolution had succeeded, rather than failed. It was not a question of the Party, as master, seeking a consensus with the subject population; rather, it was a subject population assuming the initiative and the mastery for a time. Once it had regained its confidence, the Party sought to re-establish its position by depriving the population of some of the prerogatives it had won. This would have happened even with a less conservative and authoritarian leader than Gomulka. In Poland, therefore, there was almost the opposite of an attempt at consensus. The retention of so much freedom was due to the regime's healthy respect for the Polish public and the fact that, in certain spheres, it was still not the real master of the situation. In Hungary, the situation was the opposite. The 1956 revolution had been crushed and followed by a period of grim repression. This made the need for a consensus more pressing.

For reasons stated in Chapter 1, it is possible for a retrogression to occur in Hungary or in any other country. But in no case will the retrogression mean anything like a return to the conditions that prevailed prior to 1956. The Polish and Hungarian upheavals of that year in themselves guaranteed that; in the minds of the most confident Party leaders, there was always the uncomfortable fear that something similar would happen if they ever tried to put the clock back too far. There might still be local *apparatchiks* who looked back with nostalgia on the days of coercion. In some countries, they were still strong: they could act as a powerful obstacle to progress, as in Bulgaria, or as a pressure group urging faster retrogression, as in Poland. Though they might continue to have influence for some time, it was impossible to see their representatives ever returning to power. Moreover, there is at least one feature of the Stalinist era that not even the most incorrigible old *apparatchik* would wish to see reinstituted—the supremacy of the secret police over the Party.

In addition to these political considerations, there are other fundamental factors at work—not only against serious retrogression, but also for progress toward a freer way of life. These are economic and technical forces. As the economies of all the countries in Eastern Europe become more technical and complex, "traditional" methods of government must give way to systems allowing more flexibility and freedom. The dogmatic approach must give way to empiricism. Much attention has been given in this book to the various schemes for economic reform in different East European countries. This is because those schemes are the most important symptom of the basic changes that are beginning to affect all East European societies to varying degrees. These changes; when fully implemented, will be the most important guarantee that there can be no turning back.

Fundamental changes in the East European societies, and the visible responses to them, also mean the end of Marxist-Leninist pretensions to a *Weltanschauung*. The Communist ideology has, indeed, suffered some serious blows since World War II. The defection of Yugoslavia in 1948 and the far more serious schism with China made nonsense of the supposed monolithic unity of the world Communist movement. But, in a way, the various intra-bloc disputes, couched as they were in Marxist-Leninist terms, gave ideology a new, if rather artificial, lease on life. What is really undermining it is the gradual realization that it is becoming more and more irrelevant to the problems of modern life. The growing class of technocrats realized this long ago, and most Party leaders are beginning reluctantly to admit it. Fundamentalist Gomulka, the Emperor Julian of the Communist world, is still holding out; but even Novotny and Ulbricht are swimming with the tide. Of course, there is still the practical necessity of squeezing the new empirical concepts into the old, formal strait-jacket—hence, "creative Marxism," a term made fashionable by Khrushchev. There is more deference than substance in this term; "creative Marxism" is becoming an excuse for words and deeds that would make Marx turn over in his grave.

The ideology is eroding; of that there is no doubt. Once Communism became an institution rather than a crusade, this was probably inevitable. More quickly than most religions, it has become irrelevant to the conditions and demands of its age. As a ritual, it is still important and will be so for very many years to come, but as a Weltanschauung, it is already showing its serious limitations and the false premises on which it is based. It has failed to attract the young generation in Eastern Europe, but, on the other hand, it has not been without effect. Certain of its axioms and values (or lack of them) have undoubtedly influenced the young East European mind.

Enthusiasm for the West is rife among these young people, and many observers in the West have taken a rather easy comfort from this fact, but if they stopped to analyze just what aspects of the West aroused the greatest enthusiasm, they would not be so complacent—nihilism and Louis Armstrong are, one hopes, not the best we have to offer. On subjects like the sanctity of the individual, East European youth often show an alarming ignorance or indifference.

But if the West can draw little real comfort from this fact, the East European regimes can draw none. The apathy of the young, and the Communist parties' difficulties in recruiting suitable young talent, are a serious threat to the continuing supremacy of the parties themselves. It is paradoxical, indeed, that, in the early years of the regimes, the Communist parties—Stalinist, brutal, and terror-ridden though they were—had little difficulty finding young recruits, often of the highest quality, who believed that Communism was a short cut to a better and more equitable future. Twenty years later, when the parties have reformed and are able to present a more amiable face, they are being rejected. For the youth, the disillusionment over the exposure of the Stalinist excesses and disappointment over the failure of Communism to provide a better life has been too great; the mending of ways has come too late.

This is just one of the problems that face ruling Communist parties everywhere. Perhaps the most pressing is how to retain political supremacy in an age that is fast becoming dominated by economic and technological considerations. Everybody is beginning to realize that the old formulas will not work. What, then, is to happen to the most important old formula of all—Party supremacy over every walk of life? This is now being undermined by some of the very reforms the parties are obliged to make. The new schemes for economic reorganization are the clearest case in point. They imply a great deal of power for the new technocratic class, thus pushing the Party's political officials further and further into the background. Party leaders realize the danger and have begun to fortify themselves, but it is difficult to see how the bulwarks they are erecting can withstand the pressure for long. This is, perhaps, the most encouraging prospect of all for the future of Eastern Europe.

If one were to draw up an East European balance sheet for the Khrushchev era, the credit side of the ledger would far outweigh the debit. There had been movement for the better in every field. In terms of what was ultimately desirable, the progress had been very slow, of course: personal freedom, though greater, was still tightly circumscribed; the standard of living, though higher, was still far too low; national independence, though increasing, was still narrowly restricted. But in terms of what was attainable, the progress had been quite remarkable—especially when measured against the nadir of Stalin's days. The East European peoples were aware of this, even in those states in which progress had been slowest. The tragedy of the Hungarian Revolution had taught them a bitter lesson: to seek their own salvation, and to distinguish between what they wanted and what they could get. They could face the future with some optimism, and with the reasonable hope that the progress begun would continue and accelerate.

Finally, a footnote on Khrushchev himself. Most of the changes described in this book took place while he was at the helm in the Soviet Union. Some of them were directly attributable to him; others occurred in spite, not because, of him, and he certainly would not wish to be thanked for those. However, there was one positive change, largely his doing, that has not been mentioned. Khrushchev was one of the most extraordinary personalities ever to walk across the world stage. He certainly dominated the European part of the Communist world. In doing so, he brought about a remarkable change in the psychological atmosphere and climate. The contrast between his impact and that of the brooding, distant Stalin could not have been greater. Whether the ordinary people liked or disliked, respected or despised him, they could always understand him and, to a certain degree, identify with him. What Stalin had dehumanized, Khrushchev sought to rehumanize—as far as the system would allow. This was an essential precondition for so many of the changes that occurred. Khrushchev's personality may have been one of the causes of his eventual undoing, but for Eastern Europe and the Soviet Union, it did vastly more good than harm.

APPENDIXES

State and Party Officials*

BULGARIA

STATE

Chairman of the Presidium of the National Assembly (nominal head of state)	Georgi Traykov
Chairman of the National Assembly Bureau	Ferdinand Kozovski

GOVERNMENT

Council of Ministers:

Bureau of the Council of Ministers	Todor Zhivkov Zhivko Zhivkov Stanko Todorov Ivan Mihailov Tano Tsolov Pencho Kubadinski Lachezar Avramov Apostol Pashev
Premier	Todor Zhivkov

* As of July 1, 1965.

First Deputy Premier	Zhivko Zhivkov
Deputy Premier and Chairman of the Commission for Economic and Scientific-Technical Collaboration	Stanko Todorov
Deputy Premier	Army General Ivan Mihailov
Deputy Premier and Chairman of the Council for Industry and Construction	Tano Tsolov
Deputy Premier and Minister of Transport and Communications	Pencho Kubadinski
Chairman of the Commission for Ideological and Cultural Questions	Mitko Grigorov
Chairman of the Committee for Party and State Control	Ninko Stefanov
Chairman of the Commission for Currency Questions and Trade Balances	Lachezar Avramov
Minister	Stoyan Tonchev
Minister of the Interior	Colonel-General Diko Dikov
Minister of National Defense	Colonel-General Dobri Dzhurov
Minister of Finance	Dimitar Popov
Chairman of the State Committee for Planning	Professor Engineer Apostol Pashev
Minister of Foreign Affairs	Ivan Bashev
Chairman of the State Committee for Science and Technical Progress	Professor Ivan Popov
Minister of Domestic Trade	Peko Takov
Minister of Foreign Trade	Ivan Budinov
Minister of National Education	Gancho Ganev
Chairman of the Committee for Culture and Art	Dr. Petar Vutov
Chairman of the Committee for Chemistry and Metallurgy	Georgi Pavlov
Minister of Construction	Marin Grashnov

Minister of Agricultural Production	Marin Vachkov
Minister of Justice	Petar Tanchev
Minister of Public Health and Social Welfare	Dr. Kiril Ignatov
Chairman of the State Committee for Construction and Architecture	Professor Engineer Georgi Brankov
Minister	Academician Professor Lyubomir Krastanov
Minister	Professor Evgeni Mateev

Committee Chairmen at the Council of Ministers Without the Rank of Minister:

Machine Building	Engineer Mariy Ivanov
Power and Fuel	Engineer Konstantin Popov
Light Industry	Dora Belcheva
Food Industry	Atanas Dimitrov
Labor and Labor Remuneration	Misho Mishev
Forests and Forest Industry	Professor Mako Dakov
Chief Director for Geology and Protection of the Resources of the Earth	Academician Yovcho Yovchev

COMMUNIST PARTY

Politburo:

Members	Boyan Balgaranov Boris Velchev Mitko Grigorov Zhivko Zhivkov Todor Zhivkov Ivan Mihailov Encho Staykov Stanko Todorov
Candidate Members	Dimitar Dimov Pencho Kubadinski Tano Tsolov

Central Committee:

First Secretary	Todor Zhivkov
Secretaries	Boyan Balgaranov Mitko Grigorov Boris Velchev Nacho Papazov Lachezar Avramov Ivan Pramov
Chairman of the Control Commission	Dimitar Dimov

CZECHOSLOVAKIA

STATE

President of the Republic	Antonin Novotny
Chairman of the National Assembly	Bohuslav Lastovicka

GOVERNMENT

Premier	Jozef Lenart
Deputy Premiers	Oldrich Cernik Frantisek Krajcir Jan Piller Otakar Simunek
Minister of the Interior	Josef Kuorna
Foreign Affairs	Vaclav David
National Defense	Bohumir Lomsky
Finance	Richard Dvorak
Foreign Trade	Frantisek Hamouz
Internal Trade	Jindrich Uher
Foundries and Ore Mines	Josef Krejci
General Engineering	Karel Polacek
Heavy Engineering	Josef Pesl
Chemical Industry	Jozef Pucik

Fuel	Jozef Odvarka
Construction	Samuel Takac
Food Industry	Vratislav Krutina
Consumer Goods	Bozena Machacova-Dostalova
Transport	Alois Indra
Agriculture, Forestry, and Water Economy	Jiri Burian
Justice	Alois Neuman
Health	Josef Plojhar
Education and Culture	Cestimir Cisar
Minister-Chairman of Central Office for Control and Statistics	Pavol Majling
Minister-Chairman of Central Management of Power	Josef Korcak
Minister-Chairman of State Commission for Development and Coordination of Science and Technology	Frantisek Vlasak
Minister-Chairman of State Commission for Capital Construction	Jan Piller
Ministers Without Portfolio	Michal Chudik Vincent Krahulec
Chairman of the Supreme Court	Josef Litera
Attorney General	Jan Bartuska

COMMUNIST PARTY

Presidium:

Full Members	Jaromir Dolansky Alexander Dubcek Zdenek Fierlinger Jiri Hendrych Drahomir Kolder Jozef Lenart Antonin Novotny Otakar Simunek Bohuslav Lastovicka Michal Chudik

Candidate Members	Antonin Kapek Michal Sabolcik Martin Vaculik
Central Committee:	
First Secretary	Antonin Novotny
Secretaries	Jiri Hendrych Drahomir Kolder Vladimir Koucky Frantisek Penc Lubomir Strougal
Members of Secretariat	Antonin Krcek Frantisek Zupka Ladislava Klenhova-Besserova
Chairman of the Party Control and Auditing Commission	Pavel Hron
Chairmen of Central Committee Commissions:	
Economic Commission	Drahomir Kolder
Agricultural Commission	Lubomir Strougal
Standard of Living Commission	Jaromir Dolansky
Ideological Commission	Jiri Hendrych

SLOVAK NATIONAL OFFICES

Slovak National Council:	
Chairman	Michal Chudik
Vice-Chairmen	Vincent Krahulec Jozef Kriz
Commissioners of the Slovak National Council:	
Chairman of the Slovak Planning Commission	Vincent Krahulec
Commissioner of Finance	Frantisek Hagara
Agriculture	Koloman Boda

Education and Culture	Matej Lucan
Justice	Peter Colotka
Construction	Ladislav Kompis
Health	Vladimir Zvara
Food	Jozef Gajdosik
Trade	Petronella Visnovcova

Chairmen not in the Rank of Commissioners:

Chairman of Investment Commission	Jan Marko
Control and Statistics Commission	Jan Stencl
Communal Industry Commission	Stefan Fabry
Commission for the Development of Science and Technology	Miloslav Hruskovic

SLOVAK COMMUNIST PARTY

Presidium:

Full Members	Frantisek Barbirek Vasil Bilak Michal Chudik Vojtech Daubner Alexander Dubcek Julius Loerincz Michal Sabolcik
Candidate Members	Frantisek Dvorsky Miloslav Hruskovic Jan Janik Jozef Kriz

Central Committee

First Secretary	Alexander Dubcek
Secretaries	Frantisek Barbirek Vasil Bilak Jan Janik Michal Sabolcik

Members of Secretariat	Frantisek Dvorsky Michal Chudik
Chairman of Party Control and Auditing Commission	Viliam Salgovic

EAST GERMANY

GOVERNMENT

Council of State:

Chairman	Walter Ulbricht
Deputy Chairmen	Willi Stoph Johannes Dieckmann Gerald Goetting Heinrich Homann Manfred Gerlach Hans Rietz
Secretary	Otto Gotsche (personal secretary to Ulbricht)
Chairman of the People's Chamber	Johannes Dieckmann

Council of Ministers:

Premier and Chairman of the Council	Willi Stoph
Deputy Chairmen	Alexander Abusch Dr. Erich Apel Dr. Lothar Bolz Paul Scholz Max Sefrin Dr. Max Suhrbier Dr. Margarete Wittkowski
Minister of the Interior	Friedrich Dickel
Minister of Finance	Willy Rumpf
Chairman of the National Economic Council	Alfred Neumann
Chairman of the Agricultural Council	Georg Ewald
Chairman of the Workers' and Farmers' Inspectorate	Heinz Matthes

Head of the Bureau of the Council, State Secretary	Dr. Rudi Rost
Minister Leading and Controlling District and County Councils	Kurt Seibt
Members:	
Chairman of the State Planning Commission	Dr. Erich Apel
First Deputy Chairman for Long-Term Planning	Gerhard Schuerer
First Deputy Chairman for Yearly Planning	Dr. Karl Gruenheld
Chairman of the National Economic Council	Alfred Neumann
First Deputy Chairmen	Erich Markowitsch Hans Wittik
Deputy Chairman	Dr. Kurt Fichtner
Chairman of the Agricultural Council	Georg Ewald
First Deputy Chairman	Heinz Kuhrig
Deputy Chairman	Hans Reichelt
Minister of National Defense	Karl-Heinz Hoffmann
Foreign Affairs	Otto Winzer
Foreign and Intra-German Trade	Julius Balkow
Internal Affairs	Friedrich Dickel
Finances	Willy Rumpf
National Education	Margot Honecker
State Security	Erich Mielke
Trade and Supplies	Gerhard Lucht
Health	Max Sefrin
Communications	Erich Kramer
Postal Services	Rudolf Schulze
Construction and Building	Wolfgang Junker

Culture	Hans Bentzien
Justice	Dr. Hilde Benjamin
Higher Education	Professor Ernst-Joachim Giessmann
Research and Technique	Dr. Herbert Weitz
Procurement and Purchase of Agricultural Produce	Helmut Koch
Chairman of the Workers' and Farmers' Inspectorate	Heinz Matthes
President of the German Bank	Helmut Dietrich
Chief of the Central Statistical Administration	Prof. Dr. Arno Donda

SOCIALIST UNITY PARTY

Politburo:

Members	Friedrich Ebert Paul Froehlich Kurt Hager Erich Honecker Hermann Matern Erich Mueckenberger Alfred Neumann Albert Norden Willi Stoph Walter Ulbricht Paul Verner Herbert Warnke
Candidate Members	Erich Apel Hermann Axen Georg Ewald Gerhard Grueneberg Werner Jarowinsky Guenter Mittag Margarete Mueller Horst Sindermann

Secretariat of the Central Committee:

First Secretary	Walter Ulbricht

Bureau of Agriculture	Gerhard Grueneberg
Commission for Ideology	Kurt Hager
Secretary Responsible for Questions of Security	Erich Honecker
Bureau for Industry	Guenter Mittag
Commission for Agitation	Albert Norden
First Secretary of the Berlin District	Paul Verner

Central Party Control Commission:

Chairman	Hermann Matern
Members	Ernst Altenkirch Erich Ament Elli Hempel Otto Holz Heinz Juch Otto Sepke Guenter Tenner Herbert Wittholz
Candidate Members	Richard Eyermann Hanni Glaeser Kurt Hausmann Ewald Munschke Erna Warnke

Central Auditing Commission:

Chairman	Fritz Gaebler
Deputy Chairman	Sepp Hahn

HUNGARY

STATE

Chairman of the Presidential Council (nominal head of state)	Istvan Dobi
Chairman of the National Assembly	Mrs. Istvan Vass

GOVERNMENT

Council of Ministers:

Premier	Gyula Kallai
Deputy Premiers	Jeno Fock Antal Apro Lajos Feher
Minister of State	Ferenc Munnich
Foreign Affairs	Janos Peter
Interior	Andras Benkei
Defense	Lajos Czinege
Agriculture	Pal Losonczi
Public Education	Pal Ilku
Public Health	Dr. Zoltan Szabo
Transport and Post	Dr. Gyorgy Csanadi
Finance	Matyas Timar
Justice	Ferenc Nezval
Metallurgy and the Machine Industry	Gyula Horgos
Heavy Industry	Ferenc Levardi
Light Industry	Jozsefne Nagy
Foreign Trade	Jozsef Biro
Internal Trade	Janos Tausz
Food	Imre Kovacs
Housing and Public Construction	Rezso Trautmann
Labor	Josef Veres
Chairman of Planning Board	Dr. Miklos Ajtai
Technical Development Committee	Arpad Kiss
State Office of Religious Affairs	Jozsef Prantner
National Statistical Office	Gyorgy Peter

SOCIALIST WORKERS' PARTY

Politburo:

Members	Antal Apro Bela Biszku Lajos Feher Jeno Fock Sandor Gaspar Janos Kadar Gyula Kallai Zoltan Komocsin Dr. Ferenc Munnich Dezso Nemes Sandor Ronai Miklos Somogyi Istvan Szirmai
Candidate Members	Dr. Miklos Ajtai Janos Brutyo Lajos Czinege Lajos Cseterki Pal Ilku Rezso Nyers

Secretariat of the Central Committee:

First Secretary	Janos Kadar
Secretaries	Bela Biszku Lajos Cseterki Zoltan Komocsin Dr. Mihaly Korom Rezso Nyers Istvan Szirmai Istvan Szurdi
President of Central Control Committee	Sandor Nogradi

POLAND

STATE

Chairman of the State Council (nominal head of state)	Edward Ochab
Marshal of the Sejm	Czeslaw Wycech

GOVERNMENT

Council of Ministers:

Premier	Jozef Cyrankiewicz
Deputy Premiers	Stefan Ignar Piotr Jaroszewicz Zenon Nowak Eugeniusz Szyr Julian Tokarski Franciszek Waniolka
Minister of Building Industry	Marian Olewinski
Finance	Jerzy Albrecht
Coal Mining and Power	Jan Mitrega
Municipal Economy	Stanislaw Sroka
Home Trade	Mieczyslaw Lesz
Foreign Trade	Witold Trampczynski
Transport	Piotr Lewinski
Culture and Art	Lucjan Motyka
Communications	Zygmunt Moskwa
Forestry	Roman Gesing
Defense	Marshal Marian Spychalski
Education	Waclaw Tulodziecki
Chemical Industry	Antoni Radlinski
Heavy Industry	Janusz Hrynkiewicz
Light Industry	Eugeniusz Stawinski
Food Industry and Purchases	Feliks Pisula
Agriculture	Mieczyslaw Jagielski
Interior	Mieczyslaw Moczar
Justice	Stanislaw Walczak
Higher Education	Henryk Golanski
Health and Social Welfare	Jerzy Sztachelski

Shipping	Janusz Burakiewicz
Foreign Affairs	Adam Rapacki

UNITED WORKERS' PARTY

Politburo:

Members	Jozef Cyrankiewicz Edward Gierek Wladyslaw Gomulka Stefan Jedrychowski Zenon Kliszko Ignacy Loga-Sowinski Edward Ochab Adam Rapacki Marian Spychalski Ryszard Strzelecki Eugeniusz Szyr Franciszek Waniolka
Candidate Members	Mieczyslaw Jagielski Piotr Jaroszewicz Boleslaw Jaszczuk

Secretariat of the Central Committee:

First Secretary	Wladyslaw Gomulka
Secretaries	Witold Jarosinski Zenon Kliszko Ryszard Strzelecki Boleslaw Jaszczuk Artur Starewicz Jozef Tejchma Wladyslaw Wicha
Party Control Commission Chairman	Roman Nowak

*ROMANIA**

STATE

Chairman of the Council of State	Chivu Stoica

* As of September 1, 1965.

Vice-Chairmen	Ilie Murgulescu Mihai Gere Constanta Craciun
Chairman of the Grand National Assembly	Stefan Voitec

GOVERNMENT

Council of Ministers:

Premier	Ion Gheorghe Maurer
First Deputy Premiers	Gheorghe Apostol Emil Bodnaras Alexandru Barladeanu
Deputy Premiers	Petre Blajovic Gheorghe Gaston Marin Gogu Radulescu Iosif Bank Ilie Verdet Ianos Fazekas
Minister of the Interior	Cornel Onescu
Foreign Affairs	Cornel Manescu
Armed Forces	Leontin Salajan
Finance	Aurel Vijoli
Forest Economy	Mihail Suder
Machine-Building	Mihai Marinescu
Metallurgy	Ion Marinescu
Mining	Bujor Almasan
Chemical Industry	Mihail Florescu
Building Industry	Dimitru Mosora
Light Industry	Alexandru Sencovici
Oil Industry	Alexandru Boaba
Power	Emil Draganescu
Food Industry	Bucut Schiopu

Transport and Communications	Dumitru Simulescu
Foreign Trade	Gheorghe Cioara
Home Trade	Mihai Levente
Justice	Adrian Dumitriu
Education	Stefan Balan
Health and Social Welfare	Voinea Marinescu
Chief of Rumanian State Protocol (mentioned as Chief of State Ceremonial since May, 1958)	Dionisie Ionescu
Chairman of the State Planning Committee	Roman Moldovan
President of State Committee for Culture and Art	Pompiliu Macovei
Chairman of the Supreme Agricultural Council	Nicolae Giosan

COMMUNIST PARTY

Presidium:	Chivu Stoica Gheorghe Apostol Emil Bodnaras Nicolae Ceausescu Alexandru Draghici Ion Gheorghe Maurer Alexandru Barladeanu
Executive Committee:	
Members	Nicolae Ceausescu Chivu Stoica Ion Gheorghe Maurer Gheorghe Apostol Alexandru Barladeanu Emil Bodnaras Petre Borila Alexandru Draghici Constantin Drajan Alexandru Moghioros Paul Niculescu-Mizil Gogu Radulescu

	Leonte Rautu Leontin Salajan Stefan Voitec
Candidate Members	Iosif Bank Maxim Bergheanu Petre Blajovici Dumitru Colin Florian Danalache Mihai Gere Ianos Fazekas Petre Lupu Ilie Verdet Vasile Vilcu

Secretariat of the Central Committee:

General Secretary	Nicolae Ceausescu
Secretaries	Mihai Dalea Alexandru Draghici Alexandru Moghioros Manea Manescu Vasile Patilinet Virgil Trofin Paul Niculescu-Mizil Leonte Rautu

Biographical Sketches of Party Leaders and Premiers*

BULGARIA

TODOR CHRISTOV ZHIVKOV, *Premier of Bulgaria and First Secretary of the Central Committee of the Bulgarian Communist Party.*

TODOR ZHIVKOV was born on September 7, 1911, in Pravets village, Botevgrad county, just north of Sofia. The village lies in an infertile valley in the Balkan Mountains, renowned for its warriors and anti-Turkish revolutionaries. The Zhivkov family were poor peasants, of Bulgarian ethnic stock and of the Eastern Orthodox faith.

Zhivkov had only a few years' education at an elementary school in his native village. Later, he went to an art school in Sofia and, when still very young, began work at the Sofia State Printing Office, where he remained for many years.

In 1928, at the age of seventeen, Zhivkov joined the underground Young Communist League. Four years later, he joined the Communist Party. He was initially a member of the Second Party area committee, in Sofia; from 1934 to 1936, he was Secretary of the third area committee and a member of the Sofia District Party Committee. His offi-

* Based on material provided by the Research Department of Radio Free Europe, Munich.

cial biographies do not mention his activities between 1936 and 1941, a fact indicating a period of inactivity or disfavor.

For two years during World War II (1941–43), Zhivkov was one of the leaders of the Party organization in Sofia and of the partisan movement. In 1943, he was chief organizer of the partisan movement in his native county of Botevgrad and in July, 1944, was made Deputy Commander of the first Sofia operation zone.

After the Communist assumption of power in September, 1944, Zhivkov rose steadily in the Party hierarchy. In 1945, he was elected a candidate member of the BCP Central Committee, and at the Fifth Party Congress in December, 1948, a full member. He became especially powerful in Sofia, where he simultaneously held the key posts of First Secretary of the Sofia City Party Committee, President of the Sofia City Party Committee of the Fatherland Front, and President of the Sofia City People's Council in 1948 and 1949. This is the only period during which these three positions have been in the hands of one man. In 1950, his power in the Party Central Committee increased when he became one of its secretaries and a candidate member of the Politburo. The next year, he became a full member of the Politburo and was elected First Secretary of the Central Committee at the Sixth BCP Congress, in March, 1954.

Zhivkov's 1954 appointment to the leadership of the Party was nominal rather than real. The true power still lay with his mentor, Vulko Chervenkov, who remained Premier and still dominated the Party. Zhivkov, however, slowly enlarged the base of his support. In 1957, he purged one of his great rivals, Georgi Chankov; and in November, 1961, immediately after the twenty-second CPSU Congress, he ousted Chervenkov. His triumph was completed at the BCP Eighth Congress in November, 1962, when he dramatically purged Premier Anton Yugov and took his post for himself.

In some respects, Zhivkov is similar to the Czechoslovak leader Antonin Novotny. Both are *apparatchiks* par excellence; both rose through the Party organizations of the capitals of their countries. Both acquired a great mastery of the art of Party manipulation—a mastery which, in both cases, was put to severe tests. Both are conservative and dogmatic by temperament and training. Both have proved themselves incapable of governing a modern state. Both have rather negative public personalities, and both are wretched public speakers. But despite his faults, Novotny seems, since 1962, to have acquired a stature that Zhivkov will probably never attain. One cannot deny the Bulgarian leader a certain ability and skill; but the excessive degree to which he leaned on Khrushchev, during that leader's period of power, built an image of abjectness and subservience that will probably never be eradicated.

CZECHOSLOVAKIA

ANTONIN NOVOTNY, *President of the Czechoslovak Republic and First Secretary of the Central Committee of the Czechoslovak Communist Party.*

ANTONIN NOVOTNY was born on December 10, 1904, in Letnany, then a village of about 600 inhabitants, close to some of Prague's most industrialized suburbs. A Czech by ethnic origin, Novotny was one of four children. His father, a bricklayer, was originally a member of the Social Democratic Party but later joined the Communist Party. His mother died when he was four. Novotny had eight years of elementary school, then became a mechanic and worked in several shops around Prague.

In 1919, Novotny entered the Federated Gymnastic Union, an organization sponsored by the Social Democrats. When not quite seventeen years old, he became a member of the Czechoslovak Communist Party. From 1921 to 1928, he worked mainly as an official of the Communist-sponsored United Proletarian Gymnastic Union. From 1930 to 1935, he was Chairman of the Communist Party Committee in the industrial Karlin district of Prague and became a member of the regional Party committee in Prague in 1933. He made his first visit to Moscow in July, 1935, as delegate of the Prague CP to the Seventh Congress of the Comintern. On his return, he became a paid instructor in the Prague Party organization. After a brief stint in 1937 as one of the secretaries of the Prague regional committee, he was transferred to Hodonin, in southern Moravia, as Regional Secretary and editor of the local Communist paper.

In September, 1941, Novotny was arrested by the Gestapo and sent to Mauthausen concentration camp, where he remained until the end of the war. At the end of the war, he was obviously considered to be one of the most promising of the young Czech Communists. In May, 1945, he was appointed leading Secretary of the Prague Party organization, one of the most important posts in the Party, which he held until September, 1951. In March, 1946, he became a full member of the Czechoslovak Party Central Committee, and was made a member of the National Assembly in May, 1948.

In September, 1951, Novotny broke into the top echelons of the Party by being elected to the Central Committee Secretariat. In January, 1953, he began a brief period as Deputy Premier; this, however, only lasted until September of the same year. In that month, he was elected First Secretary of the Central Committee, replacing the deceased Klement Gottwald.

On the death of Antonin Zapotocky, in November, 1957, Novotny became President of the Republic, a post to which he was re-elected in November, 1964.

Novotny seems to have entered the topmost group of the Party through his role in the deposition of Slansky. At the national Communist Party conference in December, 1952, in Prague, Karel Bacilek, then Minister of National Security, described how the Slansky group was "unmasked," as he put it. In doing so, he revealed that an apparently bitter enmity had existed between Slansky and Novotny; Slansky, he said, had been trying to remove Novotny from his position in the Regional Secretariat in Prague and to replace him with his own creature, Otto Sling, then Regional Party Secretary in Brno. (Sling was executed with Slansky in December, 1952.)

There is also an interesting piece of circumstantial evidence that suggests that Novotny's relations with Gottwald were not of the best. In January, 1953, Gottwald appointed Novotny Deputy Premier, but the latter disappeared from the list of Party secretaries at the same time. The same thing had happened to Slansky before his plunge into the abyss, and it may have meant that Gottwald wished, at least, to relegate Novotny to the background. It is highly suggestive that, immediately after Gottwald's death in March, 1953, Novotny returned to the Secretariat as its leader. It is not too difficult to see the hand of Moscow behind this manipulation.

All this suggests that during Slansky's decline, there were three factions at work among Czechoslovak Communist Party members: the Slansky group, the Gottwald group of old Bolsheviks, and a group of relatively young regional officials led by Novotny. After Slansky's execution, what might be called the Novotny group became a major new faction in the Party, beside Gottwald's followers. Novotny's rapid rise after Gottwald's death shows his factional strength and also the fact that he was fully trusted by Moscow.

Novotny's entire career, then, has been devoted to the Czechoslovak Communist Party. Having risen from the very bottom of that organization to the top, he probably understands the complex workings of its machine better than anyone. Indeed, it was this knowledge that stood him in such good stead during the hectic days of 1962 and 1963 when his position was seriously threatened.

This narrow experience as an *apparatchik* has proved to be a handicap, however, in his governing of the country. Lacking any breadth of experience, knowledge, or understanding, Novotny's only answer to most of the problems that confront him is a blind, dogmatic dependence on the rudiments of Marxism-Leninism, and particularly on the Soviet example. It was only when his own position was threatened, and when the country was in a very severe economic crisis, that he showed previously unsuspected qualities of adaptibility and flexibility.

Personally, Novotny has shown himself to be an agreeable companion in private, but a cold, almost glacial figure in public. He is a wretched public speaker, and has been completely unable to project his personality to the Czechoslovak population, by whom he is thoroughly disliked.

JOZEF LENART, *Premier of Czechoslovakia and Member of the Presidium of the Czechoslovak Communist Party.*

JOZEF LENART, a Slovak, was born on April 3, 1923, in Liptovska Porubka, Slovakia. After completing the Czechoslovak equivalent of junior high school, he began work at one of the Bata shoe factories, first as a laborer, and later in a laboratory, where he completed a course for chemical foremen.

Lenart joined the underground Communist Party in Slovakia in 1943 and took part in the 1944 Slovak uprising. After the liberation, he was appointed Party Secretary in the Svit factory (in Svit, Slovakia), which had been another branch of the Bata empire before it was nationalized. In 1946 and 1947, he was leading Secretary of the Poprad area Communist Party committee; he later worked in the offices of the Central Committee in Bratislava. In 1950, Lenart went to yet another former Bata factory, this time to the "August 29" enterprise in the Slovak town of Partizanska. From this post he was transferred, a year later, to the central government in Prague, as Deputy Minister of Light Industry. Young Lenart's capability and devotion had attracted the attention of the top men in the Czechoslovak Communist Party.

Between 1953 and 1956, Lenart studied at the Party school in Moscow and, on his return, was given the key post of leading Party secretary in Bratislava. In 1958, he was made a Secretary of the Slovak Party Central Committee, and between 1960 and 1963, was a member of the Slovak Presidium (Politburo). In 1962, at the age of 39, he was appointed Chairman of the Slovak National Council (roughly speaking, Prime Minister of Slovakia). He was to occupy this post only for about a year: Novotny, desperately trying to save his own position, was forced to dismiss Czechoslovak Premier Viliam Siroky in September, 1963, and Lenart was appointed in his place.

Though Lenart made his name mainly in Slovakia, he was by no means unknown in broader Czechoslovak Party circles. He had been a member of the Czechoslovak Party Central Committee since 1958 and of its Presidium since December, 1962. He owed his appointment as Prime Minister of Czechoslovakia chiefly to the fact that he was a Slovak untainted by close association with Prague centralism or with the Stalinist past—two counts on which his predecessor, Siroky, had been notoriously vulnerable.

Little is known about Lenart personally. He is a likable young man and clearly has real administrative ability. He is known to be among the new Czechoslovak leaders whose political approach is more flexible and moderate than that of the old guard.

EAST GERMANY

WALTER ULBRICHT, *Chairman of the Council of State of the German Democratic Republic and First Secretary of the Central Committee of the Socialist Unity Party.*

WALTER ULBRICHT was born on June 30, 1893, in Leipzig. The son of a tailor, he attended a *Volksschule* and learned the trade of carpentry. He made his political debut at the age of fifteen, when he joined the Socialist Young Workers' Educational Association. Two years later, in 1910, he became a member of the carpenters' trade union, and, in 1912, he joined the German Social Democratic Party. During the revolutionary outbreaks in Germany, at the end of World War I, Ulbricht threw in his lot with the Communists. He soon became a Party official in Saxony and was appointed editor of the Communist Party paper in that state. As early as 1923, he was elected to the German Communist Party's Central Committee; he was also a member of the Saxon state parliament.

The young Ulbricht's abilities soon attracted attention. In 1924, he was called by the Comintern for duty in Moscow, where he worked in the construction of a network of Communist Party cells, mainly in Austria. (He was known during this period as "Comrade Cell.") In late 1925, he was transferred back to Germany, where he was soon elected to the Communist Party's Politburo. In 1928, he was elected to the Reichstag, first for a Westphalian, later for a Berlin constituency. Following the Reichstag Fire, in 1933, when the Communist Party was preparing to go underground, Ulbricht went into hiding; after the new Nazi regime had declared the Communist Party illegal, he eventually escaped to Paris, thence to Moscow. For a time during the Spanish Civil War, he served at the Republican Army headquarters as one of the Comintern's political commissars. His fanatical loyalty to the Soviet Union was shown by his statements of wholehearted support for the German-Soviet Nonaggression Pact of 1939; Ulbricht urged German Communists to support "the great German army against the English imperialists." In 1943, he was one of the founders of the "National Committee for a Free Germany"; after the Battle of Stalingrad, he was the main contact man between the Paulus-Seydlitz group of captured German officers and the CPSU Politburo.

In 1945, Ulbricht returned to his native land in the van of Marshal Zhukov's armies. He now had the Soviet rank of Colonel. He was on the threshold of power—or, at least, as much power as the Soviet Army was prepared to allow him—and immediately threw his great organizational talents into the task of rebuilding the German Communist Party in the Soviet zone, and, a year later, of securing Communist predominance over the Socialists in the newly founded Socialist Unity Party.

In October, 1949, when the "German Democratic Republic" was officially founded, Ulbricht became First Deputy Prime Minister in Premier Grotewohl's cabinet. (Otto Grotewohl was the former Social Democratic leader who had brought his faction of the SPD into the SED merger with the Communists.) Despite Ulbricht's number-two position in the government, there was never any doubt that he was really the number-one man in the regime. In July, 1950, he was formally "elected" Secretary General of the Central Committee of the Socialist Unity Party, a position he has held ever since. (After the death of Stalin, the title was changed, Soviet style, to First Secretary.)

Ulbricht's rickety regime, set up in an artificial state, would have collapsed on the death of Stalin but for the active presence of Soviet troops in East Germany. In June, 1953, workers' demonstrations against the regime, in East Berlin and many other cities—sparked by an arbitrary increase of the required workers' norms set by Ulbricht himself—were put down by Soviet troops. The death of his mentor and the rise of Khrushchev then presented Ulbricht with the problem of adapting to a completely new regime in Moscow, a task he was able to accomplish mainly because of his great political skill. His personal position seemed to be in danger on a number of occasions, but he was always able to steer himself out of trouble by clever anticipation of Soviet moves. His relations with Khrushchev were outwardly good, but he no doubt regarded the Soviet leader as a menace—to himself, to his state, and to the world Communist movement.

In September, 1960, on the death of the veteran Communist Wilhelm Pieck, who had been titular head of the East German state, Ulbricht got himself elected President of the new Council of State. He thereby became head of state and relinquished his post of First Deputy Prime Minister.

Ulbricht's regime has always, and rightly, been considered a model of Stalinist inhumanity. Since the beginning of 1963, however, it has been trying to adapt itself to the new, more relaxed manner of the European Communist world—though rather belatedly and pathetically. Ulbricht himself is still the caricature of a tyrannical puppet he always was. Personally, he has never had much to recommend him: unfriendly, unsympathetic, and cowardly, he is a thoroughly dislikable man. As far as ability is concerned, however, he should not be underestimated. He has great intelligence, a rare memory, notable political skill, and talents of the highest order as an administrator and organizer. These qualities are undermined, however, by an almost complete lack of imagination and flexibility, and a rigid devotion to dogmatic Communism. As a Comintern organizer, he must have been superb. As leader of the G.D.R., he made an already impossible situation still more impossible.

Ulbricht has been married twice. He divorced his first wife, Martha, who now lives in Leipzig. (A daughter by this marriage lives in West Germany.) Ulbricht had known his second wife, Lotte, almost twenty years before he finally married her, in 1951. Lotte herself is a lifelong Communist who spent many years in exile with her first husband, Erich Wendt. (Since the end of 1963, Wendt has been the East German negotiator on the question of Berlin passes.) The Ulbrichts have an adopted daughter, Beate, to whom Ulbricht is believed to be deeply attached.

WILLI STOPH, *Premier of the German Democratic Republic and Member of the Politburo of the Central Committee of the Socialist Unity Party.*

WILLI STOPH, a native Berliner, was born on July 8, 1914, the son of a construction worker. Stoph himself had a *Volksschule* education and became a bricklayer. After the Nazis came to power, Stoph became a construction worker in Berlin.

In 1935, he was called up for two years' service in the German Army. In his official biography, this service falls within a period briefly described as one of "anti-Fascist activity." The fact remains that the impressionable young Stoph took readily to soldiering and was not unsusceptible to the magic spell exercised by the Führer himself. In 1937, he even wrote an article for a National Socialist trade magazine in which he described a birthday parade in honor of Hitler as an "experience of lasting value." His service as an *Oberkanonier* having ended, Stoph went back to bricklaying in Berlin. He was again in uniform during the war and was reportedly wounded in 1942.

The decade between 1935 and 1945 is not referred to by any of Stoph's official biographers, which implies that they were not altogether creditable from the Communist point of view. It is possible that he was a prisoner in the Soviet Union during the latter part of the war, for he is known to speak Russian well.

Immediately after the war, Stoph was an adviser to the Soviet military administration in Berlin and began to make his mark in the Socialist Unity Party. During this early period of the East German regime, he specialized in economic administration, especially in heavy industrial problems. In the fall of 1951, he became Director of the Bureau for Economic Affairs attached to the Premier's office. A year before, he had been elected to the Central Committee of the Socialist Unity Party; he was now also a member of the *Volkskammer* (East German legislative assembly).

In May, 1952, Stoph became Minister of the Interior, and it was during his tenure at this ministry that the June, 1953, East Berlin riots occurred. One month later, he was elected to the Politburo of the Central Committee of the Socialist Unity Party, and in November, 1954, he was appointed a Deputy Prime Minister. In June, 1955, he relinquished his post as Minister of the Interior and became Minister for National Defense the following January; he was made a Colonel-General in the East German army. He was to go even higher: after holding this rank for three years, during which he was also a representative to the Warsaw Pact organization, Stoph was promoted to full General in October, 1959.

In July, 1960, Stoph gave up the Defense Ministry and was made Minister responsible for "implementing and coordinating the decisions of the Party and Government"—a sign of Ulbricht's great confidence in him. It was becoming obvious that Stoph was destined for the highest pinnacles of power. In fact, ever since the end of 1960, when Premier Grotewohl became seriously ill, Stoph was virtually the prime minister. As if to legitimize his claim to the succession, he was made First Deputy Premier in July, 1962. His chance finally came in September, 1964, when Grotewohl died. At the age of fifty, Stoph became Premier of the German Democratic Republic. Twenty years younger than Ulbricht, his chances of becoming East Germany's new Führer one day look distinctly rosy.

There can be no doubt that Willi Stoph is a man of considerable executive ability who has rendered good service in the many different positions he has held. But he is a man without profile or personality, an *apparatchik* of the new, postwar order of Communists, lacking the experience and the color of the older generation. He is neither a good speaker nor a good theoretician but a man who can keep things moving. Perhaps his enthusiasm for the *Wehrmacht* when he was a young conscript supplies the real key to his personality: he enjoyed the security and the excitement of belonging to a dynamic organization greater than himself. At the head of an organization that has long ceased to be dynamic, he seems ill suited for the task of galvanizing it.

HUNGARY

GYULA KALLAI, *Premier of Hungary and Member of the Politburo of the Socialist Workers' Party.*

GYULA KALLAI was born in 1910 in Berettyoujfalu, a market town in Hajdu County, in eastern Hungary. Despite his father's humble station as a shoemaker, the young Kallai was able to pursue his education, and he became a good student. After being graduated from high school, he enrolled at the University of Budapest in the faculty of liberal arts. He soon fell in with various leftist groups among the students and joined the Social Democratic Party. In this way, he came into contact with the Communist Party, which he joined in 1931, although he still remained a member of the Social Democratic Party, whose leaders apparently did not object to this dual membership.

Kallai's intelligence was quickly recognized by the (then illegal) Communist Party: it was quite an asset to capture a gifted young man who was already a published author and journalist. In the early 1930's, Kallai was sent to Debrecen to do Party work. With the particularly able men in the Debrecen Communist group, Kallai worked to organize Communist movements among students and workers.

Toward the end of the 1930's Kallai returned to Budapest and in 1939 became a member of the editorial staff of the Social Democratic *Nepszava*, a post he retained throughout the war. But he also continued his agitation for the underground Communist Party and, together with Laszlo Rajk (who was later hanged by Rakosi in 1948), represented the Party at various anti-fascist meetings and demonstrations. In 1942, he took part in the organization of the Historical Memorial Committee and also helped to organize the March 15 demonstrations against the government. The Historical Memorial Committee was the nucleus of what later became the anti-German Independence Front and included members of different professions and political persuasions—writers, intellectuals, members of the Smallholder, Peasant, Social Democratic, and Communist Parties. Later, the Communists tried to present it as entirely their own affair, but in actual fact the main part was played by non-Communist intellectuals and the populists. After the March demonstrations, Kallai was arrested but was soon released, and he carried on his activities with the Independence Front.

After the war, Kallai became a member of the Central Committee of the Hungarian Communist Party. He was also elected to parliament, and from 1945 to 1946, he was secretary of state in the cabinet. Probably already in 1945 he had been appointed to the Communist Party agit-prop department and was on the editorial committee of the Communist Party organ *Szabad Nep*. From 1947 to 1948, Kallai was head of the Party's cultural department and played a great role in preparing for the nationalization of the schools.

It was in 1948 that Kallai became a really prominent political figure when he was appointed as *chef du cabinet* to the then President of the Republic, Arpad Szakasits. On June 10, 1949, he rose even higher in the state *apparat* by becoming Minister of Foreign Affairs in place of the arrested Laszlo Rajk. In the Party hierarchy, however, he was still only a Central Committee member, a position in which he was confirmed at the Second Party Congress held in February–March, 1951. But just one month later, he was stripped of his Party and political posts and arrested along with Kadar, Gyorgy Marosan, and Geza Losonczy. His dismissal from his ministerial post was announced on May 14.

No official reason has ever been given for Kallai's arrest. Unofficial sources state that he had aroused Rakosi's anger because of his disapproval of the methods used by Gabor Peter, chief of the secret police.

During his secret trial, it was, reportedly, alleged that as a former Social Democrat he had acted as informer for the Horthy regime's police. On the basis of this incredible accusation, he was sentenced to death. He avoided execution but spent two years in the death cell.

In 1954, during the full flowering of Premier Imre Nagy's "new course," Kallai was released, along with Kadar and Losonczy. His first appointment after his rehabilitation was to the presidency of the directorate of publishing in September or October, 1954. He also became a member of the National Council of the People's Patriotic Front. In December, Kallai was in Moscow studying publishing when the liquidation of the "new course," which led to the return of Rakosi, began.

In spite of the end of the "new course," Kallai's career continued profitably: in February, 1955, he was appointed Deputy Minister of Education. Only after the fall of Rakosi, however, on July 18, 1956, did Kallai regain his earlier Party status. He became a member of the Central Committee once again and head of the Committee's cultural department.

In this capacity, Kallai had to negotiate with an increasingly restive Writers' Association. As representative of the Party, he addressed the memorable meeting of the association on September 14, 1956 when the Stalinist writers were ousted from the organization's management. Kallai's speech was moderate in tone; he condemned the Stalinist literary policy under Rakosi and urged his audience to support the new Party leadership under Erno Gerö. He did, however, defend the Stalinist leaders in the Writers' Association and expressed the hope that some would be taken back into the management.

Kallai became a member of the Party Politburo and Secretariat on October 24, 1956, during the frantic power struggle that took place immediately after the beginning of the Revolution. He played no part in the Imre Nagy government nor in Kadar's "counter-government." He reappeared for the first time on December 11, standing alongside Kadar when he received a workers' delegation.

After this, Kallai became increasingly active. In the first days of 1957, he was a member of the Temporary Executive Committee (Politburo) of the Hungarian Socialist Workers' Party. On February 26, at a meeting of this committee, he was appointed one of the ten members of the new Executive Committee and also one of the five-member Secretariat. On February 28, he became Minister of Education.

Kallai has been among the busiest of Hungary's Communist leaders. He was made President of the Kossuth Prize Committee and in May, 1957, he was appointed to the editorial committee of *Tarsadalmi Szemle;* he later became editor of this journal. In October, 1957, he was named president of the National Council of the Patriotic People's Front. In view of the weight of his commitments, it is perhaps not surprising that he gave up his post as Minister of Education in January, 1958. But this was also at the same time that Kadar resigned from the premiership, and both he and Kallai were made Ministers of State. Later, Kallai was First Deputy Premier—from January, 1960, to September, 1961, when he became a Deputy Premier in the new Kadar government, which abolished the rank of First Deputy Premier. In June, 1965, when Kadar stepped down from the premiership for the second time, Kallai took his place. For several years he had been number-two man in the regime, and it was, therefore, no surprise.

Kallai is a serious intellectual who has not only been one of the regime's most notable ideologues but has had long and varied experience in government work. He has played a leading role in cultural affairs, in Church-State relations, and, more recently, in foreign affairs.

Kallai is a more efficient man than Kadar and will undoubtedly introduce more business-like methods than his more easy-going predecessor. This is something that Hungary very much needs. But he is less humane, less amiable, and much less popular. Certainly, his promotion was not greeted with acclamation by the Hungarian public.

JANOS KADAR, *Former Premier of Hungary and First Secretary of the Central Committee of the Socialist Workers' Party.*

JANOS KADAR was born on May 26, 1912, in Fiume (Rijeka), but was brought up in Somogy County, Hungary. Nothing is known of his father; his mother was a day laborer on a farm. In his childhood, Kadar helped on the land, worked for a swineherd, and then as a servant on a farm. Later, Kadar's mother moved to Budapest with her two sons; there she earned her living as a casual laborer, an under-janitor, and by delivering papers. After finishing primary school, Kadar attended the Vesselenyi Street higher elementary school. He also helped his mother deliver papers and run errands. At the age of fourteen, he became a toolmaker's apprentice; at seventeen, he joined the youth organization of the ironworkers' trade union. In 1929, after three years of apprenticeship, he became a toolmaker's assistant, but he was unable to get a job immediately in his trade. In the summer of 1930, he worked at the warehouse of a carpet wholesaler; in early 1931, he was unemployed. Later, he was able to obtain work in his trade.

In September, 1931, Kadar joined one of the local organizations of the Young Communist Workers' Association in Hungary (KIMSZ) and participated in its activities. This association had a structure similar to that of the Hungarian Communist Party and served as a reserve for new Party cadres; it functioned illegally.

Kadar was arrested during a demonstration in November, 1931, and remanded after three days' detention. He became a member of the Budapest north district of the KIMSZ committee and later secretary of KIMSZ for Greater Budapest.

In 1932, Kadar joined the Hungarian Communist Party and participated actively in its work. He was arrested again in 1933, after being under police surveillance since 1931, and spent seventeen months in prison. The HCP, weak and with few members, was torn by factional struggles between emigrant Communists and those in Hungary. At the beginning of 1936, the Control Committee of the Communist International held an investigation that established the culpability of the Communists in Hungary. The members of the Central Committee were dismissed and subjected to severe Party sanctions. The Party was invested with new leaders who carried out their activities abroad. Kadar was arrested again as the "black comrade" registered with the police. He was taken to the Vac prison, where he extended his Party relations and formed a close friendship with Zoltan Vas.

During the war, Kadar played an active part in the resistance movement. In 1942, he became a member of the Central Committee of the HCP, where he was very close to Laszlo Rajk, the true leader of the HCP in Hungary. In 1943, he became a Secretary of the Central Committee. After the dissolution of the Communist International, in May, 1943, the Central Committee of the HCP passed a resolution to dissolve itself. The emigrant faction did not approve of this liquidating resolution, but the Communist Party remained inactive until September, 1944.

In the meantime, the Communists formed the so-called Peace Party, and Kadar became Secretary of its Central Committee. At the beginning of December, 1944, the Peace Party, the Social Democratic Party, the Independent Smallholders Party, and the National Peasant Party combined to form the Hungarian National Independence Front. The propaganda work of the illegal Hungarian Front was shouldered by the Peace Party. Kadar participated in the editing and circulation of illegal publications, *Szabad Nep* among them. He also cooperated with Antal Apro, Karoly Kiss, and Rajk in the organization of partisan groups. In 1944, he tried to get into contact with the general staff of the Yugoslav (Communist) partisans, but was arrested near the Drava River; a warrant had been out for his arrest since 1942. Kadar, then going under the name of Lajos Luptak, fell into the hands of the Gestapo but succeeded in escaping. Around Christmastime, he went to Budapest, then left the city under Party orders and tried to establish contact with the Russian military *kommandatura* already on Hungarian territory at the time.

Between January and May, 1945, Kadar was organizing the Budapest police. (At the time, Laszlo Rajk was at the head of the police.) Kadar established close relations with the notorious Gabor Peter, head of the secret political police, and later became the Budapest Deputy Chief of Police. In 1945, the Hungarian Communist Party assigned him to the task of organizing and directing the Budapest Party organization, as Rajk's successor. He became the Secretary of the Greater Budapest Party Committee. At the 1945 parliamentary elections, Kadar was elected as representative of Heves and Nograd-Hont counties. At the Third Party Congress of the HCP (September–October, 1946), he was elected Deputy Chief Secretary, next to Rakosi. A year later, he re-entered parliament as the representative of the Greater Budapest electoral district. In June, 1948, the congress of the Hungarian Communist Party and the Social Democratic Party took place that resulted in the two parties merging in a new Hungarian Workers' Party. Kadar was given a senior position in the new Party: he became one of the fourteen members of the Political Committee and one of the eight members of the Secretariat, next to Rakosi, Gerö, Rajk, and Imre Nagy. The Party's First Secretary was Rakosi; its President was Arpad Szakasits; Mihaly Farkas, Kadar, and Marosan were Deputy Secretaries.

In August, 1948, Kadar succeeded Rajk as Minister of the Interior and, in this capacity, became supreme director of the secret police, which fell under his authority. He appointed Gabor Peter as its head. In December, 1949, the secret police became an independent organization directly subordinate to the Council of Ministers, and the Council invested Kadar, as Minister of the Interior, with the power of ultimate superintendence over it.

During Kadar's term as Minister of the Interior, the Mindszenty and Rajk trials were held. In spite of his close relations with the Rajk family, he played a sinister role in the affair. Rakosi charged him with the duty of visiting Rajk in prison and persuading him to make a false confession; Kadar was one of the four persons to sign Rajk's order of execution; and, after Rajk's death, he damned him publicly.

In June, 1950, Kadar resigned his post of Minister of the Interior, the reason given that he had been appointed to important Party work. He was awarded the gold medal of the Order of Hungarian Labor and 5,000 forint (or about $200) for "his good work carried out in the interest of strengthening the Hungarian people's democracy."

One year later, at the Third Congress of the HWP (February–March, 1951), Kadar delivered a speech on the admission of candidates to Party membership and on the Party's organizational work: he used the speech to criticize the Central Committee departments' direction and control of Party activities, the conduct of the mass organizational department, and the Budapest and county Party committees. At this point, Kadar was placed fifth in the Party Politburo, with its seventeen members and Secretariat of nine, immediately after Rakosi, Gerö, Farkas, and Revai, the so-called Muscovite foursome. In the organizing committee, he ranked just below Rakosi. But his days of power were numbered. After the Congress, the factional struggle between the Muscovites and the home groups continued to smolder; Rakosi therefore carried out another purge; and this meant Kadar's downfall. In April, he was arrested and accused of espionage, treason, and Titoism. Also among the large number arrested were Kallai, Marosan, Donath, and Losonczy. After cruel and humiliating tortures, in which Vladimir Farkas, son of the Defense Minister Mihaly Farkas, played a part, Kadar appeared in court in December. He was sent to the Vac prison, where he spent a long time in solitary confinement.

After Stalin's death, a "new course" was ushered in with the June, 1953, resolution of the Central Committee of the HWP. In July, 1954, under the Premiership of Imre Nagy, Kadar was released from prison, but a total political rehabilitation did not follow. He was given Party work as a middle cadre, becoming First Secretary of a district Party organization. At the end of October, he was elected a member of the National Council of the newly formed Patriotic People's Front; a month later, the Patriotic People's Front nominated him for the Budapest thirteenth district.

Kadar's complete political rehabilitation took place in July, 1956, when he was elected to the Central Committee, the Politburo, and the Secretariat, at the same time that Rakosi was replaced as First Party Secretary by Gerö. With his demand for Party political and organizational reforms and his condemnation of secret police atrocities, his popularity increased and his position strengthened. In September, 1956, he was head of the Hungarian delegation to the Eighth Congress of the Chinese Communist Party. At the beginning of October, he and Gerö conferred with Mikoyan and Suslov in Moscow.

With the outbreak of the 1956 revolution, Kadar replaced the dismissed Gerö and became First Secretary of the already disintegrated HWP on October 25. On October 28, a six-member Party Presidium headed by Kadar and including Nagy, Apro, Kiss, Munnich, and Szanto took over the direction of the Party. On November 1, Kadar conferred with Mikoyan and Suslov on the withdrawal of the Soviet troops that had poured into Hungary during the past days; on the same day, he spoke over Free Radio Kossuth to the participants in the "glorious uprising":

> The glorious uprising of our people has delivered the nation from the Rakosi rule, achieved the freedom of the people and the independence of the country, without which there is and can be no socialism. We can state openly that the spiritual and organizational leaders of this uprising and those who prepared it came from your ranks—the Hungarian Communist writers, journalists, university students, the young members of the Petöfi Circle,* thousands of workers, peasants, old fighters imprisoned because of false accusa-

* The Petöfi Circle, established in March, 1956, was a society of intellectuals that played an important role in the Revolution.

> tions, who fought in the first ranks against the Rakosi-ite tyranny and irresponsible policy. We are proud that in this armed uprising and in its direction you stand your own ground honorably, filled with true patriotism and faith in socialism.

Kadar also spoke of the danger of counterrevolution and announced the formation of the Hungarian Socialist Workers' Party.

Kadar had also been active in the government that took control on the first day of the revolution. On October 30, he became a member of the new Imre Nagy cabinet; a few days later, he became Minister of State. On November 4, however, during the second Soviet intervention in the Hungarian Revolution, which, indeed, crushed it, a new Revolutionary Workers and Peasants Government was imposed, headed by Kadar; among its members were Apro, Kossa, and Ferenc Munnich. On November 7, Kadar went to Moscow and then returned to Budapest via Prague. As the leader of the Party and Premier, power was now concentrated in his hands. A "reappraisal" of the armed uprising he had so recently glorified began; it became a "counterrevolution," its achievements were gradually pushed into the background, and a great purge started.

Following the October–November, 1956, events, Kadar had the full trust of Khrushchev. In its March 20, 1957, issue, *Pravda* published Kadar's portrait and an extensive biography. According to *Pravda*, Kadar was "a great personality of the Hungarian revolutionary worker and Communist movement" and "one of the most outstanding personalities among the Party and state leaders in Hungary." In April, 1958, Khrushchev, visiting Hungary at the head of a seven-member Soviet Party and government delegation, singled out Kadar, whom "he hardly knew before," for special praise, thus bolstering Kadar's position against the Hungarian Stalinists (Rakosi-ites).

Kadar's role in the Party was dominant after 1956. The leading organs of the newly organized Hungarian Socialist Workers' Party, a temporary Central Committee with twenty-three members and a smaller temporary Executive Committee, were both headed by him. On February 26, 1957, the Party's governing bodies were extended. Kadar became President of the Central Committee, a member of the Executive Committee, and head of the Secretariat. The strengthening and completion of these provisional governing bodies was finished in a few months: Kadar became one of the eleven members of the Politburo and was First Secretary of the five-member Secretariat.

In October, 1957, Kadar became Vice President of the National Council of the Patriotic People's Front. He retained his position as head of the government until the end of January, 1958, when a new "regrouping of power" took place. The government was re-formed; Kadar, in the interest of "raising the level of the work of the Party, and of the social and mass organizations," resigned as Premier but remained a member of the cabinet as Minister of State. The premiership was assumed by the veteran Communist Ferenc Munnich. Kadar was decorated by the Presidium for his work as Premier and the following winter was elected to parliament on the Budapest list of the Patriotic People's Front.

Kadar's part in the execution of Imre Nagy and his associates in June, 1958, is not clear. Whatever the details, it is true that Kadar disowned the same Imre Nagy of whom he had spoken as his friend, his honored and esteemed fellow patriot, in the days of the "glorious uprising." During the revolution, he had sanctioned Nagy's decision to withdraw from the Warsaw Pact, and he had promised Nagy immunity after the uprising, supposedly assuming that his return to political life was a possibility. Now he denied him, calling him a person who "submerged himself in the morass of treason," and approved of his execution as a well deserved punishment.

In September, 1961, Kadar once again became Premier, thus reconcentrating the leadership of both Party and government in his own hands. It would be unwise, however, to assume from such an action that he has ever held sole dictatorial power in Hungary. The evidence suggests that he believes genuinely in as much collective leadership as the Communist system of government will allow. He is receptive to advice and will change his mind if convinced that his original ideas were wrong. He depends particularly on a group of relatively young Party officials, such as Sandor Gaspar, Bela Biszku, and Istvan Szirmai, who have always supported him and whom he has rewarded with some of the top positions in the Party.

Kadar's refusal to let himself be spoiled by power has been one of the secrets of his political success. He also has the gift of projecting a simple, warm personality, and he can still identify himself with the ordinary Hungarian. Combined with a political sagacity that has often been underestimated, this at least partly explains why the man who was regarded as a traitor in 1956 later came to be considered the best leader Hungary could have had under the circumstances and why he has become the object of a considerable amount of popular affection.

POLAND

WLADYSLAW GOMULKA, *First Secretary of the Central Committee of the United Workers' Party.*

WLADYSLAW GOMULKA was born on February 6, 1905, near Krosno, a small town between Cracow and Lwow, in southern Poland. In 1905, Krosno probably had no more than 10,000 inhabitants, and its industries were mainly connected with the nearby oil fields and the production of natural gas. His parents, of Polish stock and almost certainly Roman Catholic, had emigrated to the United States, but had returned before the birth of their son. Thus the young Gomulka must have first heard of the United States from the mouth of a disillusioned emigrant—a fact that may partly explain his dislike for the United States.

On his return to Poland, Gomulka's father became a skilled mechanic in the oil industry. Gomulka himself, according to the official biography published in Poland in 1947, was employed as a cowherd when still a child. He attended primary school but never went to secondary school. Between December, 1918, and December, 1921, he was apprenticed to a locksmith in Krosno. From 1922 to 1926, he worked in the oil-products factory in Jedlicze, near Krosno. His first recorded political activities began in 1922, when he was a member of the Socialist youth association Sila ("Strength"). He was expelled from that organization in 1924 "because of activities against the rightist leadership of the Polish Socialist Party," as his official biography puts it.

In 1926, he seems to have worked on the estates of a Count Skrzynski, in Gorlice, where he had contacts with the farm workers. He became the organizer of the Samopomoc Chlopska (Peasant Self-Help) cooperative in the Krosno district. In that year, he was arrested for the first time, on a charge of distributing left-wing publications before the May 1 celebrations. He was set free almost immediately, however, and proceedings against him were dropped by the public prosecutor. His official biography ascribes his deliverance to "pressure of the masses" during the general strike in the Krosno coal basin.

By 1926, he was a member of the Polish Socialist Party—Left Wing. The *Great Soviet Encyclopedia* claims that he was also a member of the illegal Communist Party of Poland at this time.

By the end of 1926, Gomulka had become active in the trade-union movement, acting as one of the organizers of the general strike of the oil refinery workers in the Boryslaw oil basin. He was also appointed Secretary of the Chemical Workers' Union in the *voivodship* of Warsaw during this period; from January, 1928, until the end of 1930, he was a secretary of the same union in the Dabrowa Gornicza coal basin. Active in local Communist circles, he was appointed to the KPP Committee in Dabrowa Gornicza. In 1930, he was elected Secretary of the National Executive Board at the Chemical Workers' Union conference. From January, 1931, he was Secretary of the so-called Committee of Left-Wing Opposition in the unions and helped in the organization of illegal Communist cells within the miners' union in Dabrowa Gornicza, the metalworkers' union in Silesia, and the textile workers union in Lodz. At that time, his official (underground) Party position was as member of the Department of Trade Unions in the Central Committee. In 1931, he participated in the organization of the strike of streetcar workers in Warsaw, and organized the textile strike in Lodz the next year. During the Lodz strike, however, he was arrested by the police and wounded "while trying to escape." He was tried and sentenced to prison for four years. According to some sources, he was later handed over to the Soviet authorities and sent to the Soviet Union on the strength of the Polish-Soviet agreement on the exchange of political prisoners. Whether or not this is true, it is certain that he was in the Soviet Union between 1933 and 1936. The *Great Soviet Encyclopedia* states that from 1934 to 1935 he studied at the Lenin International school in Moscow, a statement which is confirmed elsewhere.

After illegally returning to Poland, Gomulka worked for a time in Silesia, where he is said to have helped to form a common front of left-wing parties. He was arrested again, however—shortly before the May 1 celebration in 1936—and sentenced to seven years' imprisonment. Thus the critical period of the Stalin's dissolution of the Polish Communist Party, the subsequent purge, and the execution in Russia of almost all its leaders, Gomulka spent in Polish jails. He knows the inside of several Polish jails well, having served time in Lodz, Warsaw, Leczyca, Bialystok, Rawicz, and Sieradz. He was released from this last jail in September, 1939. He fought in the 1939 battle of Warsaw in the Workers' Battalions for the Defense of Warsaw; after the capitulation of Warsaw, he passed into Soviet-occupied territory, where he settled in Lwow.

He returned to the German-occupied area in 1942 and began underground activities in his native Krosno. Soon, he organized the Polish Workers' Party—as the Communist Party called itself from then on—in the district of Rzeszow and led a detachment of Polish partisans. Gomulka's return to the German-occupied part of Poland seems to have been carefully timed: in January, 1942, the Polish Workers' Party was formed in Warsaw from various Communist groups; in the summer of that year, he was called to Warsaw by the new Party's Central Committee and appointed Secretary of the Party Committee of the City of Warsaw and a member of the Warsaw Command of the People's Guard, a Communist-sponsored military underground organization. In this latter capacity, he was very active. As a reprisal for the hanging of fifty Polish hostages by the Germans, he organized an attack on the Café Club, an elegant establishment reserved for Germans, and was credited with other similar resistance actions.

In October, 1942, Gomulka became a member of the Party Central Committee, with special responsibility for the supervision of the Party organization in Warsaw. He also organized liaison services and distribution of propaganda material and was responsible for publishing Party literature. He wrote many articles in the Party organ *Trybuna Wolnosci*. His official biography also credits him with writing the final draft of the Polish Workers' Party's ideological declaration.

When Pawel Finder, the Secretary General of the Party, was arrested by the Germans in November, 1943, Gomulka was elected to that position. At the end of July, 1944, when the Red Army was advancing deep into Poland, Gomulka went to Lublin, where the Soviet-established puppet Polish Committee of National Liberation (known as the Lublin Committee) was already functioning.

In January, 1945, Gomulka became First Deputy Prime Minister and Chairman of the Political Committee of the Council of Ministers in the provisional government set up by the Lublin Committee. In June, 1945, he was also Minister for Regained Territories in the "Government of National Unity," which included Peasant Party Leader Mikolajczyk. At the first postwar congress of the Polish Workers' Party, in December, 1945, he was re-elected to the Central Committee and, soon after, as Secretary-General. He was also elected to the Politburo. In January, 1947, he became a deputy to the Sejm, the lower chamber of the Polish parliament. This marked the first summit of his power. As Minister of Regained Territories, he organized the deportations of the Germans from the newly-won parts of Poland, and was also primarily responsible for crushing the Peasant Party.

To Gomulka, the Communism he was so ruthlessly introducing was a particularly Polish type of Communism. "There are two reasons why Poland cannot be a Soviet republic," he wrote in 1945, "First, this is not desired by the Polish nation; second, this is not desired by the Soviet Union. . . . The PPR, as a party participating in the coalition government and as a party most deeply connected with the Polish nation, takes over the standpoint of the sovereignty and independence of Poland from the democratic spirit of the Polish nation." The task of "reaction" was made easier he said by spreading rumors about kolkhozes. There was also mention of the subject of kolkhozes in the resolution of the Central Committee plenum of May 26, 1945:

> The Central Committee states that hostile propaganda of reaction, intimidating the peasant masses by alleging that there are tendencies and efforts of the Polish Workers' Party and of the Provisional Government toward the "Sovietization" of Poland and the collectivization of the agriculture, is made easy by the sectarian tendencies of certain members of the Party and some rash instructions by the lower authorities of the state apparatus.

These words were to be thrown in Gomulka's face after the Soviet break with Tito. But the immediate cause of Gomulka's eventual fall was his attitude toward the foundation of the Cominform in September, 1947. Later, he was accused of showing "hesitation, arising from the underestimation of the international situation," and of overcoming such hesitation "only under the pressure of the comrades from the Politburo." Gomulka showed even more "hesitation" over Yugoslavia's expulsion from the Cominform. His sympathy with the line taken by Marshal Tito—that Communist countries should retain their own internal freedom—was clearly expressed in a speech he gave to the June, 1948, plenum of the Central Committee. In a speech not previously submitted to the Politburo, he spoke strongly for the "Polish road to socialism" and dwelt on "the historic traditions of the Polish workers' movement." This speech was never published. But it was subsequently referred to by his rival, Bierut, as "undoubtedly a conscious revision of the Leninist appreciation of the history of our movement, based on the complete divorce of the struggle for national independence from the class struggle."

At a Plenum of the Central Committee several months later, Gomulka was forced to deliver a speech of severe self-criticism, in which he made the following rather ambiguous statement about Yugoslavia: "I pose the question to myself whether there was another possibility of reacting to the wrong, nationalistic, and anti-Marxist attitude and policy of the Communist Party of Yugoslavia. I must confess that I cannot find in me the decisive reply." At the Party Congress in September, Bierut delivered a crushing attack against him, and Gomulka was demoted from the position of Secretary General of the Central Committee. The decision removing him from his post alleged that he had committed the following offenses: (1) underestimation of the decisive role of the Bolshevik Party in the struggle against imperialism, and surrender to nationalistic and bourgeois influences; (2) failure to understand the necessity of the sharp class struggle against the peasant capitalists (kulaks); and (3) favoring conciliatory tactics toward the leaders of Yugoslavia's Communist Party, not realizing the essence of their deviation.

Despite the seriousness of the charges against him, Gomulka retained most of his Party positions at first, in view of his "achievements" immediately after the war in the struggle against the "class enemies" and "renascent fascism." But Bierut became Secretary General of the Party, and, at the "Unification Congress" that brought the merger of the Polish Socialist Party with the Communists in December, 1948, Gomulka was not elected to the Politburo of the new Polish United Workers' Party. In January, he was relieved of his posts as Deputy Prime Minister and Minister of the Regained Territories. Eventually, he was given a quite minor job as one of the directors of the State Social Security Fund.

His humiliation continued at the Third Party plenum, November 11–13, 1949. With Zenon Kliszko, he was dismissed from the Central Committee and deprived of the right to perform any function within the Party. On October 31, 1951, a government bulletin stated that the national assembly had "acceded to the request made by the Public Prosecutor that legal proceedings be instituted against Gomulka, who is guilty of practices contrary to the interest of the Polish People's Republic." His parliamentary immunity was withdrawn, and he was arrested.

According to Colonel Swiatlo, a senior Security Service official who escaped to the West in December, 1953, Gomulka was imprisoned in a comfortable villa maintained by the Ministry of Public Security especially for such prominent prisoners. Swiatlo also said that no member of the Central Committee had been willing to undertake the task of interrogating Gomulka; consequently, three senior officers of the Security Service were detailed to do so. He was not interrogated very intensively, however, but was questioned for only about fifteen days during the three years of his confinement. Swiatlo reported that these three years were spent by the Security Service in trying to frame a convincing case against him, but Bierut apparently was never satisfied that the case would stand scrutiny, despite pressures by Moscow for a speedy trial. The death of Stalin and the freer atmosphere that followed led to Gomulka's release in September, 1955. However, Gomulka was not officially rehabilitated until April 6, 1956.

The months after his release were full of rumors about Gomulka's return to political life. The way for his return was paved by the Poznan riots in June, 1956, which gave expression to the serious economic and political discontent prevailing throughout Poland and which threatened to set off a chain reaction that would topple the whole Communist edifice. In the tense atmosphere produced by these riots, the Party needed a popular leader whose record would at least be tolerable in the eyes of the seething anti-Soviet Polish patriots.

Only Gomulka even approximately filled the bill, and he steadily reemerged into public view. The Seventh Party plenum, in July–August, 1956, quashed all the accusations against him and restored him to Party membership. On October 15, it was announced that he had participated in a meeting of the Politburo, and on October 19, the Eighth plenum re-elected him to the Central Committee. Two days later, he was also re-elected to the Politburo and the position of First Secretary of the Party, from which Edward Ochab (who had taken over the position earlier in the year when Bierut had died) had just resigned.

These changes in leadership took place in a revolutionary atmosphere, with the whole nation ready to defy its own Communists and, above all, the Soviet Union. When news of what was going on in Poland reached Moscow, a powerful Soviet delegation headed by Khrushchev flew to Warsaw on October 19, 1956 for secret and (according to rumor) stormy discussions. Soviet troops began concentrating around Warsaw, and the workers of the capital were issued arms. In this trying situation, Gomulka undertook a number of popular actions that helped him to calm aroused tempers and to master the situation. He dismissed the unpopular Minister of National Defense, the Soviet Marshal Rokossovski, he broadcast that other Soviet "experts" were being dismissed, and he made outspoken appeals to the population.

Gomulka's next task was to restore order within the Party, now split between two hostile factions: the so-called Natolin group (Stalinists), bent on dictatorial rule and entirely subservient to the Soviet Union; and the revisionists, who advocated liberalization of political life and intellectual freedom even in interpreting the Marxist-Leninist creed. Though originally supported by the revisionists, Gomulka personally relied on a third, middle-of-the-road group, composed partly of personal followers and partly of people who disliked revisionists but who considered rule by the Natolin group impracticable. He began attacking the two hostile wings of the Party, accusing both of deviation; yet his strictures against the Stalinists were never so numerous or so vehement as were his assaults on the liberal intellectuals of the revisionist wing. At the Tenth plenum (October 24–26, 1957), he announced the "verification" campaign (or purge) within the Party; this resulted in the removal of thousands of members, mostly of lower rank.

Even before this verification campaign, Gomulka had the situation well in hand. It was precisely then, however, that he began to show the political attitudes and defects which the population had either overlooked or ignored in its enthusiasm of October, 1956.

The hallmark of Gomulka's politics has always been a simple faith in Communism—a belief that the dogmas of Marx and Lenin contain all the answers to all the problems of the modern world. He is essentially a conservative—and a self-willed, obstinate one at that. If one adds to this a strong bent toward authoritarianism and a lack of flexibility, one has the explanation for many of Poland's ills in the 1960's.

If one can overlook his growing irritability, which has also had political repercussions, there is much about Gomulka, the man, that is admirable. He is totally honest and has a broad streak of human decency. He leads a modest life, devoid of the slightest extravagance, and is a prodigiously hard worker.

JOZEF CYRANKIEWICZ, *Premier and Member of the Politburo of the United Workers' Party.*

JOZEF CYRANKIEWICZ was born in Tarnow, a small town near Cracow, on April 23, 1911. At that time, the area was part of the Austro-Hungarian empire. Cyrankiewicz was the son of a wealthy construction engineer who had built up a plant of considerable size, mainly producing heating installations. His mother boasted that she was the first woman in Cracow to drive a car. The family was middle-class, Catholic, conservative, and soberly bourgeois.

The young Cyrankiewicz received his primary education in Cracow. He continued at the Imienia Sienkiewicza secondary school (named after the famous Polish writer) and at Swietego Jacka (Saint Hyacinth's), where he passed his final examinations. The schools were conservative ones patronized by the upper classes in Cracow. He went through his military service as a volunteer in the Artillery Reserve College in Wlodzimierz Wolynski (today incorporated in the Ukraine), where he received his commission. Afterward, he studied at the Faculty of Law and Administration at the Jagiellonian University in Cracow. He finished his studies in 1935 without, however, receiving a degree.

During his studies, he developed an interest in social problems and workers' education—an interest that brought him in close contact with the Polish Socialist Party. Despite the assertions in his official biographies, there is no sign that he had any Communist contacts before World War II. He belonged to many organizations, but they were all of a socialist character—some with a distinct anti-Communist tendency. In the early 1930's he joined a socialist student organization, the Union of Independent Socialist Youth. He was elected Secretary of the Socialist Party's student circle in Cracow and wrote articles in the Cracow Socialist paper *Naprzod* (*Forward*), some of them strongly anti-Communist. He was active in the field of workers' education, first as a member, later as Deputy Chairman, of the socialist Association of Workers' Universities. He also became a member of the Socialist Party, for which he did a great deal of field work in his district. In 1935, he became Secretary of the district workers' committee of the Socialist Party in Cracow, a position he held until the outbreak of the war.

In the brief September, 1939, campaign against the invading Germans, Cyrankiewicz was a Second Lieutenant in the Artillery Reserve. Captured by the Germans, he managed to escape and returned to Cracow, where he joined the underground of the Socialist Party operating under the name Freedom-Equality-Independence. He became editor of an underground socialist paper, *Wolnosc* (*Freedom*), and wrote many articles attacking the Soviet Union and Communists. The young workers in the underground were under his strong influence at that time; he was obviously brave and a born leader of men.

In 1941, Cyrankiewicz was arrested in Cracow with thousands of other Poles and was detained in the Montelupi prison. The Socialist underground tried to rescue him, but he was transferred to the notorious Auschwitz concentration camp before he could escape. It was during his imprisonment in Auschwitz that Cyrankiewicz went over to the Communist cause. What caused him to do this is not clear, but the fact that he did so naturally disgusted his former Socialist friends, who had regarded him as a future leader of their party. Moreover, what could have been a fine record of heroism in Auschwitz was marred by a suspicion that several young Socialists were betrayed as a result of Cyrankiewicz' apostasy.

In January, 1945, Cyrankiewicz was transferred from Auschwitz to

Mauthausen with many other prisoners. There he spent a few months before being released by the American Army.

After the war, Cyrankiewicz returned to Cracow, where he contacted his former Socialist comrades and assured them that he had not changed his democratic ideas but was still a convinced Socialist. He then went to Warsaw and reported to the leaders of the Socialist Party, which already included a strong Communist element. In his first declaration, he roundly attacked the underground Socialist Party and the whole Polish underground movement. With his help, the Communists managed to split the Socialists; Cyrankiewicz emerged as Secretary General of a pro-Communist Party; the anti-Communist Socialists were prevented from resuming their activities. Thus Cyrankiewicz's career in Communist-dominated Poland began. His real task was to lead the Socialist Party into a suicidal merger with the Communists, and he consistently pursued this aim by means both fair and foul.

In November, 1946, Cyrankiewicz signed an "agreement of unity of action and cooperation" with Wladyslaw Gomulka. This meant that the Socialist Party, without a formal merger, was to be subordinated to the Communists. In the first general election, in January, 1947, it created a unity bloc with the Communists. After the elections, a decision was made to speed up the merger; and since there was considerable opposition, even in Cyrankiewicz' group, a drastic purge was carried out. But the purge did not succeed in breaking the anti-Communist opposition in the PPS and many Socialist leaders were then arrested and put on trial. Only after this opposition was destroyed or removed could the merger with the Communist Party take place. In December, 1948, the Polish United Workers' Party was born.

After successfully completing his task of destroying the Socialist Party, Cyrankiewicz became one of the leaders of the new party. At the Unity Congress in December, 1948, he was elected a member of the Central Committee, the Politburo, and the Organization Section, and became a Secretary of the Party.

Cyrankiewicz had become Premier of Poland on February 6, 1947; he was second only to Bierut, who became head of state. In 1952, Bierut also took over as Premier, but Cyrankiewicz remained his deputy, and he reassumed the Premiership in 1954. Despite the many changes in Warsaw and Moscow; despite Stalin's death and the succession of Malenkov, Bulganin, Khrushchev, and Brezhnev and Kosygin; despite Gomulka's removal and arrest, Bierut's death, the Poznan revolt, the events of October, 1956, and Gomulka's return, Cyrankiewicz has managed to remain at the head of the government. He has shown remarkable political longevity and adaptability.

It is difficult to describe the complexion of a man who has so clearly shown himself to be a political chameleon. In recent years, however, Cyrankiewicz has appeared to be a moderate and has roused the serious enmity of the Party's Partisan faction. He has a certain strength because of his leadership of the old Socialist group within the Party and because some of the progressives have come to look upon him as their protector.

In contrast to the forbidding Gomulka, Cyrankiewicz radiates a genuine warmth and friendliness and brings a much-needed touch of brightness to the Polish political scene. He is a brilliant public speaker and has achieved a certain popularity because of his friendly and gregarious personality. His private life is a scandal, and so is that of his wife, the actress Nina Andrycz. In short, what Cyrankiewicz lacks in integrity, he makes up in color and gaiety. In a way, he is a perfect counterpart to Gomulka.

ROMANIA

NICOLAE CEAUSESCU, *General Secretary of the Communist Party.*

NICOLAE CEAUSESCU is one of a group of young Communist leaders who have come to the fore in the two decades since the Communist regimes were installed in East Europe. Of peasant origin, he was born on January 26, 1918 in Scornicesti, some 75 miles northwest of Bucharest. He entered the ranks of the Communist Party in 1936 by way of its youth organization and, shortly before the outbreak of World War II, spent some time in the Brasov and Doftana (Bucharest) prisons, having been convicted of "agitation." In 1944, he was secretary of the Union of Communist Youth.

After the Communist assumption of power, in Romania, Ceausescu was assigned to Party organizational work but was reportedly soon transferred to the Political Directorate of the Army, with the rank of Brigadier General. In March, 1950, he was promoted to Major General and appointed Deputy Minister of the Armed Forces. He had been elected to the Grand National Assembly in November, 1946, and, according to some sources, he had had a brief spell as Deputy Minister of Agriculture in 1949–50.

Ceausescu climbed the first rung of the Party ladder in 1945, when he was elected a Central Committee candidate member. In 1948, according to his official biography, he became a full member of the Central Committee. At first, he was thought to be an adherent of the Pauker faction of the Party, but even if this is true, he was not slow in switching his adherence to Gheorghiu-Dej. When Pauker fell from power, he was handsomely rewarded. After becoming a full Central Committee member in May, 1952, he entered the Central Committee Secretariat and the Politburo (as a candidate member) in April, 1954. His Secretariat appointment entailed giving up his Armed Forces ministerial post, under the unwritten rule (which has since generally held good), that Party Secretariat and government functions should be separated. But this was a small sacrifice in view of the great promise of his career in the real stronghold of power.

At the Second Party Congress in December, 1955, Ceausescu became a full member of the Politburo—a considerable achievement for a man of 37. But yet a further stride forward was in store for him. In July, 1957, Josif Chisinevschi was purged from the Politburo and from the Secretariat; Ceausescu was now ranked second only to Gheorghiu-Dej in the latter body. In view of the growth in importance of the Secretariat, it becomes clear how strong Ceausescu's position was. Ceausescu's senior Party rating was also attested by the fact that he attended the November, 1957, conference in Moscow of ruling Communist parties and was present at the twenty-first CPSU Congress in January–February, 1959.

Ceausescu has also had considerable experience on various Party or "front" administrative bodies. He was a member of the Party's Organization Bureau from May, 1952 (after the fall of Pauker), to its abolition in 1954. In December, 1956, he was elected secretary of the People's Democratic Front and, for a brief period, from June to October, 1955, was a member of the Presidium of the National Assembly. In the National Assembly he represents the Pitesti district.

Ceausescu was re-elected to the Politburo and the Secretariat in June, 1960, at the Third Party Congress. He did not attend the 1960 Conference in Moscow, but in August, 1961, he accompanied Gheorghiu-Dej on a visit to the Soviet Union. Ceausescu was also a member of the Romanian delegation to the twenty-second CPSU Congress in November, 1961. He was one of Khrushchev's escorts during the latter's visit to Rumania in 1962. In November, 1962, he attended the Italian Party Congress, and an article by him on the occasion of the fifteenth anniversary of the Soviet-Romanian Treaty of Friendship and Mutual Aid was published in *Pravda* in February, 1963.

Ceausescu also escorted Nikolai Podgorny during his visit to Romania in June 1962. He accompanied Maurer and Bodnaras on their visit to Communist China in 1964 and led the Romanian Party delegation that visited Hungary in July of that year. He also headed the Romanian delegation to Palmiro Togliatti's funeral. In October, 1964, he was on hand in East Berlin for the fifteenth-anniversary festivities of the D.D.R.

Ceausescu has always been known as a young, vigorous *apparatchik*, an able and quite ruthless administrator. More recently, he was used considerably in relations with foreign Communist parties. He is reliably reported to be an eloquent advocate of a still more independent line for Romania vis-à-vis the U.S.S.R. For a number of years, he had been considered a strong candidate to succeed Gheorghiu-Dej, and, as the man responsible for Party organization and cadres, he certainly had the chance to fortify a powerful position for himself. His own hopes, and the expectations of others, were fulfilled in March, 1965, when, on the death of Gheorghiu-Dej, Ceausescu was made First Party Secretary, a title which was changed to General Secretary at the Party Congress in July, 1965.

GHEORGHE GHEORGHIU-DEJ *(1901–65), late Chairman of the Council of State and First Secretary of the Central Committee of the Workers' Party*

GHEORGHE GHEORGHIU was born on November 8, 1901, in Barlad, then a small, provincial town in the hilly southern part of Moldavia. His father was a poor worker, and he himself had only the most elementary education. He began work at the age of eleven and served in a number of small workshops during the following four years. At the age of fifteen, he joined the Steaua Romana enterprise at Moinesti as an apprentice electrician; he later worked in Campina.

It was not long before the young Gheorghiu began taking an active part in labor groups and in left-wing politics. In this, he was possibly stimulated by Russian deserters and the "revolutionary committees" they established in certain parts of Romania toward the end of World War I. At any rate, it is reported that he took an active part in "organizing unrest" among timber industry workers in the Trotus Valley in 1919. In 1921, the year of the founding of the Romanian Communist Party, he got a job in the streetcar workshops of Galati. Conscripted for military service the same year, he served with an engineer regiment at Focsani. Either during his military service or shortly afterward, he underwent his first period of imprisonment for "Bolshevist activities." On his release, he returned to the streetcar company at Galati. He was now, however, something of a marked man; he was dismissed—this time for "anarchistic activities." In 1926, after a brief period with the Goetz timber company, he went to work in the Bucharest railroad shops. Three years later, he joined the outlawed Communist Party and was assigned to agitational work in the railroad yards.

After attending a meeting of Communist unions in Bucharest in April, 1931, he was disciplined by the railway management by being rusticated to the town of Dej in central Transylvania. (It is from this town that the second part of his name originates.) Gheorghiu-Dej continued to be very active in the Communist labor movements, however. He assumed charge of a Workers' Relief Organization, issued a manifesto inciting workers to strike, and in March, 1932, took part in a clandestine meeting of Communist workers at which the publication of a newspaper was planned. In the summer of 1932, he is reported to have organized a Communist meeting at Galati that paved the way for large-scale Communist infiltration among the railway workers. His agitational work met with the most dramatic response in the February, 1933, Grivita railway strike, a violent, bitter strike which led to Gheorghiu-Dej's twelve-year imprisonment at hard labor. His colleague, Chivu Stoica, and several others were also imprisoned. (Gheorghiu-Dej had actually been arrested just before the strike started, but he brought himself [and the Party] a good deal of publicity.) In 1932, even before the Grivita strike, he had been made a Secretary of the Party's Central Committee and a member of the General Council of Communist Trade Unions. In this latter capacity, he attended an international trade-union conference in Berlin.

While serving his sentence, Gheorghiu-Dej was jailed in several Romanian prisons—Vacaresti, Craiova, Ocnele Mari, and Aiud, to name a few. (Although he was in prison, the still illegal Party kept faith by continuing to consider him a member of the Central Committee.) In 1937, he was transferred to the Doftana Prison in Bucharest. An earthquake demolished this building in 1940, and Gheorghiu-Dej was transferred to the Caransebes Prison. Here, he met more of his future colleagues (and opponents): Ana Pauker, Teohari Georgescu, and Josif Chisinevschi. In September, 1943, he was among a number of prisoners transferred to a political internment camp at Targu Jiu. In the spring of 1944, he is reported to have been contacted by Emil Bodnaras, who had just entered Romania as a Soviet agent. In mid-August, 1944, Gheorghiu-Dej escaped, through the help of Ion Gheorghe Maurer. The Soviet armies were rapidly advancing into Romania. Not only was he free; he was on the threshold of power.

In the second Sanatescu cabinet (November, 1944), Gheorghiu-Dej was appointed Minister of Communications and held the same post in the following Radescu and Groza cabinets. This position was particularly important to the Soviets because of their need to communicate with and supply their troops fighting in Hungary, Austria, and Bulgaria. It may also have given some ironic satisfaction to Gheorghiu-Dej to be directing the communications system he had tried so hard to disrupt in his early years. But much more important than his government position was his post as General Secretary of the Communist Party, with which he was invested at a national conference of the Party in October, 1945. (At about the same time, he was also made President of the government Economic Council.)

The following January, Gheorghiu-Dej visited Moscow where he strengthened his political position with the Soviets and was briefed on Soviet economic requirements and presumably on the tactics to be employed to secure speedy Communist domination in Romania. Among his technical assistants during this period were Ion Gheorghe Maurer, later to become Prime Minister, and Simion Zeigher, now one of the nation's senior economic planners.

For a short period thereafter, Gheorghiu-Dej was Minister of Construction; on December 1, 1946, after the Communist triumph in the blatantly unfair parliamentary elections, he was made Minister of the Economy in the regrouped Groza cabinet. His economic policy can be summed up by the classic Marxist theses of industrialization and proletarization. These theses have been among the pillars of the Party's policy right up to the present.

After the forced abdication of King Michael, on December 31, 1947, the state apparatus was completely reorganized; non-Communist parties were eliminated and their representatives removed from the government. In February, 1948, came the merger with the left-wing Social Democrats, the emergence of the Romanian Workers' Party, and the denunciation of Lucretiu Patrascanu for "nationalist deviation."

During this early period of consolidation of power, Gheorghiu-Dej sided with the "internationalist-Comintern" faction in the Party (Pauker, Luca) against Patrascanu, who was something of a genuine nationalist despite his Communism. It was well for Gheorghiu-Dej that he took this course, for the Pauker faction was the most powerful one in the Party at the time—so powerful, in fact, that Gheorghiu-Dej suffered the only eclipse of his career between 1949 and 1951. He had several disagreements with Pauker on agrarian problems, and such was the strength of "Red Ana" that these differences might have led to his disgrace. The Tito crisis of 1948–49 also placed him in an embarrassing position. Tito's "nationalist deviation" and the disgrace of Gomulka, Rajk, and Kostov shortly afterwards inevitably made suspect to Moscow the native Communists who had never had the benefits of direct Soviet indoctrination. Gheorghiu-Dej was such a man, and it is one of the ironies of recent Communist history that it was he who was chosen by the Kremlin to prepare the report on Yugoslavia's final exclusion from the Cominform in November, 1949. This Gheorghiu-Dej did with prudent forcefulness; he lost no opportunity in the following few years to berate Tito in the most violent terms.

Toward the end of 1951, however, it was evident that he was beginning to gain the upper hand in the struggle with the Pauker group. In the early part of 1952, the hard core of this group—Pauker, Luca, and Georgescu—were ousted from their Party positions; Ana Pauker was finally removed from her government position of Foreign Minister in July of the same year. Gheorghiu-Dej was now supreme. In June, 1952, he became Premier, succeeding Petru Groza, who was appointed titular head of state. In April, 1954, he resigned his post of First Party Secretary (Soviet style, the title had been changed from General Secretary the previous autumn) and handed it over to his trusted follower, Gheorghe Apostol. But in October, 1955, shortly before the oft-postponed Second Party Congress, he took back the position and made another close associate, Chivu Stoica, Premier. This was a game of musical chairs as far as real power was concerned, but it was a gesture against the personality cult and in favor of the fashionable concept of "collective leadership." In March, 1961, in a large government reorganization, Gheorghiu-Dej became President of the newly instituted Council of State (in other words, President of the Republic).

Gheorghiu-Dej's ruthlessness was shown by the way he dealt with opponents when the time was ripe. He did not hesitate to turn on Patrascanu and ultimately to execute him in April, 1954. He chose the right moment to pounce on Pauker, Luca, and Georgescu; and in July, 1957, in a purge closely timed with that of the anti-Party group in Moscow, he removed Chisinevschi and Miron Constantinescu from the Politburo. Each, in his different way, was a threat to Gheorghiu-Dej's supremacy. As a result of this purge, Gheorghiu-Dej finally made unassailable his own power and that of his so-called workers' group—led by himself, Stoica, and Apostol. Steps in this direction had begun very early and had received considerable impetus at the Second Party Congress in 1955, at which Gheorghiu-Dej had introduced several of his supporters into the Central Committee.

Gheorghiu-Dej was not an unattractive man. Though by no means an intellectual, he had a good deal of native ability and was a notably hard worker throughout his career. He had a slow-working, tenacious mind, was ready to admit his ignorance on any point, and persistently questioned his advisers until at least the gist of a matter was clear to him. What he lacked in intellectual ability he made up in political sagacity—a fact clearly shown by his handling of the Sino-Soviet dispute. He knew some Russian and apparently learned a little French during his long imprisonment. Gheorghiu-Dej was very much a "son of the people"; and there was no reason to doubt his devotion to the cause of Communism, even though this devotion was tempered by national feeling and, on occasion, a certain humanity.

Gheorghiu-Dej married in 1930 but was later divorced. One of his two grown daughters, Lica, is a film actress of prominence, if not of ability. Gheorghiu-Dej's private life and that of his daughters were always something of a scandal, although in his later years his health caused him to assume a more restful mode of conduct.

Gheorghiu-Dej died in March, 1965.

ION GHEORGHE MAURER, *Premier and Member of the Presidium of the Communist Party.*

ION GHEORGHE MAURER was born in Bucharest in 1902. He is very far from being a "son of the people." His father, of Saxon origin, was a foreign-language teacher in a gymnasium; his mother was of French extraction. Maurer himself was educated at the University of Bucharest, from which he graduated with a degree in law in 1923. He began his legal career as a state prosecutor but then settled down to practice in Transylvania and then Bucharest. Politics soon attracted him, and he seems to have become associated with Communism in 1931–32. During a speech of January 12, 1958, on the elevation of Maurer to the Presidency, however, Gheorghiu-Dej described him as actually having entered the Party in 1936.

Maurer was used by various prominent Communists, among them Ana Pauker, as defense counsel in political trials. On the eve of World War II, he was interned in the Targu Jiu camp along with several others among today's top Communist leaders. Maurer, however, was not to stay long in detention. Allegedly because of his close personal contacts with prominent members of General Antonescu's regime, he was soon released. This did not prevent him from continuing Communist underground activities, however. Toward the end of the war, it is said, he made possible Gheorghiu-Dej's escape from Targu Jiu. On August 20 or 21, 1944, on the eve of the "liberation," he appeared at the internment camp dressed as an air force captain and simply brought Gheorghiu-Dej out. It was perhaps this consummate act of audacity that, more than anything else, cemented the close friendship between the two men.

During the early postwar period, Maurer was also on good terms with Lucretiu Patrascanu and Ana Pauker, but he wisely did nothing to spoil his association with Gheorghiu-Dej. When Gheorghiu-Dej became Minister of Communications in 1944, Maurer was his Under Secretary; when Gheorghiu-Dej was Minister of National Economy in 1946, Maurer again was his chief assistant.

In 1947, Maurer was a member of the Romanian delegation to the peace-treaty talks in Paris. He later became Director of the Institute for Juridical Researches attached to the Romanian Academy, and Vice President of the Society for the Dissemination of Science and Culture, a position from which he was released in October, 1955.

His rise in the Party began at the First Party Congress, in 1948, at which he was elected a full member of the Central Committee. He was downgraded, however, to candidate member at the Second Party Congress, in December, 1955—a reflection of the very minor role he had played in politics during the previous few years. In fact, he almost retired completely from active life from about 1950 to 1956. This eclipse is not easy to interpret. During the period 1949–52, there was some doubt whether Gheorghiu-Dej himself would gain the upper hand in his struggle with the Pauker group; Maurer may have deliberately been lying low. After Gheorghiu-Dej's complete triumph over Pauker in 1952, Maurer did reappear in public; but there was still his early, quite close association with Patrascanu to live down. He and Patrascanu were similar types; both were well educated men who had been on speaking terms with former political opponents. Therefore, he may have continued under some degree of suspicion. It is also worth noting that Maurer was suspected of being too friendly toward Tito; if true, this would certainly account for his obscurity in the early 1950's.

But Gheorghiu-Dej did not often forget an old friend (or enemy); once the Second Congress was over and he was firmly in the saddle, Maurer's star began to rise quickly. He visited Paris early in 1956. In May of the same year, he was appointed a representative to the Permanent Court of Arbitration at The Hague; in November, 1956, he was a member of the Romanian delegation to the U.N. General Assembly. The following March, he appeared as a leading member of the Romanian group at the Inter-Parliamentary Union.

His increasing stature was indicated on March 16, 1957, when he was appointed Vice President of the National Assembly; his importance was secured the following June by his appointment as Minister of Foreign Affairs. In September, Maurer once again represented Romania at the United Nations, and on January 11, 1958, he succeeded the deceased Petru Groza as Chairman of the Presidium of the Grand National Assembly. As titular head of state, his subsequent activity and prominence suggest that he brought a good deal more weight and authority to this office than Groza had. At a Central Committee plenum in June, 1958, Maurer was elected a full member of that body, and at the Third Party Congress, in June, 1960, his triumph continued. Decorated and honored, he entered the Politburo over the heads of four candidate members who had been knocking at the door for years. His triumph was completed in the government reshuffle of March, 1961, when he was appointed Prime Minister in place of Chivu Stoica.

It is obvious that the key to Maurer's elevation was his friendship with Gheorghiu-Dej—a friendship that seems strange because of the apparent dissimilarity between the two men. Gheorghiu-Dej was the rough, self-taught son of the people; Maurer is the wellborn intellectual, well-dressed, personable, and polished, well-traveled in the West and obviously "at home" there. He has been ideally suited for his role as "chief salesman" of the Romanian regime in intra-bloc and international politics, and has done more than any other one man to raise the prestige of his country abroad.

APPENDIX III

Population and Communist Party Membership in Eastern Europe*

Country	Total Population (in millions)		Communist Party Membership (full and candidate members) (in millions)	
	1955	1965	1955	1965
Bulgaria	7.46	8.17	.42	.58
Czechoslovakia	13.03	14.11	1.45	1.68
East Germany	18.00	17.18	1.45	1.75
Hungary	9.65	10.10	.80	.60
Poland	27.01	31.30	1.34	1.73
Romania	17.04	18.98	.54	1.38
Total	92.14	99.84	6.00	7.72

* *Source:* Official government media, mainly statistical yearbooks.

APPENDIX IV

Industrial Output, Employment, and Output Per Man, 1960–64*
(*in Percentage Increases Over Preceding Year*)

	1960	*1961*	*1962*	*1963*	*1964*
Albania					
Industrial output	11.2	7.2	6.4	6.7	6.5
Bulgaria					
Industrial output	13.3	11.7	11.0	10.0	8.8
employment	10.8	2.2	3.0	5.2	4.1
output per man	2.3	9.2	7.8	4.6	4.5
Czechoslovakia					
Industrial output	11.7	8.9	6.2	— 0.6	3.6
employment	4.4	3.6	3.0	0.4	0.8
output per man	7.0	5.1	3.1	— 1.0	2.8
East Germany					
Industrial output	8.2	5.9	6.2	4.9	5.7
employment	0.7	0.6	— 0.4	—	—
output per man	7.4	5.3	6.6	6.5	—
Hungary					
Industrial output	12.8	11.0	8.4	7.0	7.0
employment	6.5	3.7	3.8	3.7	3.3
output per man	5.9	7.0	4.4	3.2	3.6
Poland					
Industrial output	11.1	10.4	8.4	5.3	6.3
employment	0.4	3.5	5.0	2.5	1.7
output per man	10.7	6.7	3.2	2.7	4.5
Romania					
Industrial output	16.4	15.3	14.8	12.5	12.0
employment	4.8	8.2	7.7	4.9	2.5
output per man	11.1	6.5	6.5	7.2	9.3
Total in Eastern Europe					
Industrial output	11.0	9.3	8.0	5.0	6.4
employment	3.1	3.3	3.4	1.7	—
output per man	7.7	5.8	4.4	3.2	—

* *Source: United Nations Economic Survey of Europe, 1963: Part I, The European Economy in 1963* (Geneva, 1964), Chapter I, page 5.

APPENDIX V

Total Agricultural Output, 1961–64*
(*in Percentage Increases Over Preceding Year*)

	1961	*1962*	*1963*	*1964*
Albania				
Total	11.7	10.0	ca. 8.0	13.4[a]
Bulgaria				
Crops	– 9.3	8.8	—	—
Livestock	8.4	–3.7	—	—
Total	– 3.5	4.2	0.4	8.6
Czechoslovakia				
Crops	– 3.1	–12.0	15	4.4
Livestock	2.9	– 3.2	–1 to –2	5.7
Total	—	– 7.6	6–7	0.6
Hungary				
Crops	– 3.9	3.9	8–9	—
Livestock	6.4	– 0.3	–1 to –2	7
Total	0.7	1.6	4–5	2
Poland				
Crops	11.6	–14.2	11.3	0.8[a]
Livestock	8.5	—	– 6.1	1.6[a]
Total	10.4	– 8.5	3.8	1.1[a]
Romania				
Crops	3.4	– 9.0	—	6.5
Livestock	18.7	– 8.5	—	—
Total	8.0	– 8.9	3–5	—

* *Source: United Nations Economic Survey of Europe 1963: Part I, The European Economy in 1963* (Geneva, 1964), Chapter I, page 15. Figures for 1964 from official government media.

[a] Plan.

Notes

Chapter 1. Political Development

1. For an economic analysis of the leap forward, see John Kalo, "The Bulgarian Economy," *Survey*, December, 1961.
2. *Rabotnichesko Delo* (Sofia), January 20, 1959.
3. *Otechestven Front* (Sofia), January 22, 1959.
4. See, for example, *Partien Zjivot* (Sofia), June, 1959, and *Novo Vreme* (Sofia), June, 1959.
5. *Rabotnichesko Delo*, April 24, 1963.
6. See J. F. Brown, "The Bulgarian Plot," *The World Today*, June, 1965.
7. The draft of the socialist constitution was published in *Rude Pravo* (Prague), April 19, 1960.
8. *Rude Pravo*, November 21, 1961.
9. See *ibid.*, October 17, 1964.
10. The interview was published on March 11, 1964, in the Hamburg SPD evening paper, *Echo am Abend*.
11. *Neues Deutschland*, October 7, 1964.
12. *Nepszabadsag* (Budapest), November 25, 1962.
13. *Ibid.*, December 10, 1961.
14. See, for example, Politburo member Istvan Szirmai in *Tarsadalmi Szemle* (Budapest), April, 1965.
15. See Hansjakob Stehle, "Polish Communism," in William E. Griffith (ed.), *Communism in Europe* (Cambridge, Mass.: M.I.T. Press, 1964), I, 97, n. 27.
16. *Nove Drogi* (Warsaw), September–October, 1948.
17. *Trybuna Ludu* (Warsaw), July 6, 1963.
18. *Ibid.*, July 27–28, 1965.
19. *Scinteia* (Bucharest), December 7, 1961.

Chapter 2. Industry and the National Economy: Development and Reform

1. *Novo Vreme,* November, 1963.
2. *Rabotnichesko Delo,* February 12, 1964.
3. *Kulturni Tvorba,* February 7, 1963.
4. *Nova Mysl* (Prague), September, 1963.
5. The proposals were published simultaneously in the Prague *Rude Pravo* and in the Bratislava *Pravda* on October 17, 1964.
6. See *Neues Deutschland,* July 17, 1963.
7. *Nepszabadsag,* February 12, 1965.
8. See Michael Gamarnikow, "Poland's Unemployment Problem," in *East Europe,* June, 1964.
9. Fourth Party Congress Theses, in *Trybuna Ludu,* March 17, 1964.
10. *Ibid.*
11. *Zycie Gospodarcze* (Warsaw), August 23, 1964.
12. *Trybuna Ludu,* July 27–28, 1965.
13. *Tygodnik Powszechny,* January 3, 1963.
14. *Probleme Economice* (Bucharest), August, 1964.
15. *Rude Pravo,* April 11, 1964.
16. *Ibid.,* July 17, 1964.
17. MTI (Hungarian wire service), October 30, 1964.
18. Radio Budapest (Homeland Service), October 9, 1964.
19. *Dziennik Ustaw* (Polish law bulletin), April 4, 1964.
20. Radio Warsaw, July 9, 1964.
21. *Polityka* (Warsaw), May 1, 1965.
22. *Darzhaven Vestnik,* June 22, 1965.
23. *Problems of Peace and Socialism,* September, 1962.
24. *Scinteia,* April 26, 1964.
25. *Neues Deutschland,* December 6, 1964.

Chapter 3. Agriculture

1. These figures are taken from official government sources and from agricultural sections of the periodic U.N. *Economic Bulletin for Europe,* published in Geneva.
2. The best discussion of the private sector in East European agriculture is by C. Z. (Carl Zoerb) in *The Performance of the Private and Public Sectors in Bloc Agriculture* (Radio Free Europe Research, January 20, 1965).
3. See special booklet published by Hungarian Ministry of Agriculture, January 10, 1963.
4. *Neues Deutschland,* February 29, and March 1, 1964.

Chapter 4. Cultural Development

1. *Narodna Kultura* (Sofia), November 10, 1962, and January 19, 1963.
2. Gomulka's speech was published in *Trybuna Ludu,* September 19, 1964.
3. For a good, short introduction see Radio Free Europe Research Department Background Report, *The Conflict of Generations in Eastern Europe Today,* March 12, 1965.
4. See, for example, the views of Alfred Kurella on the Kafka conference in

the August 4, 1963, issue of the cultural weekly *Der Sonntag*. Kurella is chairman of the SED's Central Committee Cultural Commission.

5. The January, 1964, issue of *Inostrannaya Literatura* (*Foreign Literature*) published two of Kafka's short stories, "Metamorphosis" and "In a Penal Colony."
6. See *Tarsadalmi Szemle* (Budapest), April, 1965.
7. Zhivkov gave the speech at a specially summoned meeting of representatives of the various creative arts. It was carried by *Rabotnichesko Delo*, on April 24, 1964.
8. For details on the Jar case, see *Scinteia*, May 23, 1956.
9. *Ibid.*, February 11, 1963.
10. For the discussions at this meeting, see *Gazeta Literara*, April 2, 1964.
11. *Scinteia*, May 20, 1965.
12. See *Trybuna Ludu*, July 6, 1963.

Chapter 5. Relations with the Soviet Union

1. *Rabotnichesko Delo*, August 14, 1964.
2. *Nepszabadsag*, April 12, 1964.
3. *Trybuna Ludu*, June 16, 1964.
4. Radio Warsaw, October 28, 1964.
5. *Scinteia*, April 26, 1964.
6. For example, Horst Dohlus in *Neuer Weg*, No. 32 (1964).
7. The most authoritative description of the present Yugoslav differences was given by the Croatian Party leader Vladimir Bakaric; see *Vjesnik* (Zagreb), September 21, 1964.
8. *Scinteia*, June 29, 1965.
9. See *Zeri i Popullit* (Tirana), February 2, 1965.
10. See, for example, a speech in March, 1965, by Politburo member and CC Secretary Istvan Szirmai (*Tarsadalmi Szemle*, April, 1965).
11. David J. Dallin, *Soviet Foreign Policy After Stalin* (New York: J. B. Lippincott, 1961; London: Methuen, 1962), pp. 364–65.
12. See Brown, *op. cit.*

Chapter 6. Nationalism in Albania and Romania

1. See R. V. Burks, *The Dynamics of Communism in Eastern Europe* (Princeton, N.J.: Princeton University Press, 1961; London: Oxford University Press, 1961), p. 147.
2. Vladimir Dedijer, *Tito Speaks* (London: Weidenfeld and Nicolson, 1954), p. 320.
3. See William E. Griffith, *Albania and the Sino-Soviet Rift* (Cambridge, Mass.: M.I.T. Press, 1963), p. 43.
4. *Ibid.*, p. 40.
5. *Zeri i Popullit*, October 26, 1960.
6. *Neues Deutschland*, December 18, 1960.
7. *Zeri i Popullit*, February 14, 1961.
8. John Michael Montias, "Background and Origins of the Romanian Dispute with Comecon," *Soviet Studies*, October, 1963.
9. *Scinteia*, June 26, 1963.
10. A. Otetea and S. Schwann (eds.), *K. Marx—Insemnari Despre Romani* (Bucharest: R.P.R. Academy of Science, 1964).

Chapter 7. Relations with the Western Powers

1. See, for example, A. Puiu, "World Economic Relations—An Objective Force in the Contemporary World," in *Probleme Economice*, October, 1964.
2. See *Rabotnichesko Delo*, July 10, 1964.
3. United Nations *Economic Bulletin for Europe*, XVI, No. 1 (September, 1964). All subsequent commercial statistics are taken from this source.
4. See *Borba* (Belgrade), July 13, 1964; also, the statement by GATT Secretary General Eric Wyndham White to United Press International, November 26, 1964.
5. The Bulgarian figures for 1960 are from *Information Bulgare* (Paris), January 31, 1961; for 1964, from *Narodna Mladezh*, December 3, 1964. The Czechoslovak figures for 1960 are from *Vecernik* (Bratislava), February 24, 1961; for 1964, from *Prague Newsletter*, April 3, 1965. The Hungarian figures for 1960 are from the *Hungarian Statistical Yearbook for 1960*; for 1964 from *Nepszabadsag*, October 30, 1964. The Polish figures for 1960 are from Radio Warsaw, February 3, 1961; for 1964, from Radio Warsaw (III), June 28, 1965.
6. *Privredni Pregled* (Belgrade), February 18, 1965.
7. *Express Wieczorny*, January 6, 1965.
8. *Praca* (Bratislava), January 27, 1965.
9. *Hungarian Statistical Yearbook for 1963*.
10. *Praca*, January 27, 1965.
11. *Privredni Pregled*, February 18, 1965.

Bibliography

The material in this book is based mainly on primary sources, chiefly the East European press. I have also found helpful the reports and analyses in such prominent Western newspapers as *The Times* (London), *The Guardian, Le Monde,* the *Frankfurter Allgemeine Zeitung, Die Presse* (Vienna), the *Neue Zürcher Zeitung,* and, of course, *The New York Times.*

Journals specifically devoted to East European affairs, like *Survey* and *Problems of Communism,* have been most useful, as have the background reports published by the Research Department of Radio Free Europe in Munich.

The following is a list of books in English that have been of *direct* use in writing my own book. Of course, they are not the only ones I used in preparing it.

Balassa, Bela A. *The Hungarian Experience in Economic Planning.* New Haven, Conn.: Yale University Press, 1959.

Blit, L. *The Eastern Pretender.* London: Hutchinson, 1965.

Brzezinski, Zbigniew K. *The Soviet Bloc.* Rev. ed. New York and London: Frederick A. Praeger, 1961 and 1963.

Bromke, Adam (ed.). *The Communist States at the Crossroads.* New York and London: Frederick A. Praeger, 1965.

Burks, R. V. *The Dynamics of Communism in Eastern Europe.* Princeton, N.J.: Princeton University Press; London: Oxford University Press, 1961.

Busek, Vratislav and Spulber, Nicolas. *Czechoslovakia.* New York: Frederick A. Praeger, 1957; London: Stevens, 1958.

DALLIN, DAVID J. *Soviet Foreign Policy After Stalin.* New York: J. B. Lippincott; London; Methuen, 1961.

DEDIJER, VLADIMIR. *Tito Speaks.* London: Weidenfeld & Nicolson, 1954.

DELLIN, L. A. D. (ed.). *Bulgaria.* New York: Frederick A. Praeger; London: Atlantic Press, 1957.

DZIEWANOWSKI, MARIAN K. *The Communist Party of Poland: An Outline of History.* Cambridge, Mass.: Harvard University Press; London: Oxford University Press, 1959.

FISCHER-GALATI, STEPHEN. *Eastern Europe in the Sixties.* New York and London: Frederick A. Praeger, 1963 and 1964.

——— (ed.). *Romania.* New York: Frederick A. Praeger, 1957; London: Stevens, 1958.

FLOYD, DAVID. *Rumania: Russia's Dissident Ally.* New York: Frederick A. Praeger; London: Pall Mall Press, 1965.

GRIFFITH, WILLIAM E. *Albania and the Sino-Soviet Rift.* Cambridge, Mass.: The M.I.T. Press, 1963.

———. *The Sino-Soviet Rift.* London: Allen & Unwin, 1964.

——— (ed.). *Communism in Europe.* Vol. I. Cambridge, Mass.: The M.I.T. Press, 1964.

HALECKI, OSCAR (ed.). *Poland.* New York: Frederick A. Praeger, 1957; London: Stevens, 1958.

HAMM, HARRY. *Albania—China's Beachhead in Europe.* Trans. Victor Anderson. New York: Frederick A. Praeger; London: Weidenfeld & Nicholson, 1963.

HELMREICH, ERNST CHRISTIAN (ed.). *Hungary.* New York: Frederick A. Praeger, 1957; London: Stevens, 1958.

HISCOCKS, RICHARD. *Poland: Bridge for the Abyss?* London and New York: Oxford University Press, 1963.

IONESCU, GHITA. *Communism in Rumania.* London and New York: Oxford University Press, 1964.

KASER, MICHAEL. *Comecon: Integration Problems of the Planned Economies.* London and New York: Oxford University Press, 1965.

KERTESZ, STEPHEN D. (ed.). *East Central Europe and the World.* Notre Dame, Ind.: University of Notre Dame Press, 1962.

KRAEHE, ENNO E. ET AL. *Collectivization of Agriculture in Eastern Europe.* Ed. Irwin T. Sanders. Lexington, Ky.: University of Kentucky Press, 1958.

LEWIS, FLORA. *A Case History of Hope.* New York: Doubleday & Co., 1958; London: Secker & Worburg, 1959.

MICHAL, JAN M. *Central Planning in Czechoslovakia.* Stanford, Calif.: Stanford University Press, 1960; London: Oxford University Press, 1961.

MITRANY, DAVID. *Marx Against the Peasant: A Study in Social Dogmatism.* Chapel Hill, N.C.: University of North Carolina Press, 1952; London: Weidenfeld & Nicholson, 1956.

MONTIAS, JOHN M. *Central Planning in Poland.* New Haven, Conn., and London: Yale University Press, 1962.

PRYOR, FREDERICK L. *The Communist Foreign Trade System.* Cambridge, Mass.: The M.I.T. Press; London: Allen & Unwin, 1963.

ROTHSCHILD, JOSEPH. *Communist Eastern Europe.* New York: Walker & Company, 1964.

———. *The Communist Party of Bulgaria: Origins and Development, 1883–1936.* New York: Columbia University Press, 1959; London: Oxford University Press, 1960.

SETON-WATSON, HUGH. *The East European Revolution.* New York: Frederick A. Praeger; London: Methuen, 1957.

SKENDI, STAVRO (ed.). *Albania.* New York: Frederick A. Praeger, 1956; London: Atlantic Press, 1957.

SKILLING, H. GORDON. *Communism, National and International.* Toronto: University of Toronto Press, 1964.

SPULBER, NICOLAS. *The Economics of Communist Eastern Europe.* Cambridge, Mass.: The M.I.T. Press, 1957; London: Chapman & Hall, 1958.

STAAR, RICHARD. *Poland 1944–1962: The Sovietization of a Captive People.* Baton Rouge, La.: Louisiana University Press, 1962.

STEHLE, HANSJAKOB. *The Independent Satellite: Society and Politics in Poland Since 1945.* New York: Frederick A. Praeger; London: Pall Mall Press, 1965.

STERN, CAROLA. *Ulbricht: A Political Biography.* Trans. Abe Farbstein. New York: Frederick A. Praeger; London: Pall Mall Press, 1965.

TABORSKY, E. *Communism in Czechoslovakia, 1948–1960.* Princeton, N.J.: Princeton University Press; London: Oxford University Press, 1961.

ULAM, ADAM. *Titoism and the Cominform.* Cambridge, Mass.: Harvard University Press; London: Oxford University Press, 1952.

VALI, FERENC. *Rift and Revolt in Hungary.* Cambridge, Mass.: Harvard University Press, 1961; London: Oxford University Press, 1962.

WISKEMANN, ELIZABETH. *Germany's Eastern Neighbors.* London and New York: Oxford University Press, 1956.

WOLFF, ROBERT L. *The Balkans in Our Time.* Cambridge, Mass.: Harvard University Press, 1956.

ZAGORIA, DONALD S. *The Sino-Soviet Conflict, 1956–1961.* Princeton, N.J.: Princeton University Press; London: Oxford University Press, 1962.

ZINNER, PAUL E. *Revolution in Hungary.* New York and London: Columbia University Press, 1962.

Index